ALLIGATORS OF THE NORTH

WEST & PEACHEY

ALLIGATOR

MADE ON THE LYNN RIVER • SOLD EVERYWHERE

SIMCOE
ONTARIO, CANADA

1889 ◆ 1932

Illustration produced by Robert Judd Design Co. for the launch of the *W.D. Stalker* in Simcoe, Ontario.

Robert Judd Design Co., Waterford, Ontario.

ALLIGATORS OF THE NORTH

The Story of the West & Peachey Steam Warping Tugs

Harry B. Barrett & Clarence F. Coons

Foreword by Ken Armson, R.P.F.

NATURAL HERITAGE BOOKS
A MEMBER OF THE DUNDURN GROUP
TORONTO

Published by Natural Heritage Books
A Member of The Dundurn Group
3 Church Street, Suite 500
Toronto, Ontario, M5E 1M2, Canada
www.dundurn.com

Library and Archives Canada Cataloguing in Publication

Barrett, Harry B., 1922-
Alligators of the north : the story of the West and
Peachey steam warping tugs / by Harry B. Barrett and
Clarence F. Coons.

Includes bibliographical references and index.
ISBN 978-1-55488-711-8

1. Tugboats—Ontario—History. 2. Steamboats—Ontario—
History. 3. Logging—Ontario—History. 4. West, John.
5. Peachey, James. I. Coons, C. F. II. Title.

VM464.B374 2010   386'.223209713   C2009-907456-7

Front cover: Tom Thomson, "The Alligator," Algonquin Park, 1914 (oil on book binder's board)
Gift of Stewart and Letty Bennett, donated by the Ontario Heritage Foundation to the University of Guelph, 1989; University of Guelph Collection at the Macdonald Stewart Art Centre (Ontario, Canada) – UG1989.096.

Back cover: Tom Thomson, "The Drive," circa 1916 (oil on canvas)
Ontario Agricultural College purchase with funds raised by students, faculty, and staff, 1926; University of Guelph Collection at the Macdonald Stewart Art Centre (Ontario, Canada) – UG1926.134.

Evan Caldwell, "Dead Alligator," – Courtesy of *The Forest Chronicle*, Vol. 68, No. 5 (October 1992), cover; and with the permission of Chris Lee, owner.

Text design by Beth Crane, WeMakeBooks.ca
Edited by Jane Gibson
Copy edited by Shannon Whibbs
Printed and bound in Canada by Marquis

Care has been taken to trace the ownership of copyright material used in this book. The author and the publisher welcome any information enabling them to rectify any references or credits in subsequent editions.
J. Kirk Howard, President

We acknowledge the support of the Canada Council for the Arts and the Ontario Arts Council for our publishing program. We also acknowledge the financial support of the Government of Canada through the Book Publishing Industry Development Program and The Association for the Export of Canadian Books and the Government of Canada through the Ontario Book Publishers Tax Credit Program and the Ontario Media Development Corporation.

Contents

Foreword

by Ken Armson, R.P.F.

This is a story about a Canadian invention that relatively few persons in Ontario, or for that matter in Canada, have heard of, yet it had a profound effect on the effectiveness and economics of the pine-logging industry in Ontario. The Alligator Steam Warping Tug arose from a combination of two factors. The first was a need in the northern Ontario pine-logging industry of the late nineteenth century and the second was the existence of two innovative and entrepreneurial men, John West and James Peachey, owners of a foundry in the town of Simcoe in Norfolk County in southern Ontario.

The late 1800s and the first two decades of the 1900s were a period in Ontario's history when the logging of eastern white and red pine was a major social and economic activity in the Ottawa Valley, Georgian Bay, and north shore of Lake Huron. When pine was logged in forests adjacent to fast-flowing rivers emptying into the Ottawa River and the Georgian Bay, the logs were driven down the rivers and then towed in booms to sawmills. After the accessible stands of timber were exploited, the logging moved into the hinterlands where the logs had to be moved through sequences of lakes and rivers until they arrived at the Ottawa River or Georgian Bay. The process of moving the logs in these lakes and rivers was tedious and expensive, and required much human effort.

Moving the logs down a lake involved building a cadge crib that had to be reassembled or a new one built on each lake in the chain of movement. Here was the need, and the answer to that need was to come from the energy technology of the time — steam power. Something that could move booms of logs on a lake and then be able to move overland under its own power to the next lake.

A lumberman from Norfolk County, Joseph Jackson, who had logging interests in the Georgian Bay pine country, told John West of the need and he, together with his partner James Peachey and staff at their foundry, designed and built the first steam-warping tug, which was unveiled in Simcoe in 1889. What is significant is the manner in which the need in the province's north was communicated to those with knowledge and experience in the appropriate technology of the time in the south. It came from personal contacts and a mutual understanding and respect by those involved.

The two authors of this story in a way represent another form of coming together. The late Clarence Coons, a professional forester I was privileged to know and work with, had researched the history of the Alligator Steam Warping Tug and prepared a draft manuscript. Clarence grew up in Lakefield, Ontario, and in his youth heard many stories about white-pine harvesting in the Trent watershed and of the Alligators owned by the Cavendish Lumber Company at Lakefield. In 1982–83, I was the president of the Canadian Forestry Association, and, recognizing that his manuscript deserved editing and subsequent publication, I endeavoured to find financial support to have this done — without success.

The second author, Harry B. Barrett, grew up on a farm in Norfolk County and is a long-time resident of the area. In addition to farming and later teaching agriculture, he is a noted naturalist, conservationist, and historian. He was founding chairman of the Long Point Foundation for Conservation and has published books on local history, the most recent being *They Had a Dream — A History of the St. Williams Forestry Station*. This publication coincided with the celebration of the centennial of the station's establishment in 1908.

The Canadian Forestry Association each year designates a Forestry Capital of Canada and in 2008 Norfolk County was so named. Associated with the recognition of the centennial of St. William's was, naturally, a companion one of the importance of the nearby town of Simcoe as the birthplace of the Alligator Steam Warping Tug. What more fitting tribute than for Norfolk County to continue for the year 2009 as the Forestry Capital of Canada in honour of the first Alligator tug built 120 years before in 1889. The people of Simcoe responded and reconstructed an Alligator tug, the *W.D. Stalker*, and the Canadian Forestry Association seized the opportunity to have the story of this remarkable invention made public by asking Harry B. Barrett to co-author it with the late Clarence F. Coons.

Ken Armson, R.P.F.
Toronto, Ontario

Acknowledgements

I must admit that when Dave Lemkay, of the Canadian Forestry Association and John de Witt, chairman of the Forest Capital of Canada Committee, approached me in mid September 2008, about expanding on the draft manuscript that told the story of the West & Peachey Alligator Warping Tugs by the late Clarence F. Coons, I agreed to do so with considerable trepidation.

To complete and enhance his amazingly detailed research with its complement of remarkable photographs required that I not only maintain his high standards, but do so in a manner that would have been pleasing to him and appreciated by his fellow professional foresters. Finally, it must appeal to the general reader as an interesting and informative addition to our understanding of our Canadian heritage. I hope our combined effort achieves that purpose.

I am indebted to Scott Gillies, curator, and the archives volunteers of the Eva Brook Donly Museum, as well as Ian Bell, curator of the Port Dover Harbour Museum, for their cheerful assistance in finding pictures and material that I requested of them.

The writings and stories remembered from the late Colonel Douglas Stalker and the late Bruce Pearce, both friends and one-time presidents of the Norfolk Historical Society, have made significant contributions to the story. Barbara Wright, granddaughter of James Peachey, has been most helpful with stories and pictures. James Christison, Ron, and Fred Judd, Albert Potts, and others have added anecdotes regarding the restoration of the Alligator tug, the *W.D. Stalker*.

I wish also to acknowledge the significant help from my son, Toby Barrett, MPP, and his efficient Simcoe office staff in speedily finding needed information from the Library and Ministries in Queen's Park for me. With time being of the essence they were lifesavers. Also, thank you to Jane Gibson and to Shannon Whibbs for all their editorial guidance and to Barry Penhale for his ongoing support and belief in this project. Finally to John de Witt, my sincere thanks for your keen interest and e-mailing abilities in keeping those involved in this effort informed and aware of problems and needs for action as they arose.

Harry B. Barrett
Port Dover, Ontario

I would like to extend my personal thanks to all those who assisted by providing information and photographs for this monograph. I would specifically like to thank the staff of the Public Archives of Canada and the Ontario Archives as well as all other museum staff who were so helpful.

I am very grateful for the encouragement and assistance of John Corby, curator of Industrial Technology at the Museum of Science and Technology in Ottawa, whose earlier studies and writings were most helpful. Also to John Quinsey of Mississauga, Ontario, great-grandson of John Ceburn West, whose biography of him was most useful. The memories of Colonel Douglas Stalker of Simcoe, West's grandson, were much appreciated and very informative. As a boy growing up around the factory he witnessed the events relating to the Alligators unfold before his eyes. I would also like to thank all other members of the West and Peachey families who assisted me with my research.

Finally, I would like to thank the Canadian Forestry Association and the contributing forest industries which supported the publication of this book.

Clarence F. Coons, 1983
Kemptville, Ontario (written 1983)

Introduction

by Dave Lemkay

The story you are about to read is the combined writing of two fine gentlemen who never met one another. Clarence F. Coons and Harry B. Barrett, nonetheless, are now joined as collaborators in this wonderful history of the Alligator Steam Warping Tug. Their respective personalities, professions, and life experiences would have made them great friends had their paths crossed.

Alligators of the North is now that meeting, but regrettably not in person. Clarence passed away suddenly at his home in Kemptville, Ontario, in 2006. He had retired ten years earlier from a long and colourful career as a forester with the Ontario Ministry of Natural Resources, but continued voluntarily with things he was passionate about — maple syrup, farm forestry, Stanley Steamer cars, and vintage tractors, to name a few. His work to chronicle the development of the Alligator Steam Warping Tug is perhaps the pinnacle of these endeavours.

Harry B. Barrett of Port Dover, Ontario, says that, even though he never met Clarence Coons, he has come to know him while researching the files and manuscript that Clarence had assembled on the Alligator tugs back in the 1980s. Having had this insight into the nature of the man, Harry has said that he feels honoured to be able to add his personal touch to such a worthy project. Having known Clarence Coons myself, I am sure that he, too, would be honoured to know that in these circumstances, his years and years of interviewing, cataloguing, and writing the history of the Alligator would be embellished a quarter of a century later by an esteemed historian and kindred spirit from Norfolk County. Harry's partnering in this project was initially discussed over dinner at the Erie Beach Hotel in Port Dover, Ontario, on a balmy September evening in 2008.

I had travelled down from the Ottawa Valley with boxes and binders of files and black-and-white photos extracted from the Coons's study, with the blessing of Clarence's widow, Joyce. These and a complete compilation of West & Peachey boat production by John Corby[1] were pored over and handed off to Harry. It was agreed that his challenge was to "emotionalize" this technical archive and produce a written work that was more accessible to the general public.

Strictly in technological terms, the Alligator Warping Tug, was, in its time, what we would call "high tech" today. Introduced to forest operations in 1889, it revolutionized the transportation of timber when the river drive was the only feasible way to move harvested timber from the forest to market and mill. In the 1880s, some 234 eastern Canadian rivers were being driven[2] by as many timber companies, floating millions of logs, often hundreds of miles. The vagaries of topography and ferocity of rivers or head-winds on lake tows were precursors to fierce competition at the timber slides at the rapids along the route and loading coves for right of way. It was critical that the timber got to market and that it got there early to realize the best prices. Time was money and latecomers were subjected to waning prices or no timely sale.

When the Alligator was introduced to this milieu, it catapulted the industry into the age of steam. It's fair to say that the Alligator had no less an impact on the forest industry than the post–Second World War introduction of the chainsaw and skidder, and since this manuscript was originally written, the computer that allows foresters today to scientifically manage the resource and even monitor forest health from space.

In international media coverage of the day, much was made of the Alligator's novel amphibious quality, specifically that the scow could be winched over land to the next lake or headwaters of the next tributary. In terms of time, this overland capability could drastically reduce non-productive relocation of the steamboat and its crew along the waterway. However, it is important to understand that the real value of the Alligator's warping mechanism, the winding of a mile of steel cable on the drum, was most advantageous when applied to long tows of log booms across large lakes. Utilization of the Alligator replaced the tedious, back-breaking task of kedging booms of logs by horse-power and even manpower, with the power of steam.

So much of our Canadian history is anchored in the harvest of our vast endowment of forests. We celebrate and glorify this heritage as the genesis of our country's economic well-being, the impetus to early settlement, and our reaching out to the world with fine forest products. The lumbering and sawmilling era across Canada has spawned a wealth of legend and lore and music that rings out with songs of the shanty, the bravado of the river drive, and the brawls at the stopping places along the way. Although life wasn't easy for the forest man or the river driver, it was packed with adventure and danger on a daily basis. Into this early scene came the Alligator, celebrated in this book as the iconic and ubiquitous workhorse of timbering days in the forests of much of eastern Canada. The dedication and hard work required to chronicle this saga, given by people like Clarence Coons and Harry Barrett, has finally come together to pay fitting tribute to this most significant of inventions, the Alligator Warping Tug created by West & Peachey of Simcoe, Ontario.

Enjoy.

Dave Lemkay, Ottawa Valley
General Manager, Canadian Forestry Association

The publishing of this book is a legacy project stemming from the designation of Norfolk County as Forest Capital of Canada for the years 2008 and 2009.

"This is the forest primeval, The murmuring pines and the hemlock"
—Henry Wadsworth Longfellow, "Evangeline"

1 In the Beginning

When Columbus "discovered" America in 1492, the whole of northeastern North America was covered in forest. The aboriginals living there were primarily nomadic in nature, hunting and fishing and supplementing their food supply with the berries and fruits that grew in abundance. Those living along the north shore of Lake Erie were known as the Attawandaron, or as Champlain called them, the Neutrals, who traded with both the Algonquin to the north and the Iroquois of the Mohawk Valley to the south. The Petuns, or Tobacco Indians, occupied lands southeast of Lake Huron, so called because they grew tobacco, which they traded as far west as the Pacific coast. These people lived in more permanent villages, growing corn or maize, beans, and squash, as well as pumpkins, sunflowers, and potatoes. As soil fertility declined, they would simply move on and develop a new site.

In the mid-1600s, the Neutrals were driven from their traditional lands. Those who survived were absorbed into the Wyandotte Nation, west of Lake Huron. The north shore of Lake Erie, referred to today as the Carolinian Forest Zone, was vacant and known as the Iroquoian beaver-hunting grounds, land that the British coveted for settlement. By the 1790s, when Lieutenant-Governor Simcoe was charged with bringing white settlers to what was known by then as Upper Canada, the area had been taken over by the Mississauga from north of Lake Ontario.[1]

The early settlers, many of whom were United Empire Loyalists, took up lots along the lakeshore as the lake proved to be the major access to the outside world. Roads were slow to develop and those that did exist were little more than rough, single-track forest trails in the early days of development. Simcoe encouraged men who had served in the British forces to settle in Upper Canada, as he wished to ensure a large complement of able settlers trained in the art of war and loyal to the British Crown as members of the local militia units. Simcoe did not trust the Americans, and as the War of 1812–14 demonstrated, his fears were well-founded. An enlisted man received one hundred acres of undeveloped, forested land for free, whereas captains, like Samuel Ryerse, founder of Port Ryerse, or his brother Joseph Ryerson, were granted twelve hundred acres each.

To keep his grant of land, a settler was required to clear a given amount annually, thus to many, the forest and its tree cover were considered the enemy. In many cases trees were cut and piled up to be burned, just to get rid of them. For those trees cut into logs, methods of sawing them into lumber were slow and primitive. Many were squared into beams using a broad axe, however, too many more were burned or left to rot.

As early as June 7, 1797, an official document reported to the admiralty that white pine with a diameter of 3 feet and a height of up to 175 feet existed, pine that was ideal for masting British ships. In Walsingham Township, Norfolk County, alone, 124 lots were listed with pine suitable for masting and 22 lots with oak suitable for use by the Royal Navy. This report is in the handwriting of Land Surveyor Thomas Welch of Vittoria, and titled "Report of Masting and Other Timber Fit for the Use of the Royal Navy, in the Township of Walsingham."[2] Subsequent pages in the document list suitable pine and oak in Charlotteville and Rainham townships. The best of these stands were marked, or blazed, with the King's Mark. Once marked, no logger dared cut this timber reserved for the exclusive use of British fighting ships.

In the mid-1830s, William Pope,[3] an English immigrant wildlife artist who lived in the area, commented on the miles of dark, gloomy forest as seen from the lake while sailing from Buffalo westward to Kettle Creek (Port Stanley). He also commented on the poor state of the few roads in the country as well as the fact it was almost impossible to move through much of the heavily forested country, when hunting with his fowling piece, because of the tremendous number of deadfalls blocking a person's progress. Few inroads had as yet been made into the interior forested areas of southern Ontario.

Many sawmills were being built along the streams and rivers using waterwheels as their source of power. Most of these were smaller operations, however. With the advent of the steam engine, the mill owner was no longer dependent on a good flow of water and had unlimited choice for the ideal location of his mill. By 1851, there were thirty-eight sawmills in Bayham Township, Elgin County, alone, producing 25,570,000 board feet of sawed lumber.

Slowly changes were taking place. The schooner traffic was increasing on the lakes, aided by the building, in 1825, of the Erie Canal from Buffalo to the Hudson River and some ten years later the building, in 1836, of the Welland Canal. With the opening up of our waterways came the improvement of navigational aids and harbour facilities generally. Better loading and unloading methods were being devised to handle the growing surplus of logs, lumber, shingle blocks, stave bolts, livestock, and grain being produced for shipment by a burgeoning population. The Erie Canal provided a new market and route for southwestern Ontario pine to the eastern seaboard of the United States. The Welland Canal, in turn, provided a route through Lake Ontario and the St. Lawrence River to Quebec City, and the export of timber to Great Britain.

It was about this time that a Scottish deep-sea clipper-ship captain, who had commanded his own ship on the seven seas, retired in Port Dover, Norfolk County, on Lake Erie. His name was Captain Alexander McNeilledge. Excerpts from his diary give the reader a unique insight into the lumber industry on Lake Erie as it existed at that time. Some entries from 1845 to 1867 follow:

Winter, 1845 — Number of teams drawing timber on the plank road for the [construction of] Harbour and timber to ship off [to Buffalo etc.]

Spring, 1845 — Steam boat "Kent" came in [to Port Dover] to tow Mr. Cummings timber rafts down to the Grand River to go to Quebec. (via the Feeder canal.) Number of vessels in, one timber Brig layd up.

Spring, 1845 — the vessels went out this morning bound up to [B]ear Creek for timber … The Schooner "Linnie Powell", Capt. McMannis, left for St. Catherines to get fix'd for Carring timber … Schr. "Cleopatra" from Buffalo in sight, got foggy, — ringing the town bell to guid her in.

May 25th, 1845 — I send a little parcel and letter to Captain Zealand, of Hamilton, his Schr. The "Union" being ready to sail from here for Liverpool, [England]. Cargo Staves and oak timber being the first vessel direct from this Port.

Sunday, August 7th, 1859 — Took dinner on board the Brig "Ocean" with Captain Garie … they have two horses on board being a lumber or timber vessel owned by Mr. Waters [of Port Dover]. [The horses would be used for working the capstan etc. in loading and unloading the timber.]

Monday, August 8th, 1859 — Brig "Ocean" loading square timber for Kingston.

September 22nd, 1860 — Brig "Ocean," Canadian, capsized in a gale off Rondeau, with a cargo of lumber. A total loss. Crew formed a raft and after 36 hours were picked up.

August 14th, 1863 — Captain Guskin of Bark "Mary Jane" up from Kingston loading timber at [Port] Ryerse & finish loading here for Kingston. I intend taking trip in her.

August 6th, 1866 — Mr. Lees gone to Chatham, the "Mary Jane" being thare loading timber for Tenawanda. Vessels loading barley, 58 cents/bus., for Buffalo. Square timber coming in.

January 26, 1867 — Good many Sleighs knocking round large square timber, Staves & Shingle blocks …

February 17th, 1867 — Many sleighs, large sticks of timber & Spars & Staves coming in.

April, 1867 — "Mary Jane" at anchor off the pear [pier] takeing (sic) in timber, rather rough.[4]

Among the many experienced sawyers coming into the Norfolk sand plain at this time was Collin LaFortune, who settled in the Big Creek valley of Walsingham Township in 1836. During his first winter he helped cut four hundred masts from pine each 4 feet or more in diameter. These were hauled to Big Creek by oxen and floated to the Inner Bay of Long Point for assembly into rafts, to be towed to Buffalo for export.

In 1845 LaFortune reported helping cut one of the longest masts on record from near Walsingham Centre. The tree was perfectly straight and produced a mast 110 feet long without a knot, limb, or blemish of any kind. The largest pine LaFortune ever cut was from the same area and was 7 feet in diameter and 90 feet to the first limb. Because of a small, 3-inch hollow at the top of it, it was declared unsuitable for a mast and cut into logs for shipment to Buffalo. It was declared that in the whole of both Upper and Lower Canada there was no white pine of better size or quality than that to be found in the valleys of Big and Venison creeks in the Long Point Country.

Exports of sawed lumber from Port Burwell in 1846 were about 3 million board feet, and in three short years exports had increased to 8,424,154 board feet. Demand for imports was increasing dramatically as pioneer families became more affluent.

The white pine shown here is typical of that found on the Long Point Country sand plain.

Courtesy of the Ontario Ministry of Natural Resources, E.J. Zavitz Collection.

Shipping firms prospered with their schooners carrying valuable cargo both in and out of the country.

The demand for logs and wood products was generally on the increase and methods of harvest and skidding were improving to the point where Canadian virgin stands of timber began to disappear at an alarming rate. Typical of this change were the actions of two young American fur traders for the North West Company, named Farmer and DeBlaquierre, who came into Canada from Buffalo to assess the potential for trade in furs in the Long Point Country. As they travelled the virgin wilderness they realized the tremendous potential for profit in the burgeoning lumber business.

In 1847, they returned to Woodstock in Upper Canada and began buying up lots, primarily in Walsingham Township, with heavy stands of virgin white pine. They soon had assembled some 20,000 acres of forested lands. They next mortgaged these properties to an American bank. In 1848, Farmer and DeBlaquierre used the proceeds from this transaction to build a large sawmill on Big Creek in the hamlet of Rowan Mills, on 6.5 acres purchased from William Franklin in Lot 7, Concession 1, of Walsingham Township. This steam-operated mill was capable of sawing 6 million board feet of prime lumber annually. The mill operated for nine years under the original owners until 1857 when DeBlaquierre sold it to Arnold Burrowe, a local mill operator.

Another prosperous operation was carried on at this time by the Laycock family, who had come originally from Buffalo to Cultus in Houghton Township, Norfolk County. To expedite the movement of logs from their forested properties they built a wooden-railed railway from Cultus to Big Creek. As the logs were cut they were drawn to their railroad and loaded on flatbed cars, to be drawn by horses to the bank of Big Creek. Here they were tipped into the water to be floated to the Inner Bay of Long Point, where they were made up into huge log booms and towed by steam tugs to Buffalo. A sawmill at Tonawanda, New York, was equipped to saw logs up to 80 feet in length.

It is of interest to note that by 1851, the newly established County of Norfolk had over six hundred people employed in sawmill operations and the County boasted three times as many sawmills per capita as the average number province-wide.

The West Family in Norfolk County

According to the 1861 Census, Thomas West, occupation sawyer, was living on Lot 23, Concession 14, in the Township of Walsingham, one mile west of the village of Lynedoch. He is known to have lived there prior to 1861. Born in 1817 in Glasgow, Scotland, Thomas, along with his wife, immigrated to Upper Canada where he lived to the ripe old age of ninety-eight. His wife, Margaret McGhaughey, born in 1827 in Paisley, Scotland, lived to be ninety-six years of age.[1]

The Wests emigrated from Scotland to Canada about 1843, and were known to be living in Dundas, Ontario, when their first child, John Ceburn West, was born on August 21, 1844. The young John worked in Dundas before the family moved to the Lynedoch area when he was in his early teens. Once settled there, Thomas took up employment in the lumber business. Here, they raised a family of five more boys and two girls. The youngest, Isobelle, died as a young girl.

John West, a bright and industrious lad, was soon accompanying his father to work in the woods or in the local sawmills. Their chief employer was John Charlton, a prominent lumberman of Lynedoch. John had a mechanical turn of mind and though he obtained little more than a basic formal education, he was intrigued by the steam engines that powered many of the sawmills working in the area. For a time he had worked for McKechnie and Bertram, machine toolmakers in Dundas, an experience that had sparked an early interest in machinery.

By the time he was twenty-one, West had a thorough understanding of the lumber business, having been a part of it all, from felling the trees and transporting them to the mill, to all the operations required in the mill to produce quality lumber in its many forms for the markets of the day. He is known to have worked in a sawmill near Langton in Walsingham Township, as well as many other sawmill employers in the area. However, he was not content.

John West had grown to be a big, well-proportioned man with a kind and humorous disposition. He was self-educated, ambitious, adventurous, very practical, and very well-liked by his fellow associates. He liked a good story and was himself an accomplished raconteur. But, above all, he had an uncanny ability to make anything mechanical and he loved anything powered by steam. With the advent of the railways with their powerful steam locomotives opening up the country, steam power was just coming into its own. Steam-powered freighters were also rapidly replacing the schooners and sailing vessels on the lakes and the high seas. And now mobile sawmills, powered by steam, were making the harvest of more remote forested areas more practical.

Around 1865, John West went to Simcoe where he was employed by the firm of John and George Jackson, prominent building contractors in the town. About this time he met Margaret Elliott who had recently emigrated from County Donegal in Ireland to join three older sisters now living in Norfolk County. John and Margaret were married on August 21, 1866, the date of his twenty-second birthday. West continued working for the Jacksons and gained a wide experience in methods of construction of all manner of buildings. He also expanded his contacts with tradesmen and suppliers to the building industry as the Jackson brothers gave him more and more responsibilities in their building projects. He remained in their employ for approximately ten years.

This photograph of John Ceburn West was taken circa 1875.
Courtesy of Clarence F. Coons, Mrs. Gordon Skinner Collection.

3

The West & Peachey
Partnership, 1878

While working for the Jacksons in Simcoe, John Ceburn West had been building a nest egg for himself with the intention of establishing his own business. The many sawmills in the county were busy and this meant steady work for foundries and others involved in the installation and maintenance of their equipment. With the land rapidly being cleared of its forest cover, farming was coming to the fore, and the demand for farm equipment and its maintenance was providing meaningful jobs for those with a mechanical bent. To West, the economic climate seemed favourable. On January 8, 1878, he leased the Simcoe Iron Works, a small, old foundry located on the northwest corner of Colborne and Young streets in Simcoe, and owned by Silas Montross and Donald Fisher of Fisher's Glen on Lake Erie.

Within a few weeks West formed a partnership with James Peachey, a young man with a machinist's background who had recently arrived from Brantford, Ontario. This alliance proved most successful and was destined to last for the next forty years, terminated only by the death of the senior partner. It was said that in all that time these two friends never exchanged a harsh word, nor did they have any major differences of opinion during their long business career together.

James Peachey was born in Hamilton, Ontario, on May 29, 1856, the son of Abraham Peachey, a native of England. The Peachey family moved to Brantford, Ontario, in 1860 when James was still a child. When he was seventeen years old, James Peachey was apprenticed to Charles H. Waterous. His firm, which later became the Waterous Engine Works of Brantford, would become one of Canada's leading producers of industrial and farm steam engines, as well as a leader in the production of sawmill equipment.[1]

Having successfully completed his four-year apprenticeship, James Peachey moved to Simcoe in 1877, where he met and became friends with John West. Less than a year later he joined with West to establish

A photograph of James Peachey, John West's partner, believed to have been taken circa 1882.

Courtesy of Norfolk Historical Society, File 14, Neg. 6-7.

the firm of West & Peachey, an enterprise that prospered from the very beginning. On May 26, 1881, James Peachey married Annie Weeks in Brantford, and in due course they had a family of seven children. James Peachey was an energetic, quiet-spoken, community-minded person who, like West, became one of Simcoe's most respected citizens, a man who was extremely dedicated in everything he did.

From early advertisements, it can be noted that the firm of West & Peachey was prepared to execute all orders in machine-work castings, turnings, and related repair and the like. They also offered to build many agricultural tools and implements and supply parts for such implements. Among those tools and implements offered were hand and power straw cutters, cultivators, field rollers, corn huskers, power and hand corn shellers, ploughs, and plough castings. In addition, they offered to build pumps and tuyere (a constriction in the spout to increase the water pressure) pump spouts, iron piping, saw clamps, box and coal stoves, iron fencing, and cresting. The firm proudly advertised that they had exclusive Canadian rights to the use of the celebrated diamond iron, a new iron-making process that produced a more durable product, resistant to wear, which they used in the production of quality plough points and in the building of metal shoes for bobsleighs and cutters.

Peachey's association with Charles Waterous was no doubt instrumental in their firm becoming agents for the Waterous Engine Works in Brantford, enabling them to sell the popular, portable Fireproof Champion steam farm engine. The arrangement was a coup for their budding company, as this portable steam engine was first put on the market by Waterous in 1877. That same year Waterous had received two first prizes at the provincial exhibition for this product, which was rated by experts at that time as the best overall portable steam engine. The engine could boast of having the best spark arrester on the market, a big selling point, and also of having the best boiler. The Waterous Champion Engine came in two models. The 12-horsepower engine proved the most popular; the

One of the portable steam Waterous engines, shown here mounted on a wheeled, horse-drawn carriage, is being used to thresh wheat.
Courtesy of Archival Collections, University of Guelph Library.

firm offered it for sale at $850. This price was soon lowered to $750, which was the price that was advertised by West & Peachey. The second model was a Champion 10-horse-power engine selling at $725. The commission for each sale on either model was $50.

Within a year of its founding, their business had grown to the point that they had outgrown their limited facilities. Donald Fisher had also indicated he wished to terminate the lease and so they were forced to seek new accommodations. By December 23, 1878, the partners had purchased a large lot, bounded to the north by the Lynn River, on the northwest corner of Norfolk and Union streets for $400. (Today, the site accommodates Simcoe's Federal Post Office and Customs facilities and a popular lawn bowling green.) By February 1879, Donald Fisher had resumed possession of his foundry and machine shop.

The next few months were busy ones for the partners as they prepared their new site and studied plans and made drawings for the construction of a modern factory to contain an efficient foundry, machine shop, carpentry shop, and design facility. On June 21, 1879, they were successful in obtaining a loan for $1,565 to finance construction from the Royal Loan & Savings Company of Simcoe.[2]

In 1880, the first large order for machinery to be manufactured in the new factory was received. The order was for a number of Montross anti-friction car-axle boxes for the Chicago Street Railroad. The inventor, Levi H. Montross, supervised the work, all of which was carried out in the new West & Peachey shop. Influenced by this success and by their sales of the Waterous steam portable engines, the partners were also gearing up to manufacture their own brand of steam engines and boilers on site.

In August of 1881, a further major improvement was made with the installation of a large, very powerful steam engine to power all the machinery of their shop. The following year, 1882, saw another significant first for the firm when they constructed a steam-traction engine for Findlay Butler, a local threshing-machine operator, who moved from farm to farm with a mobile grain separator. Prior to this, it would likely have been powered by a Watrous portable steam engine. This was one of the first such engines ever built in Canada. The machine was thoroughly tested on the nearby farm of John Jackson, West's former employer. Here it demonstrated the superb engineering and skilled workmanship of the firm by working flawlessly in threshing Jackson's wheat crop at the remarkable rate (for the period) of 90 bushels per hour.

In order to improve and extend their shop facilities, including the addition of $3,000 worth of improved machinery, the partners applied to the Simcoe town fathers in March 1882 for a loan of $6,000 over a ten-year period, at 6 percent. The committee of investigation,

The West & Peachey foundry and factory was located on the corner of Union and Norfolk streets in Simcoe. Photo by the Moore Studio of Simcoe, circa 1945.

Courtesy of the Eva Brook Donly Museum, Norfolk Historical Society Archives, #6-3.

finding the firm's net worth to be $8,000, produced a vote by council in favour of the loan. In accordance with town policy, a bylaw was proposed and voted on by the property owners of the town in May of that year. The result was a considerable majority in favour of the loan, and led to a mortgage for the requested amount being drawn, dated November 28, 1882. The loan allowed the improvements to go forward, including the purchase of a new universal radial drill and a punch and shear from the firm of McKechnie and Bertram of Dundas. West & Peachey was now well equipped to manufacture boilers and steam engines. In the spring of 1883, they produced a 60-horsepower boiler and a 50-horsepower steam engine for Messrs. Dease and Stearnes of Essex, Ontario. At the time this equipment was touted as the largest ever manufactured in this country.

Fire Causes Setback for the Firm

Their initial successes and the rosy future that seemed assured for the progressive firm of West & Peachey received a staggering setback on October 18, 1883, when fire heavily damaged the west end of the factory. By the time flames were seen licking the eaves and roof, considerable damage had been done to the wooden buildings. Thanks to the valiant efforts of the town's firemen, assisted by many local citizens, they were successful in saving the moulding shop and the east end of the building. The steam engine, boiler, and most of their valuable machinery were also spared from the flames.

The fire, thought to have originated from an overheated stove in the pattern-maker's room, caused a loss to the firm estimated at $9,000. All but $3,000 of this total was covered by the firm's insurance policies. The townspeople of Simcoe were both pleased and relieved to learn that the firm of West & Peachey had survived the catastrophe and were quickly making interim repairs. Within two weeks the cheery blast of the firm's steam whistle was calling employees to another busy day in the factory. What remained of the buildings were winterized to allow production to continue for the winter months. Meanwhile, the partners set to work designing a fireproof brick building with cement floors to be built the following spring.

THE WEST-MONTROSS METAL SHINGLE

Prior to the fire the partners had been working with Levi H. Montross to design and patent a metal shingle. The patent for the West-Montross metal shingle was granted on February 18, 1884, the first patented invention that West & Peachey had a share in. The company, along with Montross, established a separate firm to be known as the "West, Peachey and Montross Metallic Shingle Manufacturers."[3]

Although metal shingles were being made in the United States, theirs was the only firm in Canada manufacturing this type of shingle with srengthening ribs. The shingles were formed on a steam-operated press, with a star or a maple leaf incorporated into the centre of each that gave the square shingle an attractive, ornamental appearance. The shingles were joined together on installation by a built-in interlocking joint. The two main advantages of the metal shingles over cedar ones were their durability and the protection they gave against fire.

Once installed, the metal shingles readily conformed to the shape of the roof, were securely fastened by six barbed-wire nails, and required no repairs. Being dipped in a composition of linseed oil and iron-class paint during the production process protected them from rust. They only required repainting every six to eight years, and their original cost was little more than that of wooden shingles. Soon many homes in Simcoe were clad in the West-Montross metal shingles, and orders were being received from Nova Scotia in the east to Manitoba in the west, and as far south as Columbus, Ohio. Despite their obvious popularity, West & Peachey dissolved their partnership with Levi Montross on January 24, 1885 — barely a year after the patent was granted.

LEAN YEARS AND A NEW DIRECTION

An addition to the foundry in the fall of 1885 put West & Peachey in an ideal position to resume construction of steam engines, boilers, and a wide range of sawmill equipment. Early 1887 saw the manufacture of two steam engines. The first was built for James Marr of Port Royal, a hamlet on Big Creek, west of Port Rowan in Norfolk County. The second was built for the Simcoe carriage makers Challen and Clowes.

At a town council meeting on March 7 of that year, a financial statement was presented regarding the firm of West & Peachey and showing assets of over $2,400 and liabilities of $500. It was obvious that their assets had declined significantly since they obtained the 1882 loan from the town. With the decrease in activity at their plant, the partners built and operated a small steam-powered excursion boat on the Lynn River and nearby Crystal Lake, intended for the enjoyment of the townsfolk. The boat, launched in 1886, was named the *Little Gem*.

At the completion of the summer excursion season in 1887, the *Little Gem* was booked for a trip to Toronto. On September 9, John West transported the vessel to Port Ryerse by team and wagon and launched her in Lake Erie. That same afternoon, despite a heavy sea, she made the 4.5-mile run to Port Dover in twenty minutes. The next day with seven passengers aboard, she left for the Welland Canal and the final destination of Toronto. However, the spring of 1888 saw the end of their excursion business when West & Peachey sold *Little Gem* to the local bank manager, Henry H. Groff, who housed the boat in Turkey Point.

Meanwhile business had begun to improve with an order from the Delhi Canning Factory in Delhi, Ontario, for the largest boiler ever manufactured in Norfolk County. It was installed in June 1888. In the fall of the same year, a contract to build a steam-powered pleasure yacht for use on Lake Erie was signed, but it would appear that the yacht was never built. She was to have had a beam of 9 feet and an overall length of 45 feet and be named the *Queen of Simcoe*. In December 1888, the firm built and installed a new railway turntable for the South Norfolk Railway in Port Rowan, followed by a second turntable, which they installed in Simcoe.

In October of that year, John West's eldest son Simon John "Jack" left home to take a position with the Merchants Bank of Kitchener, and a promising young employee by the name of John Stalker joined the firm. This young man was destined to become the son-in-law of John West. Stalker married West's eldest daughter Mary Jane in 1893.

4

The Lumber Trade
in Norfolk Moves On

By 1880 the majority of the big stands of virgin pine had been harvested from the sand plains of Norfolk and the rest of the Long Point Country. The lumbermen and their families were forced to move on to often more remote areas in search of forested lands to harvest. Some turned to other parts of Ontario and Quebec where the pine-timber industry was being carried out on a much greater scale. Many others found opportunity in the forests of Michigan and beyond.

The Ottawa River watershed, which drained almost 60,000 square miles, was by far the largest area supporting white-pine timberlands in Ontario. Other areas where extensive stands of virgin pine were to be found included the Trent watershed, the Muskokas, areas around Georgian Bay, the Nipissing district, and the Rainy Lake and Lake of the Woods districts. In Quebec, in addition to their share of the Ottawa River watershed, large stands of virgin pine were to be found in the St. Maurice and Saguenay watersheds, the Lake St. John district, the north shore of the St. Lawrence from the Saguenay River to the Bersimis, and on the south shore in the Gaspé district.

By the late 1880s, the more easily harvested timber along the main water routes had been removed. Lumbermen had to work in more remote, inland areas of rough and rocky terrain, where drainage was through myriad small lakes and connecting streams and creeks. The familiar spring river drives of thousands of logs at a time were a thing of the past. Removal of logs became much more difficult, time-consuming, and expensive.

CADGE CRIB WARPING

Where pine logs had to be moved for miles, through a series of lakes and small streams, before reaching the river that would carry them to the mill, the lumbermen resorted to a method called warping. It was first necessary to build a cadge crib or warping crib. This crib was simply a raft of preferably dry, red-pine logs that were light and floated high in the water. The raft or crib, usually 40 to 50 feet square, was constructed in late winter on the shore of the lake where the logs were to be moved. A wooden capstan was next anchored to the crib and supplied with 300 to 600 feet of 2-inch manila rope. To one end was attached a heavy warping anchor.

Other floating cribs were also built to accommodate a bunkhouse for the men doing the warping, and a cookhouse where the cook on the drive could store supplies, cook, and feed the men. When the ice went out of the lake, the logs to be moved to the sawmill were assembled in a bag boom, the name applied to a mass of loose logs enclosed in a loop, or "bag," of logs chained end to end, for the purpose of towing. The ends were then brought together to enclose the remaining loose logs to be moved, and the resultant boom of logs was attached to the warping crib by a cable or chain.

A small rowboat was required to begin moving the boom. The warping anchor would be rowed out to the full 300-foot length of the manila rope to which the anchor was attached. The anchor was then dropped and the men on the crib began pushing on the bars of the capstan. As they travelled round and round the capstan, or headworks as it was called, the crib and boom were slowly drawn to the warping anchor, imbedded in the lake bottom. As the rope came aboard the crib and was coiled down, the boom was moved slowly down the lake. This procedure was repeated, as many times as required, to move the boom of logs to the opposite end of the lake being traversed.

These three men strain to operate the capstan — or headworks — on a cadge crib to move a boom of logs to a waiting sawmill. Photo circa 1891.
Courtesy of the Clarence F. Coons Collection.

The crew of a cadge crib pose for the photographer before embarking on the crib for a long day of hard work.

Courtesy of Archives of Ontario, #S 16199.

George S. Thompson, a logging superintendent for several years in the Trent watershed, provided a first-hand account of what warping a log boom was really like:

> Often I have seen a crew of forty or fifty men warping, as it is called, for days at a time, sometimes for thirty or forty consecutive hours at a stretch. This ceaseless pushing on the hand bars of a capstan, it is worse than a treadmill in a jail, the constant going round for so long a time often made men sick. To hold or coil "slacks" as the rope came in was another job even worse, for one's hands most of the time, if not freezing, would be terribly sore.[1]

When horses were used for warping, the capstan was modified and the rope lengthened to about 600 feet. This also meant that stabling for the horses had to be provided on the crib. Fewer men, from sixteen to eighteen rather than thirty or more, were needed when horses were used. Horse capstans and warping anchors were manufactured commercially by the William K. Hamilton Manufacturing Company Limited in Peterborough, Ontario.

This method of moving logs was both slow and expensive and required a workforce of many men. A further hazard was the wind, which, if in the wrong direction, could either blow the crib and boom ashore or in the opposite direction. The warping crib could not be moved from one lake to the next unless connected by a stream large enough to float the crib and its boom of logs. The alternative was to have several warping cribs to move the logs through a series of lakes. In smaller operations the cribs were disassembled and moved to the next lake, where they were reassembled.

A horse capstan, operating on the Pickerel River, is shown "at rest" as the horse and men take a breather. The man on the left coils down the manila rope as it comes off the capstan. The outboard end is attached to the anchor set ahead of the crib.
Courtesy of George E. Knight.

Once the logs had been moved through a series of lakes, rivers, rapids, and waterfalls, a crew of agile men were required to break up log jams and "sweep" shorelines for escaped logs. This called for a light, rugged, shallow-draught rowing boat. But until the 1850s no satisfactory boat could be found to perform the job to everyone's satisfaction. It is the prominent timber baron of the Ottawa area, J.R. Booth, who is credited with finding the man who designed and built the pointer boat, a boat well adapted to this very specific job.

John Cockburn, an Englishman who came to Canada to do the carvings in the woodwork of the first Parliament buildings, was a recent immigrant to the Ottawa

Marjorie Clarke, Harry Barrett's mother, Clara Gorrie, and Dorothy Clarke enjoy a canoe ride on Head Lake, while, in the background, an Alligator tug feeds logs to Haliburton's Malloy & Bryans sawmill. Photo circa 1915. The mill burned in 1919.
Courtesy of Harry B. Barrett.

Valley. He also had outstanding boat-building skills. Booth persuaded Cockburn to design a boat that met the needs of the men engaged in the log drives, gathering stray logs, and forming the booms. As a result the now famous pointer boat was born. The first of these were built in Ottawa.[2]

Cockburn pointer-boat crews are working with a log boom in Algonquin Park.

Courtesy of Bud Doering.

Cockburn's design met with instant success and soon he was building some two hundred boats a year in his shop he had established in Pembroke, on the Ottawa River. These were built of heavy pine to withstand the rough usage, with an upswept bow, and stern that allowed them to be pivoted with one tug of an oar. The largest were up to 50 feet in length, yet drew only a few inches of water and weighed more than half a ton. They ranged in size down to less than 15 feet in length. Pointer boats were still being built by John Cockburn's grandson as late as 1968. For over a century this versatile craft had made the life of the riverman a little easier on the Ottawa and its tributaries. The pointer boats were immortalized in 1916 by Tom Thomson in his striking canvas, entitled *Batteaux*, which he painted on Grand Lake, on the east side of Algonquin Park.

Dave Lemkay[3] has fond memories of seeking relief from summer heat at lunchtime in the cool, windowless, old Cockburn boat shop, with its plank floor, specialized tools, and the tantalizing fresh aromas of pine and cedar shavings and oakum. Here, too, he could relax and reminisce with Jack Cockburn, third-generation boat builder, about the great log drives on the Ottawa River watershed and the crucial part played by the pointer boats of Pembroke[4] and the men who worked them. These were tough, agile men, many of them Irish immigrants who moved into the forest camps in the fall to harvest the timber. Many came from subsistence farms to work through the winter and early spring and then return to their farms. Some brought their horses with them. Others worked as lumberjacks year round in the forests, on river drives, and in the sawmills.

There was an urgent need, however, for an improved and economical method of moving logs from the remote timber limits now being harvested. A conventional steamboat could be used, but to place one on every lake where logging was taking place was too costly and the construction of railways for the purpose was out of the question.

A logging crew operate a cadge crib, with a horse-powered headworks, anchor, and manila anchor rope, as they enter a lock on the Trent Canal at Buckhorn. Note the shelter for the horses and the second crib for cooking and sleeping accommodations.

Courtesy of Library and Archives Canada, C-27216.

5 Joseph Jackson and the Warping Tug

A formal photograph of Joseph Jackson (1831-1908), date not identified.

Courtesy of Library and Archives Canada, PA-33816.

Joseph Jackson was a native of Norfolk County, having been born in Houghton Township in 1831. By the age of thirty he was very much involved in lumbering operations in the county, an involvement that continued until 1880 when the sources of good pine timber were so depleted that it was no longer profitable for Jackson to operate there. Like many others he followed the big pine across the border into Michigan, or northward, where he continued his timber operations for a few more years.[1]

In the 1882 federal election, Joseph Jackson ran as the Liberal candidate for South Norfolk and was successful. His political career was short-lived, however, as he lost his seat in the 1887 election and turned his energies back to his interests in lumbering. That same year, he purchased the Canadian timber holdings of William F. Whitney of Bay City, Michigan. These timber limits, covering over 41 square miles, cost Jackson $130,000, and were located 60 miles inland from Georgian Bay in the south part of Patterson Township in Nipissing District in the area of Restoule Lake. Jackson wasted no time; in 1888 he harvested 3 million cubic feet of long timber in rough country.

His plan to move these logs to Georgian Bay via the French River proved much more difficult than he first thought, as the river was in essence a chain of many small lakes separated by numerous hazardous rapids. The log drive to Georgian Bay, where the timber would be rafted and towed to Tonawanda on the Niagara River, proved to be very time-consuming and expensive. Fortunately, there was a great demand for long timber in the New York market, but the experience was a very frustrating one.

On his return to Simcoe, Joseph Jackson turned to his friend John West for help. Explaining the difficulties he had experienced in his new logging enterprise, Jackson suggested to West that what was needed was a steam-powered warping tug that was not only capable of warping booms of logs through the many lakes, but also of moving overland readily from lake to lake to do it. West was immediately interested, and not only agreed to design such a craft, but promised to have it ready for operation on the Jackson timber limits by spring, in time for the 1889 season.

John West first made a trip to the Mississippi River in the United States to study the use of steamboats in rafting barges and all manner of produce up and down the river. He returned with his head full of ideas for solving his client's problem, and set to work in his drafting room in the attic of the West & Peachey foundry. With his firm already having built equipment for steam-powered boats, he had some expertise already in place. Although there is little in the way of records to mark their progress, it is known that in the winter of 1888–89, John West, James Peachey, and their chief engineer, Jonathan Awde, formerly of Cumberland, England, along with a small staff, designed and built their first steam warping tug.[2]

Already experienced in building boilers and steam engines, they had only to adapt the size of this machinery to the accommodation available in the scow, or tug. This was perhaps the least of their worries when one considers the many other technical and mechanical problems that had to be dealt with before a successful spring launch of the new vessel could be made. Since space was limited in the factory, the tug was assembled in the yard to the rear of the buildings in the late winter and early spring. The March 27, 1889, issue of Norfolk's newspaper, the *British Canadian*, announced: "Messrs West and Peachey have on the stocks a rather novel steam tug, which they are making for Joseph Jackson, Esq. For use in the lumber woods. It will be completed in about ten days."

Early reports of this novel West & Peachey tug referred to it as an amphibious craft, when it first appeared and crawled over the portages. Even before it left Simcoe for the north woods, it was being referred to as an "Alligator." With this descriptive name being deemed so suitable, the name Alligator was applied to all that followed. The success of the first warping tug set the trend for the many more that were to be built by West & Peachey.

The hull of the tug was 32 feet long and 4 feet deep with a beam of 10 feet. The tug was scow-shaped with the bottom formed from 3-inch white-oak planking.[3] A steel boiler plate protected part of the bottom of the craft and all of the bow. The chines, the reinforced sections where the sides of the vessel are joined to the bottom of the boat, were also protected by boiler plate. On the flat underside of the tug, two white-oak runners, 6 inches by 8 inches, were secured, being 6 feet apart. They were shod with iron. The sides of the hull were built up using 2-inch by 6-inch white-pine plank laid flat in white lead as a sealer. At intervals of 12 inches, bolts were run through these pine planks from top to bottom and then tightened securely.

This sturdy scow was propelled by a 20-horsepower steam engine that drove the two side-paddlewheels. This same engine also operated a heavy winch, geared 6 to 1, which translated to a pull or strain on the cable of 100-horsepower. The Clyde[4] marine-design boiler was hung horizontally on a pivot or axle in the centre. A screw arrangement on the front of the boiler enabled the fireman to tip the boiler forward or backward, so that it would always remain level as the tug was winched up and down hillsides. The boiler, if kept supplied with three-quarters of a standard cord of 4-foot wood, could supply enough steam to warp for 10 hours.

On Thursday, April 4, 1889, as black smoke rose from the stack of the tug in the factory yard, the first Alligator tug sat ready for launch. The mayor of Simcoe had declared that the occasion warranted a school holiday and an expectant horde of school children lined the riverbank. A large crowd of local citizens had joined them as the final preparations were being made. Rollers were placed under the runners of the Alligator tug, and as the cable, anchored to a tree on the opposite stream bank, tightened on the revolving winch, she moved majestically across the yard and splashed into the waters of Crystal Lake, (now Lake George) to the cheers of the onlookers. The next issue of the *British Canadian*, printed the next day, reported that: "the novel sight of the steamboat hunting for water attracted hundreds of people on Thursday, who witnessed the launch. It was a banner day for the West & Peachey firm, the people of Simcoe, and ultimately the lumber interests the Alligator was designed to serve."

The tug passed its tests as to operation of its machinery and manoeuvrability with flying colours. Joseph Jackson, proud owner of the first Alligator, was on hand on Saturday, April 13, 1889, as she winched herself out of Crystal Lake to move out onto Union Street and head west to the station of the Georgian Bay and Lake Erie Railway. Deadbolts had been previously buried at strategic locations along the route for this very purpose. Here, to the applause of the assembled spectators, the Alligator winched herself slowly up the street and into place on the bed of a waiting flatcar, to be secured for her long journey north. In reporting the event the *Norfolk Reformer*, on Friday, April 19, 1889, announced: "Mr. Jackson is greatly delighted with the success of his idea in tug building and anticipates that the unique craft will be of immense service to him in his woods handling round timber."

John West and Joseph Jackson accompanied the Alligator Warping Tug to North Bay where it was unloaded and steamed through the French and Restoule rivers to the

Jackson timber limits. Here they carried out rigorous tests of the tug's capabilities. Jackson was delighted with the Alligator's performance. He penned the following testimonial at a later date:

> The Alligator far exceeds my most sanguine expectations, it having transported itself over hills and hollows any and all distances between lakes or streams and is capable of surmounting almost any difficulty in its way and I have no hesitation in saying that the equal of these boats made by Messrs. West and Peachey for the purpose they are intended for is not on the globe today and I recommend them to one and all requiring such steam power.[5]

Joseph Jackson continued to operate a successful timber operation until 1892, when he returned to Simcoe, to be appointed sheriff of Norfolk County. In the meantime the Alligator Warping Tugs were about to revolutionize the inland logging industry. They would not only save time and labour for the lumber barons of Ontario and Quebec, but they would reduce costs of harvest and extend the areas that were economically available for the harvest of pine.

On September 11th, 1889, John West wrote the following description of his warping tug, Alligator #1:

> The invention is a warping tugboat which is arranged to propel itself overland from one lake to another by means of a steel wire cable or chain or rope anchored to a tree, rock or warping anchor. This hull may be constructed either round or square at the bow and stern, with a flat bottom having two runners or keels shod with iron. It has two rudders and two side paddle-

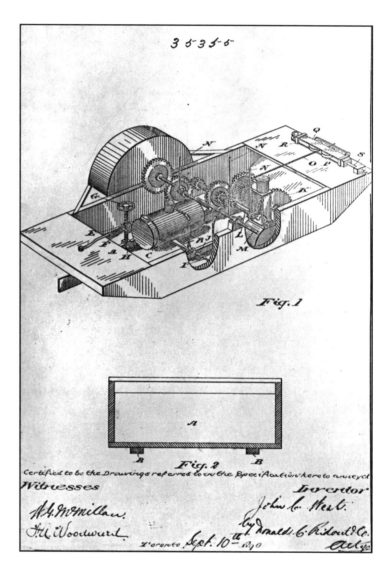

A detailed drawing by John West showing the placement of all machinery in the Alligator Warping Tug, which accompanied his application for patents submitted on September 10, 1890.

Courtesy of Eva Brook Donly Museum, Norfolk Historical Society Archives, West & Peachey Collection.

wheels which are hung on an A-frame and are raised or lowered by two screws. The boiler is hung on an axle and is kept level by a screw located at the front end of the boiler. The engine is double geared to a steel drum, 3 feet in diameter by 30 inches long, on which the cable winds when crossing portages or warping. The paddle-wheels are driven by a chain which is thrown in or out of gear at will.[6]

From this description it would appear that Alligator #1 differed in some respects from later warping tugs produced by the firm. West notes that the paddles are driven by a chain rather than by gears, as is shown in the official patent of September 10, 1890. Also the two side paddlewheels are hung in an A-frame and can be raised or lowered by two screws. (See Appendix B.)

It was soon obvious, after the completion of trials, that a strong market for the Alligator existed, and John West applied for patents for the warping tug. He obtained a Canadian patent in 1890, and in 1891 received American patents for the warping tug, as well. On November 29, 1890, John West sold a half interest in his new improved Alligator Steam Warping Tug patent for $1.00 to his partner James Peachey, making them joint owners of the patent.[7]

Optimistic estimates were made in 1894 that a thousand Alligators would be required to fill the demand for the warping tugs in inland lake areas. Although this estimate was too high, nevertheless the Alligator was soon to become a household word both in Simcoe and the vast pine forests of Ontario, Quebec, and beyond.

6

John West's Other Interests

Although John West was very much involved in the many projects being undertaken in their foundry and later in the birth of his unique invention — the amphibious Alligator Warping Tug — he always had time to assist with engineering problems that might be experienced in his hometown. Whenever problems of an engineering nature arose, John West would be the first to be consulted. He was always conscious of his civic duties and took a special interest in fire protection in the town. As a result, on March 7, 1887, John West was appointed engineer of the local fire brigade at a salary of $40 per annum.

In 1889, the town of Simcoe was in the market for a steam fire-engine. The committee of the town council had considered four different makes and had narrowed their choice down to buying either a single large Ronald Engine[1] or two smaller and less expensive Waterous engines from Brantford. The committee was leaning toward the Ronald Engine, which would provide significant initial savings in cost. The proponents of the Waterous Engine, at the council meeting of May 27, 1889, brought John West to a meeting to give his opinion of the relative merits of the two engines.

In addressing council, West demonstrated the difference between the pump valves of the Waterous and the Ronald engines. West favoured the Waterous engine, as its valves would not be affected by the sand that was present in the water in Simcoe's wells, whereas the valves of the Ronald Engine would be. He also saw as a serious defect, the fact that the Ronald Engine was often likely to stop on dead centre,[2] whereas the Waterous Engine would not. On the strength of West's testimony, council voted six to five in favour of purchasing two Waterous fire engines. They served the town well for many years.

About a year or so later the town fathers appointed a committee of William Burt, John Sutton, and F.A. Brown, all local citizens, to find a qualified head of the local fire department. They drew up terms of reference for such a position and recommended John West. On February 8, 1890, West agreed to their terms and was appointed engineer and caretaker, in other words, fire chief of Simcoe's fire brigade. His remuneration would be $250 per annum. His duties included periodic examination of all wells and cisterns, ensuring that all approaches to the river were maintained for the acquisition of water when needed for fire purposes, maintaining all equipment such as fire engines, hoses and reels, hooks and ladders, fire alarm, wagons, and other equipment. It was further noted that should any equipment fail to work due to negligence in its upkeep, West would be fined $25 for each such instance.[3]

Over the years the town sought and relied on the advice of John West regarding engineering or mechanical matters. It was always sound advice. John West also served as an alderman for many years. When the town installed water and sewer services in 1905, John West was chair of the committee overseeing the work. When the sewer system was installed, West was on the job an average of nine hours a day superintending the work with no thought of remuneration. It was acknowledged that he saved the town thousands of dollars through his foresight and practical understanding of engineering.

During West's long career he often suffered personal hardships and injury. Over and above the usual cuts and bruises experienced in the daily operations of the foundry, he suffered the occasional more serious accident. In October 1901, while operating the wheel of a hoisting machine, West's hand slipped, allowing the wheel to reverse. The handle struck him a stunning blow to the head, cutting his forehead badly. Fortunately, he was not seriously hurt. West usually travelled to and from work on a bicycle. While returning to work after lunch one August afternoon in 1905, West accidentally collided with another cyclist. He was thrown to the street and in the fall received severe cuts and bruises to his face. It was feared that he had suffered a concussion from the fall. This proved to be untrue, but he was confined to his home for a few days to recover from the experience.

An accident of a more serious nature occurred in April 1913, while West was supervising the moving of an Alligator tug from the assembly yard behind the factory. A chain, holding the taut, heavy wire cable used to move the tug, suddenly gave way. The cable spun out of control like a whip, striking West violently and knocking him down. As he fell, his head struck the door frame of the building nearby, causing severe lacerations to his ear and badly bruising his face. For a time he lay unconscious. Recovering, he later returned to work, but he was obviously badly shaken up. Many felt that West never fully recovered from that unfortunate accident.

The firm of West & Peachey was still very much involved with maintenance and repair of equipment in area sawmills and canning factories. John West obviously had an interest that went far beyond simple maintenance of equipment, for in March 1890 he received a patent for his application for "Improvements to Cannery Hoist." This consisted of an improved method of lifting containers, or retorts (also a John West innovation) of canned goods from a steam box, or cooker, by means of a travelling hoist that ran backward or forward on a track over the cooker. He explained its operation in the greatest of detail and detailed drawings accompanied the application.[4]

THE FISHING TUG *HAZARD*

In the spring of 1892, West & Peachey received an order from Edward Harris of London, Ontario, a member of the prestigious duck-hunting club known as The Long Point Company. Harris wanted machinery to operate a 65-foot fishing tug. The tug, a wooden vessel clad in spruce planking, with a beam of 11 feet, and drawing 6 feet of water, was built in Simcoe for the Company by Findlay Steinhoff. In June 1892, the tug, minus an engine, was loaded on a quartet of four-wheeled wagons and drawn to Port Dover by sixteen husky horses. Once there it was launched in Lake Erie.

After the tug was in the water, West & Peachey installed the steam engine they had built for it, and tested the vessel in trial runs on the lake. The tug handled well and the machinery worked superbly. Mayor Campbell of Simcoe had the honour of naming the tug, giving it his wife's maiden name of *Hazard.* Once in operation in the Lake Erie fishery, the *Hazard* was operated by Captain George Field.

A model of the tug was built at the time and given to the mayor's grandson. In recent years this model, on loan from Douglas Trafford of Vittoria, has been admired in the Port Dover Harbour Museum. It sold at auction on October 13, 2008, for $925.

JOHN WEST'S STEAM ROAD-MAKING SLEIGH

With the sudden popularity of the Alligator Warping Tug in harvesting the forest trees of both Ontario and Quebec, John West and James Peachey were becoming acquainted with most of the great timber barons of Canada. Soon both men were hearing of other problems in the logging industry that the proprietors of these mammoth logging firms were experiencing. One that was regularly broached to them was that of the creation of winter roads.

Each fall, timber crews went into the woods to harvest the pine. The trees were felled, cut into logs, and piled in skidways in the bush. In late December or January, when sufficient snow had accumulated to make sleighing possible, teams of horses, hitched to heavy bobsleighs piled high with pine logs, drew them out of the bush to the nearest lake or river. In preparation for moving these heavily loaded sleighs, the roads would be plowed out and the snow packed solidly on the roadbed. Next a large, wooden water tank mounted on a sleigh would be drawn over the road to water down the tracks. The water would freeze very quickly at that time of year, forming a slick running surface for the heavily loaded logging sleighs.

The water tanks had to be filled regularly from nearby lakes or streams, which often created problems for the road builders. These water-tanker sleighs were filled by using their team of horses to repeatedly pull a large, wooden barrel full of water out of a hole chopped in the lake ice and up a runway of two slanted poles. At the top, the barrel tipped, emptying its contents into the tanker sleigh. This had to be repeated one hundred times or more to obtain a full tank.

Always ready for a new challenge, John West's fertile imagination went to work. He envisaged a steam-operated sleigh that would make the water tank obsolete. At his drafting table he designed a steam road-making sleigh that would rapidly

The team of horses on right are pulling a barrel of water from a hole in the ice of a lake to fill the sleigh-mounted water tank. The water will then be used to ice the tote road. Photo taken in the Blind River area.
Courtesy of the Clarence F. Coons Collection.

clear a road through the accumulated snow, and at the same time leave a smooth, ice-hardened track behind it for the easy passage of log sleighs. In 1891 he built the first one. A vertical boiler was mounted securely on a sleigh equipped with hollow runners. A snowplow was attached to the front of his machine for clearing away surplus snow in the roadway. The steam from the boiler, in passing through the hollow runners, melted the snow. The front of the runner, being very hot from the live steam's point of entry, would melt the snow on contact. As the condensed steam passed out the rear of the

A sketch of the steam road-making sleigh in operation on a logging road.

L.A. Dool, artist. Courtesy of the Clarence F. Coons Collection.

runner it added moisture to the wet, compressed track, which rapidly froze to leave an ice-hardened track for sleighs that would follow.

In December 1891, West accompanied his first steam road-making sleigh to the woods for testing. No records of the results of these tests are to be found today. It satisfied West sufficiently for him to apply for a patent for what he described as: "An Improved Road Making Sleigh." The introduction to the detailed description and drawings that he supplied to the patent office read as follows and described its purpose: "A sleigh capable of rapidly clearing a road through snow, leaving behind it a smooth, hard track for the passage of other vehicles."[5]

On November 22, 1893, West was granted a patent for his novel invention. The machine was on the market for a few years, but it would appear that not many of them were sold. For those that did go into operation, they used too much steam in melting the snow and the majority of the logging roads proved to be too long to make the elaborate sleighs practical.

7 Evolution of the Alligator Warping Tug

The success of Jackson's Alligator, when at work, was soon noted, and in January 1890 West & Peachey received orders for two more Alligators. One was ordered by the Moore Lumber Company of Detroit (Alligator #2) for use in their limits on the French and Pickerel rivers in Ontario, The other was ordered by R.H. Klock and Company (Alligator #3) for use on Lake Kipawa and the Ottawa River in the province of Quebec. Both Alligators were shipped out to their new owners in March 1890. John West followed them a few days later to instruct those responsible for them on their operation.

The *H. Trudel*, Alligator #3, shown here tied to a dock, was built in 1890 for R.H. Klock & Co. of Klock's Mills. Note the pointer boat tied astern, the passenger steamer, and the steam engine sitting at the railroad terminal.

This became standard practice with each Alligator tug that West & Peachey built. The tugs were normally shipped to their destinations in early spring to arrive in time for the spring log drives. This allowed time for the firm to test them thoroughly in the Lynn River before shipment to their final destination. Then John West, James Peachey, or one of the senior members of the firm would follow the warping tug to its destination, where they would put it into service for the new owner. Obviously this attention to detail and the interest of the firm in seeing that their client had a sound working knowledge of the tugs capabilities and operation payed off. The following testimonials bear this out.

Alligator #2 — Did All That Was Claimed Of It.
No. 4 Buhl Block,
Detroit, Mich,.
January 7th, 1891.

Messrs. West & Peachey, Simcoe, Ont.

Gentlemen, —

In reply to your request for a testimonial as to the working of the steam warping tug you built for us, we have pleasure in saying that the tug has given entire satisfaction; that it has done all the work that you claimed it would do, and that it has saved us, at least, one half its cost the past season in men and time.

Yours truly,
MOORE LUMBER CO.,
A. H. Fleming, Sec.[1]

Alligator #3 — Has Given Entire Satisfaction
Klock's Mills, Ont.,
December 29th, 1890

Messrs West and Peachey, Simcoe, Ont.

Dear Sirs,

The steam warping tug which we purchased from you has given us entire satisfaction. It has, indeed, done all that is claimed for it; and we have much pleasure in recommending it to all parties doing business of this nature.

We remain,

Yours very truly,

R.H. Klock & Co.[2]

West & Peachey were soon making claims for the versatility of the Alligator Warping Tug to lumbermen and mill owners, as this statement implies:

> It will climb hills and go through swamps and woods or up small streams from one lake to another. After warping a boom of logs it will return with the empty boom doing the work cheaply and thoroughly with a great saving of time and number of men … It is also useful in taking in supplies to the lumber camps, or in towing scows bearing horses and provender.[3]

The Alligator also proved useful in breaking rollways of logs. Many mill owners found it to be most useful in their mill ponds, as well, for towing small booms of logs to the jack-ladder, which carried the logs up to the waiting saw carriage. The long, steel cable and winch on the tug was used also for skidding heavy timber out of the woods efficiently from shoreline locations.

West & Peachey also developed and manufactured a small, portable sawmill that could be operated on location anywhere by the versatile Alligator tug. In replacing the old cadge crib and its horses and sixteen to eighteen men, the Alligator only required four or five men for warping, namely: the captain or pilot, an engineer, an engineer's assistant, a fireman, and one or two deckhands or logmen.

The Canadian Lumberman and Woodworker, in its June 7, 1893, issue, noted that: "Messrs. Shepard, Morse and Company had the Alligator tug 'North River' on the Kippawa and the way this Alligator tug brought out a tow of logs astonished all old-time river men."

The Alligator #10, *North River*, was purchased by Shepard & Morse Lumber Company of Ottawa in 1893 and sold in 1898 to the McLachlin Bros. of Arnprior. She is shown frozen in for the winter on a lake in Algonquin Park, circa 1900.

Courtesy of Archives of Ontario, #S-5145.

WARPING WITH AN ALLIGATOR WARPING TUG

Woodsmen spent the winter months felling trees. Bucking crews cut them into logs and trimmed the branches and knots. Teamsters hooked skidding tongs into the logs and snaked them out of the bush to a yarding point, called a skidway. Beginning in January, while in the yard or skidway, scalers would use a log rule to scale or estimate the number of board feet in each log and record it on their tally-boards. They would also identify each log with the owner's mark, using a scaling hammer.

Skidders then positioned the logs for loaders, or cant-hook men, to load them onto sleighs. They and the "skyloader," who had to be an agile, sure-footed man, loaded and directed the logs onto sleighs. This was done with the help of a tall wooden crane called a "jammer," powered by the sleigh team of horses.

Edmund Zavitz's huge, wooden box camera captures a typical stand of white pine.

Courtesy of Ontario Ministry of Natural Resources, E.J. Zavitz Collection, #808.

Teamsters and their horses assemble outside the camp's "camboose shanty" in preparation for the day's work.

Courtesy of the Clarence F. Coons Collection.

A skidding crew loads a sleigh with logs for transport to water.

Courtesy of Library and Archives Canada, PA-12942.

A "Brag Load." Here, a bobsleigh load of almost ninety logs are secured with logging chains and are ready to be moved out. The men are unknown, but the team of horses bear the names "Kid" and "Farmer."

Courtesy of Haliburton Highlands Museum, #L 984-4-216.

The team pulled a cable attached by hooks, or "pig's feet" jammed into either end of the log to be loaded. Two men, known as "bull-ropers," guided the logs into position over the sleigh. The skyloader stood on top of the sleighload of logs to position them for safe travel. This was always a dangerous job. A fully loaded sleigh carried from 15 to 20 tons of logs piled high on the sturdy bunks of the sleigh bobs.

Once loaded and the logs made secure, the sleighs were drawn out by the team of horses, over the tote roads, to the nearest lake or riverbank to be piled on the shore or stream bank to await spring breakup. At times the logs were piled directly on the ice of the lake or river. Upon the breakup of the ice, those logs not already in a lake would be broken out of their winter piles on shore to be driven downstream to the nearest lake by the spring freshets.

As lake currents usually were not strong enough to move logs along, they were assembled in bag booms that consisted of a series of pine logs of sufficient length to enclose the number of logs to be moved, chained end to end. Once enclosed, the boom was closed and made ready for warping. At this point the Alligator tug, equipped with a powerful winch on the drum of which ½ to 1 mile of ⅝-inch steel cable was wound, was made ready. Two methods were used.

In one, the tug would engage her paddlewheels and steam down the lake in the direction the logs were to be moved. When a mile had been covered, the large warping anchor, attached to the steel cable wound on the drum, would be dropped to the bottom of the lake. If a shore-hold, in the form of

Evolution of the Alligator Warping Tug

a rock or tree, was available, the cable would be attached to it. The Alligator would then reverse her paddlewheels and back up to the boom, paying out the warping cable as she did so. On reaching the bag boom, the Alligator was securely hooked to it by chains. The paddlewheels were then disengaged and the drive for the winch from the engine put in gear. As the cable was wound onto the drum of the winch, the Alligator tug and her boom of logs were drawn to the warping anchor embedded in the lake bottom, or, to the shore-hold. The chains to the log boom were then unhooked, the paddlewheels put in gear, the warping anchor pulled aboard, and the whole process was repeated until the boom had been moved to the opposite end of the lake. Here the boom would be opened and the logs sent into the connecting stream, or flume, to the next lake. The Alligator would winch itself overland along the prepared portage into the next lake where the logs had been caught in a bag boom that awaited them. The whole process would be repeated in this way until the logs finally reached a main river, where they became part of a major log drive down river to the company's sawmill.

The Gilmour & Company's Alligator #18, *Nipissing*, is shown preparing to warp sawlogs held in the bag boom, circa 1895.

Courtesy of the Clarence F. Coons Collection.

This method of warping was also used where a bag boom of logs had to be rolled through a narrows, since fresh holds could be taken along the boom without disturbing the anchorage until the tug and the boom were winched up to it. Then the warping anchor would be raised and a fresh hold taken or another snub or shore-hold could be taken.

In the second method of warping, the bow of the Alligator was run up to the boom and the winch cable was fastened securely to it. The Alligator would then be reversed until the cable had all been paid out from the drum of the winch. The Alligator tug would then be chained to some suitable anchorage, such as a rock or tree on the bank.

The winch would then be engaged and the bag boom of logs would be winched down the lake to the stationary Alligator tug.

Using these methods an Alligator could move up to 60,000 logs in a single bag boom in calm weather. Even under adverse conditions, with a strong headwind, the Alligator could still move 30,000 logs in a boom. This was a big improvement over the old cadge-crib method, which normally could not operate under adverse wind conditions. This meant that between 2 and 3 million board feet of material could be warped by the Alligator in a single bag boom. This, in turn, amounted to a significant percentage of the total annual cut of many of the sawmills. The Alligator, under ideal conditions, with a full bag boom of 60,000 logs, travelled at a speed of about 1 mile per hour. With fewer logs or adverse weather conditions, the speed would vary up or down. With no tow, an Alligator could reach speeds of 5 to 6 miles per hour.

In 1891, West & Peachey built a Alligator Warping Tug, named the *Saginaw*, for J.W. Howry and Sons of Saginaw, Michigan. It was the fourth one built by the firm and was ordered for warping logs in timber limits being logged along the Whitefish River on the north shore of Georgian Bay. The following testimonial attests to the tugs merits and the satisfaction of its owners:

> Alligator #4
> Saginaw, E.S. Michigan
> November 16, 1891
>
> Messrs West and Peachey, Simcoe, Ontario
>
> Gentlemen,
>
> In reply to yours of recent date in which you ask for a testimonial in regard to the working of the steam warping tug — "Saginaw" which we purchased of your firm last spring we are pleased to say that after using the boat for one season and having thoroughly tested it, we find that it does all and more than you claim. It is certainly worthy of our most hearty recommendation and we shall be pleased to reply to any parties whom you may refer to us. — We, this year, handled 300,000 logs with the "Saginaw", and consider that she saved her cost to us in this one season's work. The above number of logs were moved with the assistance of eight men, in one half the time it took us the previous year to move 126,000 pieces with cadj crib and sixteen men. We took the boat out on land and around dams and riffles and went up grades where the rise was one foot in three. We find the

"Saginaw" very useful in breaking in high "rollways" and also in towing scows loaded with supplies, up the creeks.

Yours truly,
(Signed) J.W. Howry & Sons[4]

ALLIGATOR #5

The fifth Alligator Warping Tug to be built was ordered by the Saginaw Salt and Lumber Company, who were operating on the Wanapitei River in northern Ontario. As work progressed on it during the winter of 1891–92, several improvements and modifications were introduced into its construction. As changes were made, all were incorporated into the tugs that followed. On March 31, 1892, the fifth Alligator Warping Tug, this one named *Lorne*, was shipped by rail to a northern destination.

An interesting description of the West & Peachey foundry as it appeared to a casual visitor in the spring of 1892 is to be found in the March 23, 1892, edition of the *British Canadian*, a Norfolk County newspaper. Written by Captain John Spain of Port Dover who wrote under the *nom de plume* of the "Rambler," his account reports:

Alligators

Your rambling scribe called on Messrs. West and Peachey recently and found everybody; from the unassuming proprietors down to the apprentice boys, as busy as bees. Both flats, the yard and the street are strewn with disjointed parts of steam alligators or warping tugs. The second flat is used for the manufacture of pilot houses, steering gear, paddle wheels, boxes etc., which are nicely painted, then numbered and packed, with the name of each alligator marked on the boxes and cases containing the various parts. In the large machine shop you are bewildered with what is going on there in the shape of boring, drilling, trimming and polishing iron and steel.

The clanking sledge and clinking hammer talking with the ringing anvil to outvie the humming machinery, puts all other conversation out of the question, but your eyes can feast on huge wheels, steam boilers and bright engines. In the centre of the room is a templet or matrix, where the boilers and engines, together with their connections, are fitted exactly the same as if in the boat; they are then numbered, as above stated, knocked down and packed, ready for shipment. The hull of the boat is treated in the same way. Every bolt, spike or nail is got ready here, and each alligator is shipped in this knocked down style to its destination.

Then Mr. West, with a gang of men, will go and put them together and start them through lakes and over portages to do the work for which they are so well adapted. Messrs West and Peachey are going to complete one of these alligator boats, put life in it, and make it crawl to the station and creep up onto a flat car, notice of which will appear in the town papers …

ORDERS FOR MACHINERY ONLY

In 1892, West & Peachey received their first request, for the machinery only, for construction of an Alligator Warping Tug. The request came from the McLachlin Bros., who were Ottawa River lumbermen located in Arnprior, Ontario. They, and some others, preferred to buy the steam engine and machinery and then construct their own warping tug on site.

Alligator #6, the *Madawaska*, was the first order received by the West & Peachey foundry for machinery only. The hull was built in Arnprior in 1892, by McLachlin Bros. of Arnprior, Ontario. The Alligator tug is shown hauled up on bank of Ottawa River, circa 1900.
Courtesy of Archives of Ontario, #S 4854.

West & Peachey considered this first request, and as they did not feel that it violated their patents, they agreed to co-operate. The machinery was shipped to Arnprior, and the McLachlins built their own hull in which the machinery was installed. They next installed their own superstructure and named the resultant Alligator the *Madawaska*. She was Alligator #6.

As other such arrangements were requested, West & Peachey found they were at times supplying machinery only, while others would request all machinery plus the lumber and other materials for the buyer to assemble their own tug. If requested, West & Peachey would also supply the plans for construction and assembly of an Alligator tug. By 1897, they were offering all machinery for building an Alligator Warping Tug for $2,300.

The *Alligator*, paddlewheeler #13, built in 1893, is shown warping herself up Union Street in Simcoe en route to the Georgian Bay and Lake Erie Railway siding at Metcalfe Street to be shipped to Gilmour & Company in Trenton, Ontario. This is the oldest known surviving photograph of an Alligator taken in Simcoe.

Courtesy of Norfolk Historical Society Archives, West & Peachey Collection, L 11191.

During the Alligator's heyday, West & Peachey filled many contracts to supply machinery only. The chief buyers of machinery for tugs, in addition to the McLachlin Bros., were the Upper Ottawa Improvement Company of Ottawa, Ontario, and W.C. Edwards, also of Ottawa. Later on, during the production of twin-screw Alligators, West & Peachey would supply owners with the machinery to convert the tug with a paddle-wheel drive to a twin-screw drive.

One is left to wonder if the attempt by McLachlin Bros. to build their own hull and install the machinery, bought from West & Peachey, did not save them as much as expected? Did they find building the hull and superstructure was a more difficult undertaking than they anticipated? We may never know the answer, but we do know that later the same year, 1892, two orders for complete Alligator tugs were received from the McLachlin Bros. These were Alligator #7, the *Bonnechére*, and Alligator #8, the *Amable du Fond*.

The first order for a complete tug in 1893 was for Alligator #9, the *Ballantyne*, also from the McLachlin Bros. Three 1893 orders for Alligator tugs were received from Gilmour and Company of Trenton, Ontario. In fact, Alligator tug #13 through to Alligator tug #18 were all built for this large lumbering firm. Those constructed in 1893 were tug #13, the *Alligator*; tug #14, the *Trent*; and tug #15, the *Muskoka*. In 1894, the orders from Gilmour and Company continued, with Alligator tug #16, the *Hunter*; tug #17, the *Peck*; and tug #18, the *Nipissing*. These Alligator Warping Tugs were all destined for use in the harvest of the timber limits of the lucrative Trent River and Trent Canal territory.

By March 1893, twenty men were working at the West & Peachey factory, and six Alligator tugs were under construction. Business had never been better, enabling the retirement of the factory mortgage. Both John West and his partner, James Peachey, were able to pay off their respective mortgages on their homes, as well. In that same year John West attended the Chicago World Fair where he picked up many good ideas from exhibits of the latest technology. He also purchased a new iron shaper, which was on display in the Canadian Machinery Hall, for use in their factory. And, from an American firm, he purchased a jacksaw used for cutting iron bars to their desired lengths. These he would use at his home base, but West was very adept at designing and manufacturing his own equipment, which he would then install in their company facilities. One such piece of equipment was a mill head with which they could cut threads on bolts and iron rods with automatic dies. At this time he also designed a piece of machinery for cutting key sets in wheels, gears, and the like.

In September 1893, due to the lack of space for the increased workload the firm was experiencing, West and Peachey decided to build a large, brick building adjacent to their foundry. It was put to good use immediately. By the spring of 1894, they had received orders for eleven more Alligator tugs. The firm was now operating day and night with forty men working in their shops. The weekly payroll had risen to $300. The previous year they had operated the shops on a ten-hour day with a weekly payroll of less than $75 to their employees. By the mid-1890s, an Alligator Warping Tug brought the firm $2,800 apiece. With the increase in demand for Alligator tugs came an increase need for lumber and other construction materials. As a result, during July and August of 1894, West & Peachey built a new steam-driven portable sawmill on the property.

With their own sawmill, the firm now was able to saw up to 10,000 board feet of lumber daily.

ALLIGATOR TUG PORTAGING.

The ability to portage overland was an essential feature in the success of the Alligator Warping Tug, which was also the reason for their name. The tug could safely move up an incline of 1:3 (or a rise of 1 foot for every 3 feet of movement forward) and over very rough terrain. Much of the work required of it involved moving between lakes when no navigable stream existed between them. It was also essential for getting around dams, waterfalls, and flumes that provided for the passage of logs, but not for boats.

A level, graded road was not required, only the placing of logs under the heavy oak steel-shod runners, set about 6 to 8 feet apart, to keep the runners from grinding over the rocks. A heavy block pulley was attached to a chain near the bottom of the bow of the Alligator. Another single block pulley was attached to a tree on the side of the portage road. The cable was run out, passed through the block at the tree and returned to the tug to be passed through the pulley block attached to the chain on the bow of the tug. From there the cable was run forward and anchored to a tree on the opposite side of the portage road and across from the first pulley block. When the winch was put in operation, the cable rewinding on the drum pulled the Alligator forward on a straight course between the two anchors. In this way the Alligator could be moved at least a mile a day, and, if conditions were good, as much as three miles a day. In one case, an Alligator was known to haul itself overland for 40 miles, taking almost a month to accomplish the feat.

Portaging proved very hard on the wooden hulls of the tugs and a hull's life span was dependent on the amount of portaging it was subjected to. Some tugs required new hulls within a year or two of their building and many Alligators had several new replacement hulls during their lifetime.

8 Alligator-Operated Portable Sawmills and Other Ventures

By 1897, West & Peachey was offering a portable sawmill for use with the Alligator Warping Tug. The complete mill weighed 4,500 pounds and was offered for $350 f.o.b. (free on board), Simcoe. The saw carriage was mounted on three bunks and operated with a rope feed. The Alligator would be set up on shore where needed and the tug's steam engine provided the power to drive the saw. A 75-foot-long rubber drive belt from the tug drove a 54-inch circular saw. A pair of idlers were mounted on the bow of the Alligator, which the drive belt passed over. The saw was able to cut mill timber up to 30 feet in length. The portable sawmill was of interest to lumbermen wishing to square timber or saw logs into lumber on site, particularly in remote areas, for the construction of camps and other buildings. They were also in demand on inland locations for the construction of dams and flumes to expedite the movement of logs through a network of small lakes and connecting streams. West & Peachey had sold four Alligator sawmills to the following lumber companies, R.H. Klock and Company in Mattawa, Ontario; Gilmour and Company in Trenton; J.R. Booth of Ottawa; and to Robert Hurdman, also of Ottawa, by the end of 1905.

A sketch by artist L.A. Dool illustrates the operation of portable sawmill using an Alligator tug's steam engine to supply the power.

Courtesy of Clarence F. Coons Collection.

FEATURES OF PADDLEWHEEL ALLIGATORS, 1889–1900

Normally all Alligators were painted red and white. Although the colour combinations varied over the years, these colours were used throughout the entire production of the popular tugs. The name of each Alligator was usually painted on the circumference of the paddlewheel box, with a sea horse painted at each end of the name.

There were several distinctive features of the early paddlewheel Alligators manufactured between 1889 and the turn of the century. The tugs could be purchased in two sizes. The first one built, Alligator #1, was only 32 feet in length. The standard after that was an Alligator with a length overall of 37 feet and a beam of 10 feet. The standard drew 30 inches of water. A larger Alligator could be supplied having a length of 45 feet and a beam of 11 feet, with a draught of only 26 inches.

Each Alligator was equipped with two 7-foot-diameter paddlewheels consisting of eight 26-inch-wide paddles. The paddle-drive gear, the largest gear in the tug, was 46 inches in diameter and 4 inches wide. When travelling without a load or boom in tow the Alligator moved at a speed of 5 to 6 miles per hour. A gantry, a curved metal arm mounted on the bow of a tug that swung inboard or outboard for raising or lowering the anchor, mounted on the foredeck, was

used to lift the warping anchor aboard and swing it behind the cable-guiding device for storage when not in use. All the early Alligators had the paddlewheel box supported on the outside by three struts. Those built after 1900 used four and often five struts to support this box.

The factory equipped early Alligator tugs with a small wheelhouse large enough to accommodate the wheel and the captain. Sleeping facilities were provided in the bow

Alligator #26, *Weslemkoon*, was built in 1896 for use in the timber limits of John Ferguson, the MPP for South Renfrew. The tug is shown on Lake Weslemkoon with a full cargo of picnickers, circa 1896.

Courtesy of the Clarence F. Coons Collection.

of the vessel for four men. Many lumbermen extended the wheelhouse to the rear to provide room for additional bunks.

All Alligators were built with a large, hinged rudder that could be lifted clear of booms, logs, and other obstructions the tug might pass over. The rudder was controlled from the wheelhouse by the steering wheel and attached cables. The tugs were all equipped with a standard steam engine with a 9-inch bore and a 9-inch stroke. The best production years prior to the turn of the century were 1893 and 1894, when a total of fifteen Alligators were manufactured.

John West continued to work on an improved rudder on the Alligator tugs to alleviate damage often suffered because of their rigid installation. He was also experimenting with the design of the bow davit to increase its efficiency. On October 31, 1895, a patent was issued to West for a rudder that tilted, allowing it to ride over obstructions without damage. The patent also covered a combined winch and davit so that one man could lift and carry a load with this new and much improved arrangement.

ALLIGATOR WARPING TUG SHIPPING METHODS AND PROBLEMS

Many Alligator tugs were required to be delivered to locations miles from any railway lines, which meant that early in the building of them they had to be shipped in sections. John West's solution to this problem was to load the sections on a railway flatcar to be shipped to the station nearest to their final delivery point. They were then unloaded and placed on several sleighs to be drawn by horses over winter logging roads to their final destination.

The shipping of Alligators in sections required much more work and expense for the builder. West had a template or matrix installed on the main floor of the large machine shop of the factory. Here the boilers and engines, together with all their connections, were fitted exactly as if in the tug. The parts were then all numbered, disassembled, and placed ready for packing and shipment. The second floor of the factory was used for the manufacture of the pilot houses, steering gear, paddlewheels, boxes, and the like.

The hull of the tug was treated in the same way. Every bolt, spike, and nail was packed in cases. Packed, uncrated, were six pieces of oak 26 feet long for runners and ninety-five pieces of 2-inch by 6-inch pine, 18 feet to 24 feet long, to be used in the construction of the hull on site. Also uncrated was the boiler weighing 3,200 pounds, and a mile of steel warping cable weighing almost 3,300 pounds.

The weight of other major parts of an Alligator tug were as follows: the steam engine, 1,500 pounds; the winch, 1,500 pounds; the steel shoes, sheeting, and rudder, 1,600 pounds; and the paddlewheels, 1,200 pounds. When all these individual parts were assembled as a finished standard Alligator Warping Tug they represented a total weight of 13 tons. The moving of a knocked-down tug from a railhead up to 100 miles and more over rough logging roads, or tote roads as they were called, with teams of horses drawing the loaded sleighs was no mean feat.

An example of the extra charges involved were illustrated when, in 1895, the Gilmour and Hughson Lumber Company of Hull, Quebec, requested that Alligator #25, named the *Baskatong*, be shipped in sections. To pack and crate all parts at the factory triggered an immediate extra charge of $100. In addition, the buyer was responsible for providing transportation for West & Peachey's men who accompanied the tug and assembled it at its final destination. The buyer was also responsible for all costs to team the parts to their point of assembly, as well. The West & Peachey assembly team, in such cases, consisted of either West himself or Peachey or a senior staff member, accompanied by two or three employees who travelled to the remote destination, assembled the tug, and ensured its satisfactory operation for the customer.

Upon arrival at the site, the West & Peachey team would pitch a tent and begin to assemble the tug. Once the tug's cabin was completed, they would move into it, relying on the fired-up boiler to provide welcome warmth as they completed the assembly. The team carried their own supplies, much of their food being in canned and dried form. They were usually on site for about three weeks before the finished tug could be turned over to the company crew.

Members of the assembly crew found these excursions exciting, as they often travelled into remote wilderness that had never before been opened up. These trips were not for the faint-hearted, however, as the trip from the railhead was often long and fraught with unexpected hazards. For example, an order destined for a remote northern Quebec lake had to be hauled for nearly 100 miles by horses and sleighs. Twenty sleighs were needed, and each sleigh required one to three teams of horses to move it over the hazards of the rough tote road. In some of the worst places, up to six teams of horses struggled to keep the heavy sleighs moving. The trip involved several days of hard slugging for everyone involved. To have some ideas of costs involved, in 1895 the average monthly wage drawn by workers in the woods were as follows; loggers and teamsters, $20 to $35; sawyers, $22 to $26; swampers, $20.

Many amusing stories were told by the men upon their return from these excursions, all of which enhanced the camaraderie and friendly, good-humoured working conditions that existed between management and employees. Doug Stalker remembers a story that his father delighted in telling of being awakened on a remote site in northern Quebec by what he first thought was a bear attempting to break into their tent. Leaping up, intent on repelling the invader, he discovered that his father-in-law, John West, still half asleep, was thrashing around in a most peculiar manner. On closer examination he found that during the night West's beard had frozen solidly to the wall of the tent and he was unable to free himself, despite all his considerable efforts to do so.

On another occasion West was returning with his crew from assembling an Alligator when his money ran out. He managed to find sufficient train fare to get all hands to Jarvis, 10 miles east of Simcoe, but that was it. As soon as they stopped in Jarvis, West made a beeline for the nearby American Hotel, where, being no stranger, he was able to borrow $10 from his friend the hotelkeeper, though they had no time for a leisurely drink. Rushing back to the station, he was just in time to get everyone aboard and safely home on the same train.

Although these unique tug boats that could swim in the water and crawl on land were known by everyone in the lumber industry as Alligators from the very beginning, they were also referred to as the "Bull of the Woods" by some and as "Slough Hogs" by others.

THE LAUNCH OF ALLIGATOR #24, THE *VICTORIA*

May 24, 1894, was a day long remembered by the County of Norfolk and the good people of the county town of Simcoe. The occasion marked the seventy-fifth birthday of the Commonwealth's beloved sovereign, Queen Victoria, and the Queen's birthday celebration committee were sparing no effort or expense in planning a celebration fitting for the occasion. Several major attractions were planned as part of the day's activities. Simcoe had its own bicycle club and the committee had invited two of the great bicycle riders of the day, Hyslop and Moore of Toronto, to attend. A special train from Toronto had been laid on for the occasion. Bicycle races were a feature attraction on the program and members of bicycle clubs from Toronto, Hamilton, Brantford, Ingersoll, Aylmer, Norwich, and Tillsonburg were in attendance.

Shortly after daybreak, the booming of a cannon heralded the beginning of the festivities, awakening the soundest sleepers from their slumbers. By 9:00 a.m., the banks of Crystal Lake were host to masses of holidaymakers, expectantly awaiting the feature attraction for the day. West & Peachey's fame, as makers of the Alligator Warping Tug, had spread far and wide throughout the Dominion and beyond. Today the local citizens and their visitors could see one of these famous Alligators take to the water before their very eyes. The firm had been busy building the tugs the previous winter, and on this day, May 24, and at this hour, 9:00 a.m., the twenty-fourth Alligator to be ordered had been built and most appropriately named *Victoria,* the name proudly appearing in large letters. She now sat in all her splendour, puffing black smoke from her stack as she rested on her rollers, waiting to be launched.

The tug launched herself into Crystal Lake, as the small body of water north of the West & Peachey yard was called. The crowd stood in awe as she winched herself toward Norfolk Street, crept out of the water, crossed the road, and launched herself again into the river below the high school, where she was tied to the bank. During the launch into the river the 39th Battalion brass band belted out "Britannia Rules the Waves" as the enthusiastic crowd cheered. Mounting the deck of the *Victoria,* Mayor McCall addressed the crowd and officially opened the day's celebrations. Rides aboard the Alligator tug were offered throughout the day and hundreds of spectators took advantage of the free trips on the river.

At 10:00 a.m. the next popular event took place with the launch of Professor Bartholomew's hot-air balloon from Beaupre's Square. The professor was well prepared and the airship quickly rose into the air to the collective gasps of amazement from the assembled crowd. Meanwhile, foot races, bicycle races, and horse races entertained many during the rest of the day. Dress balls and dances in the evening rounded out the day's activities. The Queen's birthday celebrations in Simcoe in 1894 would be remembered as a resounding success and fondly treasured for many years to come.

The *Victoria* remained in the river or the West & Peachey yard until June 8, 1895, when she was shipped by rail to Trout Creek, Ontario. There, her new owner, the Hardy Lumber Company, planned to put her to work replacing Alligator #1. They had acquired the very first Alligator, but unfortunately, while in the service of the company she had sunk at the Persia Rapids on the French River and could not be recovered.

Alligator #24, *Victoria,* was built 1894 and launched in the Lynn River as part of Queen Victoria's seventy-fifth birthday celebrations in Simcoe, Ontario. The Simcoe high school is shown in the background.

Courtesy of Norfolk Historical Society.

The Gilmour Dynasty: Their Tramway and the Alligator

One of the largest white-pine logging dynasties in Canada was the Gilmour Company, established in Trenton, Ontario, in 1825.[1] They also operated a successful timber-importing business in Glasgow, Scotland, and a timber-exporting facility in Quebec City. In addition to sawmills operating in Trenton they also owned sawmills in Hull and in Chelsea, Quebec. In the heyday of the wooden, sailing ships, Gilmour and Company were said to be one of the largest shipowners in the world.

On May 18, 1881, their main Trenton sawmill was totally destroyed by a fire. Replaced a year later, the mill was touted as having the greatest sawing capacity of any mill ever to be built on the Trent River system. The new Gilmour mill was driven by an enormous 1,500-horsepower twin steam engine powered by sixteen boilers and was capable of turning out 350,000 board feet of lumber in a 10-hour day. Their smaller Trenton mill produced 50,000 board feet daily. Thus, in a single day the Gilmour Company produced 400,000 board feet of pine lumber and deals (boards 3 inches thick or more). Despite having huge timber limits on the Trent and Moira river systems, the Gilmour mills were rapidly depleting the supply of available pine timber in those watersheds, and there were no other large stands nearby to depend on for future development.

In September 1890, brothers Allan and David Gilmour took over the company as a new partnership. With their immediate concern being the acquisition of additional timber limits, on October 13, 1892, David attended an Ontario govern-

A work crew are busy constructing an extensive log sluiceway.
Courtesy of the Clarence F. Coons Collection.

ment auction of timber limits in Toronto. He was the successful bidder on 86.75 square miles of timber cutting rights in the townships of Hunter and McLaughlin in the Parry Sound District and in Peck Township in Algonquin Park at a total cost to the company of $704,145. These new limits did not drain into the Trent River system, however, but into Georgian Bay.

After intensive study of how to economically transfer their timber from the Muskoka limits into the Trent River system, the Gilmours devised a log jack, a device to elevate logs over a rise or height of land, and sluiceway combination they felt would accomplish their purpose. The contract for construction of what soon became known as the Gilmour Tramway or Logway was awarded to the William Hamilton Manufacturing Company of Peterborough, Ontario. To begin with, moving their logs over the height of land separating the Trent River system from the rivers flowing into Georgian Bay required 5,780 feet of chain. The tramway would carry the logs from the Lake of Bays in the Muskoka system over the height of land at Dorset and into the backwaters of Raven Lake, a part of the Trent drainage basin. The tramway was designed to handle a total of 10,000 logs daily. It was certainly the most complicated and expensive scheme yet devised for the transport of logs to the mill.[2]

To expedite the movement of logs to and from the tramway and then down the Trent River system to their Trenton sawmill, the Gilmour partners placed orders and took delivery of six Alligator Warping Tugs in 1893 and 1894. That winter, they operated ten logging camps on their new timber limits, harvesting about 20 million board feet of pine timber. This was all transported over the new tramway, which was completed and in operation by June 1894.

It became apparent at the beginning of this ambitious undertaking that operations would need to be carried out on a twenty-four-hour basis. The Gilmours contacted John West to ask if his firm could supply a small steam engine to run a dynamo to power an electric searchlight. They planned to install the searchlight on one of

The Gilmour tramway or logway near Dorset was 5,780 feet in length. It was built in 1893-94 by the William Hamilton Manufacturing Company of Peterborough, Ontario. Loggers are taking a break from moving logs over a height of land in the system.
Courtesy of Library and Archives Canada, C-21212.

their Alligator Warping Tugs, so that it would be able to continue operating after dark. West solved the problem by installing a 25-horsepower boiler, instead of the standard 22-horsepower type. This larger boiler would produce the extra steam required to power the dynamo installed in the Alligator with the night-light. Once a reliable source of electric power was assured, in 1893 Gilmour and Company purchased an electric searchlight from The Trenton Electric Company Limited. This was one of the celebrated carbon-arc lamps made by the Brush Electric Company of Cleveland, Ohio. The light proved so satisfactory during nighttime operations that West & Peachey were asked to equip two additional Alligator tugs with the larger boiler, small steam engine, dynamo, and powerful searchlight.

The *Peterborough Review* reported the success of the searchlight on a Gilmour Alligator tug in an 1894 edition of the paper:

The *Peck*, Alligator #17, owned by Gilmour & Company of Trenton, Ontario, was one of first tugs to be equipped with a carbon-arc searchlight for warping at night. Note the gantry and heavy warping anchor, circa 1895.

Courtesy of Library and Archives Canada, C-11455.

The Gilmour Company's drive of 60,000 logs is being taken through Sturgeon Lake this week. The drive is one of the largest that has ever passed down the lake and the apparent ease with which it is handled by the alligator boat which accompanies it is marvelous. The drive is kept moving day and night. At night the operations are conducted by the aid of an electric light on the alligator boat. [The men eat and sleep on shore in well-appointed tents.]

It would appear that the sleeping accommodations of the Alligators located in the fore part of the tug proved unsatisfactory, due to the excessive noise of the machinery while the tug and the winch were in operation at night. For this reason tents ashore were supplied. A fourth Alligator, known as the *Nipissing* and also owned by the Gilmours, had a large, railway-locomotive-type calcium-carbide lantern installed for night operations.

The details of the Gilmour Company tramway were described in a book written by Captain George Thompson in 1895. His account follows:

> First they harnessed a waterpower on the shore of the Lake of Bays and thus secured power to raise the logs out of the lake sixty feet almost straight up the side of a mountain; then they built a slide or sluiceway, which takes the logs on the first mile of their journey. The water to supply this slide also had to be pumped up out of the Lake of Bays. When the logs leave the slide an endless chain or a tram carries them on nearly another mile, and then deposits them into a canal which is two miles long (made by flooding Raven Lake). An Alligator steamboat then tows them through a canal to Senoras (St. Nora's) Lake, where the logs are made up into rafts or drives of about fourty [sic] thousand pieces each and they are then started on their long journey over two hundred miles to Trenton.[3]

Along with other river improvements made in addition to the tramway, it was estimated that the Gilmours had spent nearly $200,000 on their logway project. Although it worked well, it still took up to two years to get the logs, once they were cut, to their sawmill in Trenton. In the end, it proved to be a costly error for one of Canada's greatest lumbering families. As a result, the tramway was closed at the end of the 1895 season.

The Gilmours constructed a sawmill on Canoe Lake in Algonquin Park close to the transportation facilities of the Canada Atlantic Railway, which was under construction at that same time. Two of the Gilmour Alligators were offered for sale for $2,200 apiece. The electric searchlight apparatus was offered for an additional $400. If anyone profited from this whole exercise it was the firm of West & Peachey, for it did much to publicize the successful role played by the Alligator tugs in the tramway experiment.

10 Steamboats for South America

The Barney and Stevens Railway Car Works of Dayton, Ohio, learned of the Alligator tugs built by West & Peachey in Simcoe and became interested in them. They operated a transportation company in Colombia, South America, and saw the Alligator as a means of solving some of the problems they were experiencing in moving goods inland on the shallow Magdalena River.

In August 1895, Robert Rochester, a foreman for Barney and Stevens, accompanied by other members of the firm, met with West & Peachey to discuss the details and sign a contract for the construction of the largest and most powerful Alligator tug ever attempted. In order to inspect a working Alligator and assess its potential for the job they required of it, John West accompanied them to Fenelon Falls, Ontario, to see the *Hamilton H.*, owned by J. W. Howry and Sons. Impressed by what they saw, they immediately placed an order for a new tug.

The Alligator tug, to be named the *Ohio*, would be 57 feet in length, with a beam of 11 feet. Twin duplex steam engines producing 40 horsepower were to be

A drawing of the *Ohio* shows the Alligator tug under way during pre-shipment trials on October 9, 1895.
Courtesy of the Clarence F. Coons Collection.

installed in the craft. The tug was launched for its trials in Crystal Lake, adjacent to the factory, on October 9, 1895. It performed beautifully, and many townsmen enjoyed a ride on it during its testing. The tug was then disassembled, crated, and loaded on railway flatcars for shipping to New York City. It was then transferred to the steamship *Mexico* for delivery in Cartegena, Colombia. John West and his brother James followed the tug to its destination where they would assemble it and put it in operation for the new owners. James Peachey travelled with them as far as New York City, where he accepted payment in full for the tug in the form of gold coin.

Once they arrived in Cartegena, John West wrote a long and intriguing letter to the editor of the Simcoe newspaper, recounting their experiences in detail. West did not use paragraphs, but instead inserted a great many semicolons. Most of the letter is shown here with paragraphs created to assist with reading, but the actual wording has been left intact.[1] His account is not only very descriptive, but provides an intimate insight into the thinking and character of John C. West:

Cartegena, Republic of Colombia,
December 28, 1895

To the Editor:

According to promise I write you a few lines, giving some items of interest from leaving Simcoe until we arrived here. We were 24 days getting over 5,000 miles and making five stops. Our first experience was getting dumped out of our berths in the middle of the night on the fast mail train on the New York Central, which was wrecked by four boys; [they stole tools from a locked shed and removed the fish plates from the rails. Engine No. 888, traveling at 75 miles an hour, was thrown down an embankment into a ditch and almost submerged in water. The accident, at 4:25 a.m. near Rome, N.Y., smashed the windows of their sleeper, but fortunately it did not topple down the embankment] and we came out first best and arrived in New York City right side up.

We took passage in the steamer Mexico of the Spanish Line for Cartegena. The crew numbered about 80 from cabin boy to captain and out of the whole lot there was only one man who could talk English and he was the chief engineer. He was a good fellow and came from London where the ship was built; he helped us all the way by acting as interpreter, or we would have had some trouble. We sailed out of

New York onto the ocean and everything was lovely. There were 12 passengers beside us going to Havana; they could all talk English and everyone enjoyed the ever-waving swell of the Atlantic.

All went well until the next day in the afternoon; we were nearing Cape Hatteras, when the wind began to blow a little at first; at midnight it was blowing a heavy gale, which got up a big sea and heaved us about in great shape. When daylight broke the waves were a sight to see; but there were very few able to hold up their heads, your humble servant amongst the rest; but the sickness did not last long and in six hours I was over it entirely. From start to finish I could not get over the Spanish cooking; they cook with olive oil and garlic and none but a Spaniard could relish the food; we had to eat it or starve.

We arrived at Havana and were an eye witness of Spain landing 15,000 soldiers in the city. We were in the centre of the anchorage and the seven Spanish troop ships cast anchor around us. We had a good chance to see them land. Havana is a very old town; the houses are built of stone or a kind of hard red brick and plastered on the outside and covered with tile. The streets are very narrow, many of them not more than 16 feet from wall to wall. The sidewalks are about 18 inches wide. There are no piers or docks that steamers can lie alongside; everything has to be taken off with lighters.

The people are the slowest class I have ever seen; they move like the wheels of an eight-day clock. Well, after the earth had turned around a few times and they got good and ready and we had taken about 60 passengers on board, all Spaniards, we set out for Sanago, on the east side of Cuba where the war is going on. We made it in two days; we stopped there over night, and next morning started for La Guayra, on the coast of Venezuela. The wind was blowing a little fresh when we got under way, but kept increasing until it blew a hurricane and the night was as dark as the crew; the waves rolled over our decks so you could not find a dry spot to stand on and everything that was not lashed fast was going at a 2.40 race from one side of the ship to the other. The seas smashed and carried away the bow bulwarks and then made a clean sweep over her bows; strange to say we were not troubled with as much water in the middle of the ship after that. I have never seen before such a wild crowd as was on that ship. They were both sick and frightened. The storm went down some the next day but the sea was something grand. It was stormy all the way until we got to La Guayra, where there was grand scenery.

The mountain rises from the water's edge until the top is lost in the clouds and the town is built one tier above another up the face of the mountain for hundreds of feet; to see the lights at night up that steep side was beautiful. The next morning our party went on the shore to see the sights and I may say right here that we were in great danger of not getting on board again on account of a row the natives had with the English the day before we landed …

We then sailed for Cartegena which was about three days' sail. It was a little stormy all the next day but in the evening it got a little calmer and we all turned in for a good night's sleep.

When about the middle of the night a steamer ran into us striking us between the engine and the boilers and dumping us all out of our berths and then one of the wildest times had arrived that we have had and the good-for-nothing sailors were the worst; the officers did not know which end they stood on. I went to the engineer and he took me down to the engine room and showed me where the steamer had struck us and we looked it all over; we were somewhat bruised but not broken; and then we could look around and take notes. The steamer that struck us had drifted astern and soon we lost her lights and were just putting on steam when we heard someone shouting and soon three men came alongside and said the steamer was sinking and wanted help; but our captain was such a coward he would not let them come on board for some time; by this time the steamer had gone down.

We lay there until daylight and then we picked up another boat with eight men; we then sailed through the wreckage and picked up 17 men floating on hatches and ice boxes; another steamer picked up 10 men; there were 18 men drowned. The name of the steamer was Nansemond of the Red D Line. She was a wooden ship and ours was of iron. So we came out of that scrape first best and right side up and now I am waiting for an earthquake and then I will have been through the mill.

I like this place with its old wall. I have had two or three walks upon it. It is as solid as when it was first built. Except in a few places the streets are wider than in any of the other places I have seen. The natives are clothed and some of them very well. But it looks comical to see colored women wearing low-necked dresses and bunches of bright ribbons tied to each shoulder and in their wool. Their skin is as black as jet and they weigh anywhere from 150 to 300 pounds. But I think I can pass for a North American Indian now and if I were to stay here long I could compare with any of them for color. It is awful hot at noon. The sun burns like a ball of fire.

The harbor is a land-locked sheet of water. The water is very clear; you can see shoals of fine fish 20 feet down. We saw large numbers of flying fish; they are a make-up between bird and fish and can fly about 50 yards; they are fitted out with two pair of wings and do most of the propelling through the air with their tails; they are a silver-gray color and glisten like silver when they raise out of the water; they appear to be from 4 to 12 inches in length. One or two nights we sailed through phosphers (sic); a little insect that makes the water look like gold. They would light up the sides of the steamer like fire.

Well, it is nice to walk through the cocoa-nut groves and see the nuts on top of the stems. The stem grows about 30 feet high and the leaves are about 15 feet long and 4 feet wide. We had a shade of them on poles over our boat; they reach across and hang down on each side. I am writing under difficulties so I guess I will have to close. I am in the best of health. Wishing your readers the compliments of the season,

I remain yours truly,

J.C. West[2]

The Wests finally arrived at their destination, Barranquilla, Colombia, which was about 18 miles up the Magdalena River from the seaport of Savanilla. Barney and Stevens of Dayton, Ohio, were doing a large and profitable trading business along the Honda, Nevia, and Magdalena rivers in Colombia. Huge amounts of merchandise were being taken up the rivers by boat. On the Magdalena River trade was carried on in Mississippi riverboats and boats of a similar style from Germany.

The boats were being towed up river by Native men, which proved a very unreliable method for getting the cargos to their destination. When conditions were ideal, a trip could be accomplished in fourteen days, but this was rare. One big problem was navigating shallows and in other places rapids in the rivers involved. Transport was so unreliable that often supplies could be left at various locations awaiting transport for up to two years.

Barney and Stevens felt sure that the Alligator tug *Ohio* could overcome these delays and could also navigate the river inland successfully for 200 miles more inland than any of the craft they presently were using. The Wests assembled the *Ohio* and successfully tested her for service by the middle of January 1896. John West then left for home, travelling by trading steamer from Cartagena to New Orleans at the mouth of the Mississippi River. From there he continued by rail to Simcoe, arriving home on January 25, 1896. James West remained in South America, to operate the Alligator tug for her new owners until their crew was thoroughly familiar with its operation, when he, too, returned. He arrived in Simcoe on or close to October 1, 1896.

THE PASSENGER VESSEL *FERNANDO NETOS*

While on the Magdalena River, in Colombia, John West met and discussed the construction of a steel-hulled, light-draught passenger steamer with businessman Neto Harmonas. This was not to be an Alligator-type vessel, but a regular steamer of 110 feet in length, with a beam of 20 feet. It would be put in service to transport passengers on the Magdalena River and would be driven by a single-stern paddlewheel 14 feet in height and 14 feet wide. For its passengers' comfort, the steamer would provide eleven staterooms and twenty-two berths.

These discussions were confirmed on October 17, 1896, when an order for the vessel was received from Harmonas. It would be the largest steam vessel undertaken by West & Peachey to date. The builder would deliver the steamer by rail and absorb the costs to New York City, where the buyers would be responsible for paying all duties and the transportation costs from New York to Colombia.

West & Peachey set to work. They built the 200-horsepower engine and installed it in the vessel. However, West had the steamer's huge boiler made by the Bertram Engine Works of Toronto. The boiler was a Roberts patent water-tube-type unit. On March 23, 1897, it arrived in Simcoe, having been shipped from Toronto by train. The boiler weighed 14 tons, and required four teams of horses to haul it to the West & Peachey factory for installation in the new steamer. The huge stern-drive paddlewheel had already been built and put in place. The contract price for the steamer, delivered to New York City, was $13,500.

The now completed vessel was thoroughly tested and everything about her proved to be satisfactory. All the machinery and other materials for the big craft were loaded on five railway cars for shipment to New York. Once all were en route, arrangements were made for John and James West, James Peachey, Orlando Scott, J.B. Robbins, and D. Lindsay of the firm to travel to Barranquilla, Colombia, where the passenger steamer would be assembled, tested, and put in service on the Magdalena River.

The boat was constructed in the same city where the *Ohio* had been put in service earlier, then taken for a test run on the river by John Chegun and Christiansen Jasen, Harmonas' employees who would be responsible for the new boat and its operation. They were very pleased with her trial results. The steamer was capable of a speed of 13 miles per hour under a boiler pressure of 140 to 180 pounds on the steam-pressure gauge. In their estimation, she handled the strong currents of the river surprisingly well. Chegun and Jasen ran a distance of about 20 miles upriver during these tests. Once the test runs were completed to everyone's satisfaction, all of the West & Peachey crew, except James West, returned to New York City on the steamer *Atlai* of the Atlas Steamship Line. From there they continued home to Simcoe by railway coach, arriving on July 20, 1897.

John Stalker had been left in charge of the West & Peachey shops when the partners left for South America and had no idea when they would be returning to Simcoe. According to a story John Stalker's son, Colonel Douglas Stalker, delighted in telling, his father was busy at his bench on that July day in 1897. Hearing a commotion, he looked up and to his surprise saw Grandfather West and Mr. Peachey entering the shop. Grandfather was carrying a parrot in a cage and Mr. Peachey had a monkey. John Stalker welcomed them home asking, "Well! How did things go?"

To which John West replied, laconically, "Very well, Boat worked well."

Colonel Stalker comments at this point that his grandfather West was all technical in his interests and ability, saying, that on his own he would never have managed to make a decent living. Mr. Peachey, on the other hand, had the financial interests of the firm in mind and managed that end of the business very well. As proof of this point Mr. Peachey walked up to John Stalker's bench, plunked down a canvas sack of gold coin with the comment, "We got our money!"[3] They had insisted that payment be made upon delivery of the vessel to New York, in gold coin, and were greatly relieved to have arrived home safely when carrying so much gold with them. The parrot lived a long life in its new home in Simcoe, but the Peachey monkey, unhappily, did not last long in its new quarters.

James West remained in Colombia for some time to run the boat for the new owners until their crew members were completely familiar with all aspects of her operation. The trip had proved to be resounding success for everyone and further orders were anticipated from South America. However, this never happened.

11

The Diverse Enterprises of West & Peachey, 1897–99

The two South American steamboats had occupied much of the firm's time during part of 1896 through the first half of 1897. Only one additional Alligator Warping Tug was built in that year, Tug #34, named the *Kegebongo* and built for the Gilmour and Hughson Lumber Company of Hull, Quebec. She was shipped knocked-down from Simcoe to the end of the rail line at Gracefield, Quebec, on March 3, 1897.

John Stalker, West's son-in-law, along with William Monteith and J. Yeomans, accompanied the tug, which had to be hauled on sleighs by teams of horses for 100 miles to Bark Lake, then on to an assembly point near Lake Kegebongo. Here, the team assembled and tested the vessel during the time that John West and James Peachey were in South America.

Although Alligator construction was in a bit of a doldrums at this time, the firm was engaged in several other specialty projects. In fact, the only year in their forty-year history of building Alligators (from 1889 to 1929) that no Alligator tugs were built was in 1898. They were kept very busy manufacturing steam engines and boilers for yachts, cheese factories, printing offices, and mills. They also were still engaged in manufacturing complete sawmills for their customers in the lumber business.

The firm of West & Peachey was now the major ironworks in Simcoe operating that part of the business under the name of The Simcoe Iron Works. By this time the main building on the West & Peachey property was a two-storey, board-and-batten, timber-frame building 40 feet wide by 100 feet long. The first floor consisted of a well-equipped machine shop. At one end was a blacksmith shop and equipment for manufacturing boilers. A large steam engine drove an overhead line shaft from which all equipment in the machine shop was belt-driven. The belts were attached to various lathes, drill presses, and other equipment necessary to the operation of an efficient machine shop.

An equally well-equipped woodworking shop was located on the second floor. Here, all patterns were made of clear white pine for moulding the many castings they required. It was also the place where cabins, decks, and wheelhouses for the Alligator tugs were cut and prepared for assembly. John West maintained his drafting room in the attic of this building.

To the north of the main building was the business office. To the north of it again was the foundry, a large brick building. Here, all the castings were poured for the machinery they were making. All the moulding sand, flasks, and patterns were stored in an extension on the end of this building. Many custom-made castings were poured when customers requested them, as well. Adjoining buildings on the property housed a planing mill and a sawmill. The portable sawmill, with a circular saw, could turn out 10,000 feet of lumber a day. This mill cut all the oak and pine required for the construction of the Alligator tugs as well as doing a great deal of business in custom-sawing work. Each spring the Kent Street road allowance, which dead-ended west of the West & Peachey property at that time, was piled high with logs delivered from their own and surrounding woodlots and awaiting transformation into useful lumber in the nearby sawmill.

Alex Landon,[1] a longtime Simcoe area local resident, remembered his father keeping regular reports of logs cut in their Charlotteville Township (Norfolk County) woodlot in his diary from 1903 onward. Good white oak and pine logs were normally teamed into the West & Peachey yard where they were scaled and sold. In some cases, sawn lumber was brought back to their farm for their own use. The Landon farm is now within the southern limits of the town of Simcoe. At that time it was in Woodhouse Township, and farther west was Charlotteville Township.

The planing mill was established primarily for sizing and dressing material for their Alligator tug construction, but a considerable business had developed, as with the sawmill, in custom planing, as well. This mill was equipped with every kind of equipment one would need in the form of planing and matching machines, lathes, bandsaws, whipsaws, and cut-off saws. The boiler house to run the big steam engine in the machine shop was located at the rear of the main building, adjacent to the steam engine, and fired by slabs and edgings surplus to the operation of the sawmill.

The name of William Monteith as an employee of the West & Peachey firm in the 1890s is a reminder of a persistent story of an Alligator Warping Tug being used in connection with the Kualt Mill, on Shuswap Lake, in the Salmon Arm area of British Columbia. The author's grandfather[2] and other relatives lived in the Armstrong area of the Okanagan valley at that time and they, too, talked vaguely of such a craft being used in the Shuswap Lake logging enterprise. An inland steamboat captain and Salmon Arm's first blacksmith, named Monteith, is credited with bringing an Alligator to the lake in 1897. Captain Monteith and Jack West were cousins, which lends credibility to the story, although no record of this Alligator or its name has come to light. One of the early sawmills on Shuswap Lake was the Genelle Brothers mill. It later became the Columbia River Lumber Company. However, in 1907, the records do indicate that a twin-screw Alligator #84, named *Nellie*, was shipped to the Shuswap Lumber Company of Shuswap, British Columbia. Perhaps this is the actual basis for the story, although rumours would indicate it was earlier than that date.

Even without an Alligator tug order in 1898, the firm was kept busy with a wide range of other work. They manufactured a large boiler for the Simcoe Canning Company, installed a steel bulkhead in the town's water pumping station, and built and

John West is testing horizontal marine engines in the West & Peachey factory yard. This type of engine may have been used in the *Bersimis*, the large Alligator #101.
Courtesy of Norfolk Historical Society.

installed a new steel bridge at Sutton's Mill in Simcoe. Other canning factories in the area kept them occupied manufacturing retorts, large, heavy, perforated iron containers to hold produce-filled cans being cooked in tank of boiling water, and all manner of equipment used in the canning process. In addition to this kind of work, their many customers in several fields kept them busy making repairs on steam, threshing engines, agricultural implements, flour and gristmill equipment, as well as sawmill machinery in Norfolk County and neighbouring counties. In fact, by the turn of the century the firm of West & Peachey had grown to be one of the largest and most successful companies in Norfolk County.

12

West & Peachey Enter the Twentieth Century

Both John West and James Peachey were by now well established and respected businessmen of their community. The latter had built the first summer cottage on the beach in Port Ryerse and each summer the family would travel by team and wagon to spend the summer there. James Peachey enjoyed getting away from the stress of business at the foundry and having the weekends to himself, being with his family, swimming, and cavorting in the sand.

The second cottage in Port Ryerse was built by the Gunton family. John Gunton was a well-known builder who constructed his cottage in the backyard of his home in Vittoria. He may have originated the idea of the prefabricated home, for he then took it all apart, transported it by team and wagon to the beach site in Port Ryerse, and reassembled it next to the Peachey cottage.

Not long after, John West built his cottage adjacent to that of his partner in Port Ryerse. The roads at the time were little more than tracks in the sand and the safest, most reliable mode of travel was by sturdy wagons drawn by heavy draught horses, or by light, high-wheeled buggies or democrats. In due course, John West, with his love for all things powered by steam, purchased a small, used Locomobile Steamer, a "dos-a-dos" roadster model. For several years he was a common sight driving his steam car on the streets of Simcoe. Colonel Douglas Stalker, West's grandson, describes it as a topless contraption with two passenger seats back-to-back like an Irish jaunting car. The driver and companion in front saw where they were going, the two in the back seat saw where they had been. The boiler and engine were below the seats and smoke was vented from the fire box to each side. It was steered by a curved handle and a foot pedal rang a bell (the bulb horn was yet to come) to warn others of the approaching vehicle. A lever on the driver's side operated a steam throttle to control the speed.

Doug Stalker remembers a trip to Port Dover with Grandfather West and father, John Stalker, in the Locomobile with nostalgic pleasure. At least twenty minutes before a trip could begin it was necessary to fire up the kerosene-fed copper-tube boiler in order to build a head of steam. The water tank had to be filled at frequent intervals to ensure safety and sufficient steam to operate the quiet and efficient engine. They set out with Doug in the rear seat. As they approached a large hill on the deeply rutted sand road, West paused to make sure they had a full head of steam, about 300 psi being required, then they charged ahead.

Upon reaching the Halfway House (at the intersection of today's Highways 6 and 24) the men went in for a drink, leaving Doug to proudly attend to the car's many lubrication points with a large oil can. As Doug comments, "They lubricated inside while I lubricated outside!"[1] On their way again they stopped at Hay Creek to take on water, using the pail that was always carried for dipping water when needed. A short break was required to wait for the steam pressure to build sufficiently to navigate the rutted track into Port Dover. Doug notes, "It was a big trip for the little Locomobile, although only eight miles away and an experience a young boy was not about to forget."[2]

On another occasion James Peachey travelled to their Port Ryerse cottages with West driving the Locomobile. Having arrived safely that evening, they turned west into the lane along the beach heading for the cottage. The steamer, however, became stuck in the deep sand on the beach. They both jumped out to push the car, and soon it was free, but to their chagrin it now took off on its own as West had left the throttle open. The men ran after the car, but it was outdistancing them in the rutted track to the cottage. Then to their horror, it suddenly jumped the track and headed for the lake. "Goodbye car!" exclaimed West, visualizing the hot boiler of his prized possession blowing up as it plunged into the cold waters of the lake. Providentially, one front wheel struck a

John West's big 1912 Model 26 Russell-Knight automobile, circa 1915, is adorned with two unidentified ladies on the running board.

Courtesy of the Mrs. Gordon Skinner Collection.

stone and turned the car back toward the cottages, where it crossed the lane and crashed into the hand pump between the two buildings. The little car just sat there vibrating violently, as if out of breath following its hair-raising ordeal.[3]

Around 1908 John West sold the little steam Locomobile and bought a gasoline-powered Russell, which was made in Toronto. Four years later, West purchased a big Russell Knight, which was his pride and joy. It was also his most expensive pleasure — a most luxurious automobile for the period, costing $3,400, or roughly the price of a new Alligator tug at that time. James Peachey had purchased a new Everitt automobile the previous year.

As Clarence Coons points out in his extensive research into the history of the Alligator tugs:

> While John West and James Peachey lived comfortably they did not enjoy the wealth and prosperity that many of the timber barons they dealt with did. Their outlook was truly conservative and they took great pride in producing Alligators cheaply and in offering them to customers for a modest markup. Production of top quality machinery and a satisfied customer seemed more important to them than big profits.
>
> They were two of Simcoe's most successful businessmen, building their business on quality workmanship, honesty and integrity into one of Norfolk County's largest. Their success was not one of riches, holidays and mansions. Theirs was a business success; success in doing something that others had not accomplished. The team of West & Peachey was a solid, dedicated partnership, which, it seemed, would never fail. Both men lived in modest homes in Simcoe and had cottages in nearby Port Ryerse on Lake Erie.
>
> Depending on demand for Alligator tugs the factory staff varied from seventeen to forty employees. It was important to them that their staff demonstrate the same qualities of excellence and interest in their

This Peachey family photograph was taken circa 1902 (l–r): William, Arthur, Mrs. Annie (Weeks) Peachey, Edward, Harry, Evelyn, James Peachey, and Mary Bell.

Courtesy of Barbara Peachey Wright.

work. Wages were modest. In the 1890s the average wage was about $1.25 per day. John Stalker, West's son-in-law, received $9 per week at that time.

Some of the dedicated staff who worked during the production of the Alligator tugs are remembered as follows: George Adams, Jonathon Awde, Theodore Brown, Jack Churchill, Robert Coates, J.B. Edmondson, D. Lindsay, William Monteith, Harry Peachey, Ted Peachey, Webber Piette, Archie Piette, J. B. Robbins, O. Scott, Robert Stewart Sr., Robert Stewart Jr., George Stringer, Alfred Winter, J. Yeomans, and others remembered only as Masterson and Stegmire. Having satisfied employees seemed equally as important to the partners as having satisfied customers. The fact that several employees spent most of their working careers with West & Peachey attests to this fact.[4]

By the beginning of the twentieth century, thirty-six Alligator Warping Tugs had been manufactured by the firm of West & Peachey. Minor modifications and improvements had been made over the years, but they all followed the original design and all were of the side-paddlewheel type. The lull in production of the previous three years was abruptly reversed in 1900 when four Alligator tugs were ordered and produced for that spring.

In January 1900, West & Peachey received two orders for Alligator Warping Tugs. The first was from a McLaurin and a McLaren of the East Templeton Lumber Company in East Templeton, Quebec. At that time the firm was operating a sawmill there in addition to three large logging camps at the headwaters of the Coulonge River in Quebec. Their timber limits were on the height of land from which water flowed to the Coulonge, Black, and Gatineau rivers. All three rivers eventually flowed into the Ottawa River.

Their order for the Alligator tug, *Emma*, requested that it be shipped deep into the Quebec wilderness, north of the Ottawa River, to the Coulonge River timber limits. In March, the unassembled tug was sent in sections by rail to Pembroke, to be hauled by teams of horses over winter tote roads to a remote inland lake near the headwaters of the river. John West and a small crew from the factory left a few days later to assemble the tug on site and put it into operation. John West sent the following letter to the local paper, the *British Canadian*, describing his experiences after he arrived in Pembroke. It was printed in full on March 25, 1900:

To the *British Canadian*:

I thought I would write a few lines to let you know something of my trip. I arrived in Pembroke on Friday at noon. I went up to the curling rink at night and had a game. The outfit here is nothing like ours. They use cast iron blocks (curling stones) from 60 to 62 pounds apiece, they are about 8 inches wide and 4 inches high. Lots of players in Pembroke never saw a pair of stone blocks. There are one hundred members in the club. The rink is only wide enough for two rinks, and the ice was the worst I ever played on, but we had a lovely time.

We left Pembroke Saturday noon, crossed the Ottawa River and travelled north up the Black River. The first half day we made 32 miles. We crossed the island, which is well settled, and is on the north side of the lake. As we went up the Black River there were some very nice houses for 10 or 15 miles, but soon the farms became poor and the buildings were merely log shacks, and before we got to the first stopping place they disappeared.

These stopping places are log buildings, built in the rough, notched at the corners, and chinked and stopped with hay or moss, are one storey high and covered with scoops, which are small trees about 12 or 15 inches in diameter, split in two pieces and hollowed out, one row laid with their faces up and another course with their hollow sides down, and they make a watertight roof. As we got up the river some of the buildings were so low your head would hardly clear when you would stand straight. The floors are round poles flattened a little on one side. Some of them have pole platforms raised one side, or both, as the case may be. But you must find your own blankets and fit yourself on the poles the best way you can for sleep. The first place was the last place we got a bed that you could call a bed. We could not find fault with our conveyance. It was a long sleigh and a light pair of horses. The sleigh was fitted with two seats as near the centre as possible, so that the pitching and jumping motion would not throw us out of the sleigh in going over cradle knolls, pitch holes, and rocks which are enough to give you a lame back.

The next day we travelled 50 miles. We now could see deer tracks and before we got to the stopping place we saw wolf, moose, and a great many other tracks. At last we came to one place where there were three dead wolves lying alongside the road. They had been poisoned by eating a dead horse which had been poisoned by the shantymen. There are a great many wolves around there and are giving some trouble; they have treed two gangs of men travelling into the camps. You can hear them howling at night while chasing the small deer. But we have got a long way above them now. We are in the land of the caribou, moose and beaver. Wolves do not tackle caribou or moose, as their kicking ability drives the wolves off.

We got to the second stopping place at dusk. There we got our supper of bread and pork and laid down on our pole bed until morning. Got another feed of fat pork and bread and started for the next stopping place, which was 35 miles through a very rough and wild country. Fire had run through, burned up all the valuable timber, and it had grown up with silver birch and poplar. After a hard day's ride we made the third stopping place. There we got pork, beans and moose meat for supper; the same bill of fare for breakfast, and started for the fourth stopping place, which was about 25 miles, and the hardest part of our journey.

We had travelled up the Black River so far, but now we had to cross over the mountains to the head waters of the Calaunge [sic] River, where we were to build the boat which was following us up with 20 teams, all in one string. We were half of the day climbing up hill and the other half going down, and it was going down with a vengeance. The horses would set back on their haunches, with their feet straight out before them, and would slide down 15 to 20 feet at an angle of 45 degrees. You would think the sleigh would go on top of them but the horses here are used to it.

Finally we got down to the lake just as it was getting dark. It had been snowing but now it turned to rain. By the time we got to the camp we were wet through, and the camp was covered with poles and brush, so it leaked nearly as bad as it rained outside, but it was warmer. We took our pork and bread and took to the poles for sleep. We now had 20 miles to go, and it was through an unbroken wilderness — not even the mark of an axe, except where the trail was cut over the portages.

The most of the travelling is done on the lakes. The ice is three feet thick and the snow is five feet deep. The temperature is nearly down to zero [Fahrenheit] All the time; but they expect a thaw any day. We have got a comfortable camp here. It is wild and that is putting it mild. I forgot to mention that they measure the miles with a long sleigh and they throw the tongue in every time. There are some Indians near here; they come to the camp to trade furs for the things they want. I bought a black beaver skin the other day, it is a beauty. I also got a nice fisher skin. We get a good deal of moose meat; it is nice, sweet, juicy meat. This is a hunter's paradise; but you have to do your walking on snow shoes.

Well, I guess I have said about all I can think of.
Yours truly,

J.C. West

The *Emma* arrived in due course and John West and his crew assembled and tested her on the Coulonge limits before returning to Simcoe. The Alligator tug served her owners well for several years in that same area. In 1910, the *Emma* was sold to the Gilmour and Hughson Lumber Company of Hull, Quebec for $700. The tug was moved to their Bark Lake operations. Little else is known of the *Emma* or the *Kealy*, which was also owned by the East Templeton Lumber Company. They were both sold to the Gilmour and Hughson Company in 1910 for a combined total of $1,300.

13

The Alligator Warping Tug in Newfoundland

The first order ever received from Newfoundland came in May of 1900 for the larger of the two Alligator Warping Tugs built by the firm of West & Peachey. Lewis Miller of Millertown, Newfoundland, requested that the tug be shipped in sections. For the past eighteen years he had been operating a sawmill in Sweden, but by the turn of the century his timber limits in that country had become exhausted. Upon visiting Newfoundland to assess its potential, he found that the heart of the island possessed a considerable stand of good timber. After having bought up timber limits there, he began building a large sawmill on Red Indian Lake, located about 20 miles from the main line of the Newfoundland Railway.

Alligator #40, a large tug to be named *Annie*, was shipped from the factory in Simcoe in late August of 1900. John West and O. Scott booked passage to Newfoundland to assemble the tug and put it into operation. Their memorable venture into the wilds of that rugged island involved travel on several trains and steamboats. From Hamilton, Ontario, they boarded the steamship *Hamilton* for Montreal, where they transferred to another steamship bound for Quebec City. Here they caught a train to North Sydney, Nova Scotia. In North Sydney they took passage on the steamer *Bruce* for Port Aux Basques, Newfoundland.

Once on the island they booked seats on the narrow-gauge Newfoundland Railway and travelled for another fifteen hours, through small fishing villages and beautiful but rugged terrain, to the junction that led to Millertown, 20 more miles into the wilderness. The final leg of the trip was made on the Cannonball Express. For the last section of the trip, West and Scott rode on a railway tie for a seat that was anchored to the bed of an open flatcar. With at least some consideration for their passenger's comfort, the flatcar was pushed ahead of the steam engine, so that ash from the smokestack would not get in their eyes.

Upon arrival in Millertown they found that, physically, it was as yet non-existent. On setting up their 8-by-10-foot tent, West and Scott became Millertown's first and only inhabitants. About half a mile away, some fifty men were chopping the trees down and clearing a tract of land on the shore of Red Indian Lake where the railway emerged from the forest. This was to be Millertown.

Red Indian Lake was a narrow body of water about 40 miles in length. The timber in the area of the lake was primarily spruce, but Miller's timber limits also contained a considerable amount of white pine and tamarack. John West was enthralled by what he saw, describing the country as, "beyond conception, it's a hunter's paradise with caribou in abundance. There are thousands of them."[1] West and Scott wasted no time in completing the Alligator *Annie*, and once the testing and training of her operators was complete, they returned home. They arrived back in Simcoe on October 15, 1900.

Lewis Miller worked his Red Indian Lake timber limits until the spring of 1903, when an American syndicate made him an offer he could not refuse. He sold his entire Newfoundland limits to them. In October 1903, Miller purchased properties owned by the Dominion Lumber Company of Nova Scotia. That purchase included a sawmill at Ingram Docks, 25 miles distant from Halifax, and 80,000 acres of heavily timbered forest lands. Much of these limits contained good spruce, hemlock, and white pine.

In 1920, West & Peachey again heard from Lewis Miller, when he ordered a small twin-screw Alligator Warping Tug from the firm. This was Alligator #158, and was named the *W.A. Christie*. It was shipped to Nova Scotia to be used on the original Dominion Lumber Company limits that Miller had acquired in 1903. The two tugs, *Annie* and *W.A. Christie*, were the only Alligator Warping Tugs sold in the Maritime Provinces. Both were purchased, twenty years apart, by Lewis Miller.

By 1901, West & Peachey's production had increased to eight orders for tugs. In fact that year the firm had to refuse three orders, knowing that it would be impossible to have them completed in time for that year's spring log drive. They did build and ship the *E.B. Eddy* to E.B. Eddy & Company of Hull, Quebec; the *Hercules* to the Upper Ottawa Improvement Company, Ottawa; the *Holland & Graves* to the company of that name in Buffalo, New York; the *Sweepstake* and the *Traveller* to the Turner Lumber Company of Midland, Ontario; the *Victoria* shipped in May to Victoria Harbour Lumber Company of Toronto; the *Coulonge* in August to Gillies Brothers in Braeside, Ontario; and the *Beaver* in August to the Georgian Bay Lumber Company in Waubaushene, Ontario.

Alligator tug buyers were very pleased with the operation of their vessels and were not hesitant to write glowing testimonials to West & Peachey, to that effect. The Hull

Lumber Company of Hull, Quebec, now owned three Alligators, and the letter that follows speaks for itself:

Ottawa, Ontario, Canada
November 16, 1901

Messrs. West and Peachey, Simcoe, Ontario

Gentlemen —

In reply to your favor of the 14th, inst., in which you ask us if the Alligator warping tugs we have purchased from you have given satisfaction, we beg to state that we are now using three of these tugs and that they are giving every satisfaction in fact, as the writer has often stated, they are something like the telephone in one respect, that we used to be able to get along without them but now that we have them we do not see how we ever did.

Yours very truly,

The Hull Lumber Co. Ltd.
Chas. E. Reid, Man. Dir.[2]

The Alligator Warping Tugs owned by the Hull Lumber Company at that time were: Tug #19, the *C.S. Reid* (1893); Tug #30, the *F.W. Avery* (1896); and Tug #39, the *W.T. White* (1900). Such glowing testimonials by a company like The Hull Lumber Company were a major factor in promoting sales of the tugs to other lumbermen.

Those among the lumbering companies and timber barons of the day who were using the Alligator tugs included: John R. Booth of Ottawa, Ontario; Ezra B. Eddy of Hull, Quebec; James B. and Robert A. Klock of Klock's Mills, Ontario; the McLachlin Bros. of Arnprior, Ontario; W.C. Edwards of Rockland, Ontario; John Waldie of Victoria Harbour, Ontario;[3] The Gillies Brothers of Braeside, Ontario; and David and Allan Gilmour of Trenton, Ontario.

In addition to the performance of the Alligator Warping Tugs and the testimonials from satisfied timber companies, which certainly played a role in the successful sale of these versatile craft, West & Peachey advertised their warping tugs in other ways. In 1895, they placed their first commercial advertisement in *Canadian Lumberman and*

Woodworker. From that time forward, the West & Peachey advertisements appeared frequently in the magazine throughout the whole period of production of the Alligators.

The firm never produced any sales catalogues for the Alligator tugs. However, soon after the production of the first Alligators, West & Peachey did print and distribute a circular that described the Alligator Warping Tug and its operation to any lumbermen who made enquiry. Around 1902, a large and colourful wall calendar, measuring 24 by 35 inches, was produced. The calendar featured a large watercolour of two Alligators and was issued annually until 1915, with only the year and daily dates being changed. On the back of each of these calendars was a description of the tug and its operation, as well as a list of all buyers of the tug to date. Only one good copy of this annual calendar, issued in 1909, is known to exist.

The majority of the Alligator tugs produced were sold to buyers in Ontario and Quebec and then only after an order was received by the firm, as in most cases they were built individually to the buyer's own specifications. Primarily, buyers were influenced to invest in an Alligator because of its superb performance for other owners. As West & Peachey pointed out in one of their advertising slogans, placed in the *Canadian Lumberman and Woodworker* — "Not altogether what we say but what users say!"

A West & Peachey advertising calendar showing Alligator tugs warping and portaging. From 1902 to 1915 the same image was used on their annual calendar.

Courtesy of the Eva Brook Donly Museum, Norfolk Historical Society Archives, R1 17A.

Not altogether what we say but what Users say

"We have used the Alligator or Warping Tug manufactured by you for the last 7 or 8 years, and consider them indispensable to lumbermen on waters of French River or similar streams."

Will move a bag containing 60,000 logs, in calm weather, 30,000 in a head wind.

WEST & PEACHEY
SIMCOE - - - ONTARIO

An advertisement placed in *The Canadian Lumberman and Woodworker* issue of August 1910, features an Alligator tug hauling itself overland.

Courtesy of the Eva Brook Donly Museum, Norfolk Historical Society Archives, F1 8A.

14

Turn-of-the-Century Improvements and Modifications

An improvement in sleeping accommodation on the Alligator tugs was made around 1901, when the small wheelhouses were enlarged and extended to the rear, allowing bunks to be placed in them. This provided better sleeping quarters for the crew, even when the tugs were in operation.[1]

In 1902, the Hawkesbury Lumber Company ordered Alligator #51 to be named the *D. Lunam*. She proved to be one of the most transitional tugs the firm manufactured, as several improvements and modifications were incorporated into her construction. She was equipped with the first steam engine to have a short crankshaft. She also had split paddlewheel gearing, which allowed each paddlewheel to be turned independently. This greatly improved the Alligator's manoeuvrability when in a confined space.

The *D. Lunam* was the first Alligator to have West's newly designed automatic cable-winding device installed on her bow. All earlier tugs had the cable guided back and forth across the face of the cable drum by two sheaves attached to a transverse screw on the bow of the tug, just behind the bow roller. When being wound in, the cable ran between the sheaves quite satisfactorily, but, to keep it winding evenly across the drum, a crewman had to be in constant attendance inside to operate the screw.

This, in turn, meant that the anchor could not be hauled up over the bow without hitting the cable carriage. For this reason, all earlier Alligator tugs had been equipped with a gantry to lift the anchor out of the water and clear of the bow, to be swung inboard, and stowed on deck behind the cable guide. John West's new automatic cable-winding device, unlike the old guide, was mounted on the deck just in front of the cabin. This allowed the anchor to be winched in over the bow roller without striking the cable guide. Not only could the gantry be removed, but a crewman was no longer needed to tend the screw that guided the cable as it was wound in on the cable drum when warping.

EXPLOSION AND FIRE AT THE WEST & PEACHEY WORKS

A loud explosion, followed by prolonged blasts on the factory steam whistle shortly after 7:00 a.m. on Saturday morning, October 19, 1901, alarmed the good citizens of Simcoe. At the same time, it alerted them to some serious accident at the West & Peachey Foundry. Within minutes the firm's oil house was a roaring mass of flame.

This small wooden building was located at the northeast corner of the property adjoining the new brick moulding shop. It served as storage for large quantities of paints and oils. Also a great many moulding flasks had been stored there temporarily during the construction of the shop. A hastily formed bucket brigade was credited with preventing the spread of the fire, until the Simcoe steam fire pumpers arrived to bring the blaze under control. Fortunately, the new brick moulding shop had shielded the large wooden, and highly flammable, older building from harm.

Simcoe Fire Department's Waterous Fire Engine, operated by John West's son, Charles T. West. Photo circa 1900.

Courtesy of the Eva Brook Donly Museum, Norfolk Historical Society Archives, File 12 Neg. 10A-11.

Later it was learned that an employee, Alfred Winter, had entered the oil house to draw some Japan varnish from the barrel in which it was stored. The varnish came out so slowly that Winter, unaware of its volatility, lit a match to check the level of varnish in the barrel. The fumes ignited immediately and Winter was knocked down by the resultant violent explosion. George Adams, who was working nearby, rushed to the aid of the dazed and injured Alfred Winter, and miraculously, they both escaped the burning building without further injury.

In time, Winter recovered from his injuries from the mishap. The oil building was not insured, causing a loss of $600 to West & Peachey. They replaced the building with a brick addition later. On June 11, 1904, fire again threatened when a spark from the cupola started a fire in the shingles of the roof of the main building. Thanks to quick discovery and action taken by employees, the fire was extinguished with little damage being incurred.

WEST & PEACHEY MOVE TO TWIN-SCREW ALLIGATOR TUGS

The first sixty-six Alligator Warping Tugs built by West & Peachey were all equipped with two side paddlewheels. The paddlewheel models had the advantage of working well in shallow, weedy water and in amongst logs and booms.

In the fall of 1904, West & Peachey introduced the first Alligator tug with twin screws on drive shafts with flexible joints, which allowed the raising of the propellers out of harm's way when portaging. A lever was used to accomplish this. The propellers were protected from floating logs or other sunken hazards by guard irons, fixed to the hull, around them. The buyer had a choice of three- or four-bladed propellers in sizes ranging from 28 inches to 34 inches in diameter. A standard-size Alligator tug equipped with twin propellers, rather than side paddlewheels, was reduced to 10 feet in width, making it much easier to move over narrow portages or run through floating logs. The paddlewheel tugs were 16 feet in width. Propeller-equipped Alligator tugs also provided more room below decks and allowed for better light and ventilation in the engine compartment.

Alligator #67, the first with twin screws and named the *St. Maurice No. 3*, was purchased by the Department of Public Works in Ottawa for service on the St. Maurice River in Quebec. The tug was shipped from the factory on April 10, 1905, to Trois-Rivières. It performed to everyone's satisfaction for the next seven years until it was destroyed by fire on October 12, 1912, with the loss of one crewman's life. The *St. Maurice No. 3* was salvaged and finally rebuilt on site at Trois-Rivières in 1914. It continued in operation there until 1925 when it was rebuilt again to continue to in service for the department. Finally, Alligator #67 was scrapped in 1941.

West & Peachey, at a later date, supplied Alligators with fixed twin-screw propellers. These proved more popular with buyers in the 1920s and 1930s. The firm built a total of ninety-four twin-screw Alligator Warping Tugs from 1905 until the last tug was built by the firm in 1934. During that period many of the original side-paddlewheel Alligator tugs were converted to twin-screw models. West & Peachey supplied a package of all the machinery necessary to convert from paddlewheels to propellers for about $540. They would also do a conversion for any owners not prepared to make the changes themselves. In some cases old paddlewheel Alligators, or their machinery, were returned to the factory for rebuilding by employees of the firm.

INTRODUCTION OF THE BABY ALLIGATOR WARPING TUG

In 1907 West & Peachey introduced a smaller Alligator tug to the industry. These proved popular with lumbermen wanting a smaller, lighter Alligator for portaging and with those operators without large quantities of logs or pulpwood to be rafted and moved. This smaller tug, first introduced as a paddlewheel model, was 35 feet long with an 8 foot beam. Several were also 37 feet in length. These Alligators had only a small wheelhouse for the captain and no above-deck sleeping accommodation or cooking facilities. The baby Alligator tug was normally supplied with a smaller engine having a 7-inch bore and stroke. Small-size, return-flue boilers, 40 inches by 58 inches, were standard equipment as well. They also carried only 3,500 feet of half-inch steel warping cable. A smaller, 250-pound warping anchor was also made available for them.

The *Chapleau*, Alligator #77, was the first small, or "Baby Alligator" tug built in 1907. Here, it is working a log boom for owners Mageau LeBlanc Lumber Company of Chapleau, Ontario.

Courtesy of the Clarence F. Coons Collection.

Alligator #77 was the first of these baby tugs built by West & Peachey. She was named the *Chapleau* and was sold to Mageau LeBlanc Lumber Company of Chapleau, Ontario. West & Peachey went on to build ten paddlewheel models of this smaller style. By 1923, they had built ten additional twin-screw tugs, for a total of twenty of the baby Alligator models. The last two of this type were built in 1923 for a cost to the buyer of $3,767. By comparison, the price of a standard Alligator Warping Tug by this time was approximately $5,050.

ALLIGATOR WARPING TUG #101, THE *BERSIMIS*

In April 1910, West & Peachey contracted with the sawmill owners, Howard & Craig of Sherbrooke, Quebec, to build an extra-large paddlewheel Alligator Warping Tug. She would be Alligator #101, to be named the *Bersimis*, and to be used on the Rimouski River in Quebec. The agreed upon price was $7,000.00, or almost twice that of a standard Alligator of that time. As the finished tug would be too large to ship to Quebec by rail, it was decided to assemble it in Port Ryerse harbour, directly south of Simcoe, on Lake Erie. Once tested and approved for delivery, it could sail under its own power through the lakes to its destination in Rimouski on the St. Lawrence River. She was to be built with a stem post and pointed bow rather than the normal scow-type found on other Alligator tugs.

The *Bersimis* was launched and tested successfully at Port Ryerse on June 30, 1910. Finally, on August 4, she set out with ten men on board, including Captain Amundson, as pilot and R. Howard Jr. representing the owners, Howard & Craig of Sherbrooke. John West and James Peachey's son, Arthur, with a crew of James Brock, Alfred Winters, and Charles Hart representing the builders, were also on board. As well, three prominent Simcoe citizens were

The *Bersimis*, the extra-large Alligator #101, is being assembled at the Port Ryerse pier on Lake Erie, in 1910.
Courtesy of Barbara Peachey Wright.

on board as passengers: George H. Luscombe, A.T. Sihler, and W.C. McCall. They spent their first night in nearby Port Dover. Leaving the port the next day, they delivered the Alligator to her new owners in Montreal eight days later. Once the new crew was familiar with the operation of the tug, they took charge and set out for her home port in Rimouski. The West & Peachey contingent returned to Simcoe by train.

The Story of the Cavendish Lumber Company's Alligator Tugs

In the winter of 1910–11, woodsmen employed by the Cavendish Lumber Company of Lakefield, Ontario, harvested the last of the white pine timber to be cut by that firm in the whole of Peterborough County. It was also the last extensive cut of virgin white pine in the Trent Valley watershed. At the time of settlement some of the finest white pine in all of Canada was growing in this watershed, an area covering roughly 6,000 square miles of southeastern Ontario. By 1840, the cutting of timber and settlement had extended north of Lakefield.

By the turn of the twentieth century, most of the old-growth white pine in the Trent watershed had been harvested. Only the extensive white pine stands on the Scott limits[1] of Peterborough County survived, and that was only due to a lengthy and costly legal battle that was not settled until 1889. At that time Scott's rich timber limits, covering 105 square miles in Cavendish, Anstruther, and Harvey townships in Peterborough County, were acquired by the Dickson Lumber Company of Peterborough. In 1893, they also purchased the sawmill at Lakefield from the Lakefield Lumber and Manufacturing Company. This was a water-powered sawmill previously owned by the former timber barons of the Trent watershed, Roland and George Strickland.

Late in 1893, Dickson Lumber sold the Scott timber limits to J.W. Howry and Sons of Saginaw, Michigan, who had only recently acquired a sawmill at Fenelon Falls, Ontario. In 1897, however, the Howry company failed financially and the Dickson Lumber Company regained control of the Scott timber limits. In 1898, they purchased one of the Howry's Alligator tugs, then called the *Dickson*. This tug is thought to be the old Alligator tug *Saginaw* originally sold by West & Peachey to J.W. Howry and Sons in 1891. At that time it was to be used in their logging enterprise in the Whitefish Bay area, on Georgian Bay's north shore. In 1898, the Dickson Company also built a new sawmill in Lakefield on the same site as that of old Lakefield Lumber Company. The tug *Dickson* was to be used to move logs from the Scott limits to this new mill. The Dickson company had not been in operation long before it became apparent that if they were to move roughly 10 million board feet of lumber annually to the Lakefield sawmill, they needed an additional Alligator Warping Tug. As a result, the Alligator #49, *Hazlitt*, was ordered from West & Peachey for delivery in spring 1902.

The new paddlewheel *Hazlitt* arrived in Lakefield by train and was launched into the Trent River on May 7, 1902. Trials were carried out on the Trent as far as Young's Point, and every one proved to be satisfactory. The two Alligator tugs would be used to assist in the removal of the last extensive virgin stands of white pine left in the Trent watershed. The *Dickson* would operate on the upper lakes, warping logs from the timber limits in Cavendish and Anstruther townships through Bottle, Catchacoma, and Mississaugua lakes. The logs would be driven down the Mississaugua River to Buckhorn Lake. The *Hazlitt* would then take charge to move the logs from Buckhorn Lake down the Trent River system to Lakefield, through Lower Buckhorn, Lovesick, Stoney, Clear, and Katchawanooka lakes. Here, the logs were to be stored in the large holding booms above Lakefield. The *Hazlitt* would also tow small booms of logs on down to the mill in the village. The Dickson Lumber Company operated their Lakefield sawmill for eight years.

The *Hazlitt*, Alligator #49, is shown working in the Trent River, north of Lakefield, with a pointer boat and boom logs in tow, circa 1909.
Courtesy of the Clarence F. Coons Collection.

Lumber stacked on either side of the rail siding awaiting shipment from the Cavendish Lumber Company mill, Lakefield, Ontario.
Courtesy of Mrs. John Twist.

In 1906, a new company, the Cavendish Lumber Company, was formed. They purchased the Scott timber limits and the two Alligator tugs, but leased the Lakefield sawmill. It was estimated at that time that the Scott limits still contained about 50 million board feet of standing pine timber. The final assault was about to be made on what little remained of the old-growth white pine forest in the Trent watershed. Since the Lakefield sawmill could saw 80,000 to 90,000 board feet of lumber a day, it would take only five years, sawing 10 million board feet annually, to remove the last vestige of remaining good pine timber from that vast watershed. During those five remaining years of timber harvest, the *Hazlitt* was a familiar sight as she steamed between Buckhorn Lake and Lakefield, piloted by Captain Ott Wanamaker, while Art Payne served as engineer and Ed Payne fired her boilers.

Fire rages through the Cavendish Lumber yards on July 27, 1907.
Courtesy of Mrs. John Twist.

During the winter of 1910–11, the last of the white pine was removed from the Scott timber limits and the *Hazlitt* was sold to the Munn Lumber Company of Orillia. The *Dickson* Alligator continued warping logs to the Lakefield mill until September 4, 1913, when the last log was sawn into lumber and the humming saws and busy mill fell silent. It spelled the end of an era. Once the cheery whistle and chuffing engines of the Alligators ceased, the great river drives were no more, and the Lakefield mill closed, never to open again.

In November 1913, the *Dickson* was sold to the Peterborough Lumber Company. Four years later, the *Dickson* was again sold, this time to leave the barren, denuded, rock-strewn Trent watershed, with its subsistence farms being all that remained where the once proud forest stood. The Alligator moved north to be operated by the French River Boom Company Limited.

THE PLACE OF YELLOW BIRCH AND OTHER HARDWOODS

When the timber barons first came to the fore in the harvest of our Canadian forests they sought only white pine, and for good reason. It was plentiful, suited for a multitude of uses, and, where water was in abundance, the buoyancy of pine lent itself to easy transport to distant sawmills. Although yellow birch preferred the same general forest region as white pine, the nineteenth-century lumbermen bypassed it.

During the first decade of the twentieth century, with the expansion of railways, sawmills utilizing hardwoods, notably maple, oak, and yellow birch, began to establish themselves in proximity to rail service. These heavy, hardwood sawlogs did not lend themselves to water transport as 50 percent of them would sink and be lost before they reached the mill. Most were sleigh-hauled overland to the mills. Some lumbermen, preferring water transport, partially peeled the logs to dry them out before floating them. Others resorted to chaining each hardwood log to a lighter, buoyant pine or cedar log to ensure that it would reach the sawmill. Despite these methods, wherever birch logs were "boomed up," slow but steady sinkage took its toll.

The richly coloured finished product from yellow birch was coveted by flooring and furniture manufacturers and by 1915 it was very much in demand. Yellow birch veneer was also in demand particularly during the Second World War, when it was substituted for scarce aluminum in the manufacture of the skin of the deadly Mosquito fighter planes, which came into their own during the Battle of Britain. To this day, salvagers of hardwood logs scour the old log booming sites to haul up the long-drowned logs to produce popular old-growth lumber for a lucrative market.

16

The Role of the Alligator in the Ottawa Valley

The valley of the Ottawa River and its tributaries supported the most extensive pine forests in the whole of Canada. The mighty Ottawa River extends northwesterly from its juncture with the St. Lawrence River, inland to its source some 700 miles distant. During the timbering era, millions upon millions of squared white-pine logs would be floated out of the watershed and rafted to Quebec City. The last drive of squared timber, in 1908, originated in the Coulonge River in J.R. Booth's limits. For almost a century, saw timber was driven and tugged down the Ottawa to sawmills at Pembroke, Braeside, Arnprior, Rockland, and Hawksbury, with the last tow taking place in 1990 to Braeside.

GILLIES BROTHERS: A TYPICAL LUMBER COMPANY

By 1871, it is known that over 1,200 saws were in operation in the Ottawa region alone. The mills in Ottawa itself were estimated to be sawing between 250 and 260 million board feet of lumber annually. From the beginning, all the logs had to be moved by means of river drives from their forest limits where they had been cut, to the mill that would saw them, often many, many miles away. By 1860, the many mill owners driving logs to their mills had increased to the point where identifying the logs of the various owners was becoming a major problem. Better organization of the river drives was becoming a major issue for the lumber companies.

One such company with a long and respected history was that of the Gillies Brothers of Braeside, on the Ontario side of the Ottawa River. As Mary Campbell, fifth-generation member of pioneer Scottish settlers and mayor of McNab-Braeside Township, points out, the Gillies sawmill was begun in about 1850 by Henry Usborne, a minister who came from a famous lumbering family with a well-established lumber brokerage firm in London, England. Their lumber was supplied and marketed through the firm of Atkinson & Usborne of Quebec City. The firm also owned a sawmill in Quebec, which they disposed of in 1854.

Henry Usborne built his Braeside sawmill in 1857 along the Ottawa River at Red Pine Bay. In 1873, John Gillies of Carleton Place purchased this mill. John Gillies Sr. had been born in Sterlingshire, Scotland, in 1811. In 1821, at the age of ten, he came to Canada with his parents, James and Helen Stark Gillies, as part of the immigration of the Lanark Society settlers. John married Mary Bain, and, in 1840, after having carried a 90-pound saw on his back the 50 miles from Brockville, he established a sawmill on the Clyde River. He soon acquired extensive timber limits, and, in 1843, built a gristmill. By 1873, the Gillies were a large, well-known and prosperous family in Carleton Place. Their sawmill, operated by son John Jr. since 1867, was producing 100 thousand feet of lumber a day. The mill employed a hundred men. The Gillies also owned the gristmill, a tannery, a woollen mill, and the machine and engine works there. John Gillies later sold his share in the Carleton Place sawmill to Peter McLaren.[1] In 1873, John Sr. established his sons James, William, and David, as operators of the Usborne sawmill at Braeside. With the purchase came 250 square miles of timber limits on the Coulonge River in Quebec. John Jr., as a partner with his brothers, remained in Carleton Place to manage their interests there.

The Gillies brothers as they appeared, circa 1875, (l-r): George, William, David, James, and John. A brother, Alexander, had drowned earlier.

Courtesy of the Clarence F. Coons Collection.

Due to a severe depression for the next three years following the end of the Crimean War, the mill was closed during 1875 and 1876, but the family survived to become a major producer of squared timber for the Quebec trade. In 1893, they rebuilt the Braeside mill, replacing the circular saws with the more efficient bandsaws and increasing annual production to 35 million board feet. They also incorporated as Gillies Brothers Limited. As the railways expanded, so did the Gillies Brothers' markets, as well as their output of lumber, shingles, and railway ties. In 1910, a fire destroyed almost 30 million feet of lumber, and, in 1919, fire destroyed the Braeside mill. Deciding to adopt a preventative approach, they opened a fireproof modern facility in

1921. This mill, powered by electricity, soon established a reputation as one of the better known mills of the area, and continued to operate until 1963 when the company was purchased by Consolidated Bathurst Incorporated of Braeside.

In 1901, Gillies Brothers ordered the large-sized Alligator paddlewheel-driven tug #47, which they named *Coulonge*. They had timber limits in the Lake Nipissing area, which meant a long drive before their logs reached the Braeside mill. John "Bud" Doering[2] tells stories of his father Stanley operating a gas-powered ferry boat on Cedar Lake for Gillies Brothers lumber camps operations.

Bud Doering grew up in Brent, on Cedar Lake in the northern part of Algonquin Park. As a teenager in 1946, he worked in the summer on a Gillies-owned Alligator tug, the *William M.*, which was originally built as the *Max* in 1905. (This boat has been restored and is on display at the Logging Museum near the east gate of Algonquin Park today.) He claimed he was low man on the totem as crewman. His main duties were to hook up and unhook the tow ropes from the Alligator to the log booms and row a pointer to shore to load the firewood for the engine. He was also the cook on board, using a small gas stove on which he could fry eggs and other simple fare for Captain "Black Bill" Paquette and the other crew members. Another constant duty was to watch that sparks from the smokestack didn't ignite the coils of manila rope on the Alligator's deck. He had to have a pail of water at the ready to douse the occasional flare-up.

When working a boom of logs, Doering was involved with warping. If the logs caught on anything, he was sent with the pointer boat and a pike pole to free them up. Along with the rest of the crew, he slept on board. Doering enjoyed the life, but claimed he could swim faster than the tug itself moved through the water.

The logs were floated from the company limits, which were 30 miles west of Cedar Lake on the Nipissing River. As they reached the mouth of the river, the Alligator tug warped them in a boom for 11 miles down the lake to the entrance to the Petawawa River. From that point they began their 200-mile run to the Ottawa River, and eventually a year or more after being cut, they reached the Braeside mill to be sawn into lumber. It was recognized by all the mill owners that in moving logs those great distances, 8 to 10 percent of the logs were lost. Many became waterlogged and sank, while others escaped the boom, or were left behind in the wild rides through rapids and falls in the rivers they traversed. The Braeside mill burned in 1919, and was replaced with a new mill, also built on the Ottawa River, but closer to Arnprior than the original location.

Tom Stephenson, a Pembroke resident, worked in the logging camps for the Gillies Brothers, and had many interesting stories relating to the business. He became interested in the way in which company logs were identified and eventually sorted out according to the company marks they carried. Each company had their own identity stamp, which was "hammered" into the ends of each log they owned. In 1984, under the direction of the late Dr. Terry Honer, a book was published by the Canadian Forestry Service, titled *Registered Timber Marks of Eastern Canada from 1870 to 1884*. This enormous undertaking, compiled by Dianne Aldred, featured over 2,000 marks and the many hundreds of companies who registered them in chronological order. As an example, the Gillies Brothers registered the complete alphabet and numbers one to twenty-five for their exclusive use in identifying their logs. In addition to their mark hammered into the ends of the logs, they would chop a blaze a short distance in from the end of each log and scratch the following identification mark, "IXXI," on the face of the blaze.

In an attempt to solve the growing problem of identifying and sorting the company logs, the Upper Ottawa Drive Association, made up of all the principal mill owners, was formed in 1863. Their mandate was to take charge of all the logs coming into the Des Joachims boom on the upper Ottawa River and see that the logs got to their respective owners. Previous to this, each company brought their logs down in separate drives. As members of the new association, the mill owners had agreed to pay the cost of moving their logs in proportion to the number of logs moved that each of them owned.

In 1868, the association obtained a Dominion charter that recognized the Upper Ottawa Improvement Company, which took over the responsibilities of the association and commenced building improvements along the river that would expedite the movement of logs to the member's sawmills. At the same time they assumed responsibility for booming and driving of logs from Des Joachims to the Chaudière Rapids at Ottawa. By 1886, it was estimated that the company would handle 2.75 million logs on the river annually. Large rings were anchored in the rock up and down the length of the Ottawa River to allow booms of a company's logs to be secured to the shore when they reached their final destination, or, to hold them if the weather was against moving them on.

At first, the company sublet the towing of the logs in their charge. Several firms were involved in towing logs in the various lakes in the system. Included among them was the Union Forwarding Company, under Captain Murphy and the Upper Ottawa Steamboat Company under Captain Goulet. In 1889, the Upper Ottawa Improvement Company took charge of all towing between Des Joachims and Ottawa. As the independently owned, big towing tugs had been built in the lakes they had operated in and could not be readily moved elsewhere, the Improvement Company bought them from their owners. Later, the company acquired the towing rights north to Lake Temiskaming, which had previously been the responsibility of the Lumsden Company of Lumsden Mills, Quebec. This gave the Improvement Company control of all towing of logs, from the head of Lake Temiskaming to Ottawa, a total distance of 325 miles. This whole river route was more accurately described as a chain of lakes varying in length from 10 to 30 miles and in width from 1 to 5 miles. In almost every case they were linked to one another by either turbulent rapids or waterfalls. By 1896, the cost of moving logs over that considerable distance was about $1.30 per 1,000 board feet of lumber. The drives required to move this huge volume of logs involved hiring from four hundred to six hundred rivermen annually.

ALLIGATORS ON THE OTTAWA

In 1890, Alligator #3, named the *H. Trudel*, was purchased by R.H. Klock and Company from West & Peachey for use on Lake Kipawa and the Ottawa River. This was the first Alligator Warping Tug to work in the Ottawa River watershed, and its capabilities were soon being discussed by many of the lumbermen up and down the river, including members of the Improvement Company.

The first operator to order a tug from West & Peachey in 1893 was Alex Lumsden, whose company was in charge of towing on the Upper Ottawa. He took ownership of Alligator #11, named the *Beaver*, which was delivered to him at Lumsden Mills. Alex Lumsden was so pleased with the *Beaver* that he placed an order for a second tug in 1894. This was Alligator #27, named the *Otter*. The tugs proved invaluable to Lumsden as he was responsible for moving all logs in the upper reaches of the Ottawa River system as far north as Lake Temiskaming.

The second tug order in 1893 came from the Upper Ottawa Improvement Company, who took delivery of Alligator #12, the *Samson*, in Ottawa. These three Alligator tugs now operating in the Ottawa River system were all standard, side-paddlewheel craft. All had been completed in the West & Peachey factory in Simcoe. These initial three Alligators, the *H. Trudel*, the *Beaver*, and the *Samson* performed so amazingly well for their owners that it was only a matter of time before others on the river saw the need for them and orders were placed. Following the shipping of the *Samson*, West & Peachey were deluged with requests for Alligator tugs.

In 1901, the Upper Ottawa Improvement Company placed an order for a large-sized Alligator #42, named *Hercules*. Only the machinery was ordered, which was shipped to

Ottawa on February 18, 1901. The hull was built by the company. In 1903, they acquired the shipyards and workshops and other assets of the Lumsden Steam Boat Lines, including the large Alligator, built in 1896 and known as the *Mink*. Millionaire Alex Lumsden died on August 5, 1904, at the age of sixty-five, the head of a large, progressive business empire. At his funeral were hundreds of mourners including Sir Wilfred Laurier, Mayor Ellis of Ottawa, and lumbering giants J.R. Booth, F.H. Bronson, David McLean, and others.

The *Hercules*, Alligator #42. The order for machinery only, came in 1912 from the Upper Ottawa Improvement Company, who built the hull of the tug in their own yard. Here, the *Hercules* is shown taking a group on a Sunday outing on a sunny day. Note the pointer boat in tow.

Courtesy of Library and Archives Canada, #PA-111596. Preire De Mentionner, photographer.

Alex's widow, Margaret Lumsden, and their son John ran the business for another two years, eventually selling the large steamboats, the *Meteor*, *Temiscaming*, and *City of Haileybury* in 1906 to the newly formed Temiscaming Navigation Company. This company of investors from Mattawa and Ottawa was headed by Ottawa lumberman George Hamilton Rochester as president. Other partners included miners Henry Timmins and his brother-in-law Arthur Ferland, Joseph Larochelle, the steamboat operator and contractor for Lumsden who rebuilt the Alligator *Beaver*, John Loughin, Dr. Charles Haentschel, and Charles McCool.

By 1906, the Upper Ottawa Improvement Company realized that the large volume of logs being handled on the river meant larger Alligators were required to handle the drives. They requested a larger engine, and West & Peachey supplied the first 10-inch bore by 10-inch stroke steam engine to them for each of two Alligator tugs. The machinery only for this order was shipped from Simcoe to Pembroke in April 1907. The two tugs were Alligator #80, the *Pollux*, and Alligator #79, named the *Castor*. The hulls of these two tugs were larger than normal and constructed of steel in Toronto by the Canadian Ship Building Company. The next year, the Improvement Company ordered the larger machinery for Alligator #90, the *Fisher*. On April 27, 1908, this shipment left Simcoe, headed for Témiscamingue, Quebec. The *Fisher* was rebuilt later, in 1919, with a hull 48 feet long and a beam of 10 feet, 4 inches. She was rebuilt later at Temiskaming and renamed the *Muskrat*.

In 1912, the Upper Ottawa Improvement Company also ordered machinery only for a large Alligator #114, named, as their first Alligator had been, the *Samson*. The hull of this oversized tug was 50 feet long, with a beam of 16 feet. It was built for them by the Collingwood Shipbuilding Company Limited of Collingwood on Georgian Bay. In 1923 and 1924, the company rebuilt two older unknown Alligator tugs, using their machinery in larger, newly built hulls. They were renamed the *Martin* and the *Seal*, respectively.

John R. Booth:
A Distinguished Ottawa River Client

Timber baron John Rudolphus Booth, regarded by all as the dean of Canadian lumbermen, was the largest timber-limit owner in the British Empire.[1] He also owned the largest sawmill on the continent, located in Ottawa. By the beginning of the twentieth century, John R. Booth controlled over 4,000 square miles of prime forested land in Ontario and Quebec, most of which was within the Ottawa River watershed. Booth's sawmill at Ottawa had the capacity to turn out 2 million board feet of lumber and deals, daily. It required about 2 million saw logs or more annually to keep his Ottawa mill operating at capacity.

When news of the West & Peachey Alligator Warping Tugs and their phenomenal performance in the moving of large numbers of logs, over all kinds of terrain, reached the ears of J.R. Booth, he was quick to realize their potential in his extensive operations. Realizing that it often took up to two years to move logs from remote timber limits to his mill, Booth saw the Alligator tug as an answer to one of his biggest problems. Not only would the use of the Alligator tugs speed up delivery of logs, but it would also be a significant labour saver. Labour savings alone could pay for an Alligator tug in one year in his far-flung logging empire.

J.R. Booth purchased his first Alligator Warping Tug in 1894. She was Alligator #20, named the *Joseph Taylor*. The tug was shipped in sections to Quebec where it was teamed overland to Lake Dumoine, and assembled by the West & Peachey crew. The *Joseph Taylor* was a standard tug with a 9-inch stroke by 9-inch bore engine.

John Rudolphus Booth, known as "King of the Timber Barons," was the largest timber-limit owner in the British Empire.

John Stalker had been in charge of the West & Peachey crew that assembled the *Joseph Taylor* at Lake Dumoine. Once it was assembled and tested, he sent the crew back to Simcoe, their part of the bargain completed. He had been instructed, as part of the original contract, to remain with the new Alligator, however, until the French-Canadian crew was comfortable operating it. This meant staying with them until their first boom of logs had been warped out to the Ottawa River and then down river to the sawmill. He soon learned that the men he was meant to train were a lazy, disinterested lot, who left him to do most of the work. By the time they reached the Ottawa River with a boom of 60,000 logs in tow, he was exhausted from lack of sleep. They soon reached a lake, and after about two hours of work, had a mile of cable out, the outer end anchored to a tree stump on a point along the shore. Stalker hooked the Alligator to the boom, put the winch in gear, and slowly the tug began winching the huge boom of logs toward the point, a mile distant.

A Booth logging crew pose outside their camboose shanty.

Courtesy of Library and Archives Canada, C-75264.

As it would take an hour or more to rewind the mile of cable, Stalker instructed the French Canadians to keep watch, and he stretched out in the bunk in the wheelhouse to catch up on his lost sleep. All the rest of the crew, seeing Stalker lie down, lay down and went to sleep, as well. The sturdy engine chuffed away, slowly winding in the cable. The exhausted Stalker, feeling he had just dropped off to sleep moments before, was suddenly rudely awakened by a tremendous bang as a shudder ran through the whole tug. This was followed by a steady thumping in the bow. Thinking the tug had struck a rock, he lept from his bunk and rushed on deck, expecting to find the tug sinking in mid-lake. While the crew rushed about excitedly and in complete and sleepy confusion, Stalker realized that the tug had completely rewound its cable, crashed into the rocky shore, and was unsuccessfully attempting to mount the anchoring stump.

Convinced that the Alligator would be stove in and suspecting other damage, as well, Stalker disengaged the winch. He then reorganized his less-than-competent crew,

This sawmill in Ottawa, belonging to J.R. Booth, was reputed to have the largest sawing capacity in the world. It produced 2 million board feet daily. Here, sawn lumber is sized on wagons for stacking.

Courtesy of Library and Archives Canada, C-27621.

and, using the winch and another nearby stump, dragged the *Joseph Taylor* back into the lake, half expecting it to take on water and sink. Finding nothing amiss, a very relieved John Stalker returned to the task of warping the boom of logs toward the J.R. Booth mill in Ottawa. Mr. Booth, the millionaire owner, was busying himself around the mill at the time of their arrival and was delighted to meet Stalker and accept possession of his new acquisition, an Alligator Warping Tug.

Colonel W.D. "Doug" Stalker, grandson of John West, who had obviously inherited his grandfather's storytelling abilities, used to delight in telling of his father expecting to meet more formally with the great timber baron Booth at his Ottawa headquarters in the late 1890s. However, that first meeting with Booth occurred on a remote site in northern Quebec. Booth, always very much a hand's-on owner, had no doubt visited the site to learn first-hand about the much-touted craft he had purchased. During his site visit he questioned Stalker about the firm and the capabilities of the now famous Alligators.

While passing through Ottawa at a much later date, John Stalker decided to pay a visit to Mr. Booth at his head office on Duke Street. Expecting to find the great man busy in a panelled office of grand proportions, in keeping with his reputation in the industry, John asked Booth's secretary if he might speak to him. To his surprise, the secretary informed him that Mr. Booth was out working in the yard at the rear of the building. Upon entering the large, open space at the back, the first person John Stalker saw was Mr. Booth, in old, well-worn, grubby overalls, wheeling a wheelbarrow of cement toward him. He was helping a construction crew pour a foundation for an addition to his building. It is likely that John Stalker's jaw dropped, if only momentarily, when he realized that the richest lumberman in Canada was working shoulder-to-shoulder in this muddy yard with a rough gang of men, forming a building foundation.

He soon realized, however, that J.R. Booth was not unlike his own boss and father-in-law, John West, who had no great love of paperwork and was rarely to be found in his office. West was always happiest and most likely to be found in the thick of things on the shop floor of his factory, or, in the far north country, assembling one of his beloved Alligator tugs. James Peachey, although he carried out a good deal of the office work necessary to the successful operation of the business, was also happiest when working on the superstructures of the Alligator tugs or at other tasks in the shops.

On February 4, 1904, Alligator #58, named the *J.W. Hennesy*, was shipped to Eau Claire Station, as ordered by J.R. Booth of Ottawa. She was a standard paddlewheel tug and the first with a 3⁷⁄₁₆-inch paddlewheel shaft not turned down. She served her master well for many years, being rebuilt by West & Peachey at their factory in 1920–21. At that time the machinery of the *J.W. Hennesy* was installed in the new tug, and she was converted to a twin-screw propulsion system. She was also renumbered Alligator #167 and renamed the *J.R. Booth No. 4*. On April 4, 1921, she was shipped from Simcoe to Kiosk, Ontario, for J.R. Booth, Ottawa. Booth was charged $3,387 f.o.b. Simcoe, for the reconstruction.

Three J.R. Booth Alligator tugs are ready for testing in the Lynn River, Simcoe, in the spring of 1921. Shown here are (l-r): *J.R. Booth No. 1*, *J.R. Booth No. 4*, and, on the shore, *J.R. Booth No. 2*, along with Alligator #172, *Teddy Bear*, built for the Abitibi Power and Paper Company of Montreal.

Photo by the Moore Studio of Simcoe. Courtesy of the Eva Brook Donly Museum, Norfolk Historical Society Archives, PS 541.

Also in 1921, on April 1, Alligator #164, named *J.R. Booth No. 1*, and Alligator #165, named *J.R. Booth No.2*, both of which had been completed and tested at the West & Peachey yard, were shipped to Kenny Station, Ontario, as ordered by J.R. Booth. Both were completed as standard-size tugs, 10 feet by 42 feet, with a dry-back boiler, 48 inches by 72 inches. The engines were 9 inches by 9 inches, driving twin 30-inch, 3-blade propellers. The winches carried 5,000 feet of ⁵⁄₈-inch cable on a cast-iron drum with bevel gears and automatic cable guide. These two tugs were practically identical, the only recorded difference being that Alligator #164 was equipped with boiler No. 2509 and a 2-inch Powell Gate throttle valve, while Alligator No. 165 was equipped with boiler No. 2501 and a West & Peachey slide-throttle valve. The cabin roofs of both tugs were felt covered and false decked. They sold for $6,600.00, f.o.b., Simcoe.

A third tug had been ordered at the same time as the above, but with different delivery instructions. She too was a twin-screw Alligator tug #166 and named *J.R. Booth No 3*. She was ordered knocked down and was shipped on January 25, 1921, to Kipawa, Quebec. She was identical to tugs #164 and #165, with the exception that her boiler was No. 2502 and she had a Morrison throttle valve. The charge for breaking the tug down and packing all the components for shipment in a knocked-down state was $200, making the selling price f.o.b., Simcoe, $6,800.

It is also known that on March 4, 1920, machinery was ordered from West & Peachey to convert the paddlewheel Alligator #50, named *James Thompson*, to a twin-screw drive propulsion system. The *James Thompson* had been built by West & Peachey in 1902 for Robert Hurdman of Ottawa. New material for the hull, cabin, and wheelhouse were included in the order, which came from J.R. Booth. The order requested that everything be shipped to Kipawa in Quebec.

In January 1921, J.R. Booth decided it was time to delegate some of the considerable responsibilities of managing his lumbering operations. As a result, a joint stock company was formed and came to be known as J.R. Booth Limited. Up until this time the entire Booth empire had been owned and controlled by Booth. He alone had built it up to the amazingly successful position it held at that time. Mr. Booth was by this time ninety-four years of age, which made his achievements even more amazing to all who knew and respected him. There is little indication that Booth was slowing down, however, for it is at this same time that he ordered more Alligator Warping Tugs — three new and one rebuilt — designated #164 through to #167.

Following a brief illness, John Rudolphus Booth passed away in December 1925. He was in his ninety-ninth year. In no small measure his extensive use of the West & Peachey Alligator Warping tugs in his logging operations had contributed to his phenomenal success in business. Of equal importance, and a great source of pride to the firm of West & Peachey, was the confidence that John R. Booth placed in their product, service and integrity.

The firm of J.R. Booth Limited continued their lumber business on the Ottawa River and they still had faith in the capabilities of the workhorses of their logging enterprises, the Alligator Warping Tugs. These sturdy, plain-looking, amphibious scows continued to economically and efficiently bring logs to their mill, often from otherwise inaccessible corners of their vast timber limits in the Ottawa watershed.

On April 7, 1931, the second-last Alligator that West & Peachey built was shipped to Kipawa, Quebec, to fill an order from J.R. Booth Limited, Ottawa. This was a complete rebuild of one of the earlier Booth warping tugs, identified as Alligator #206, and renamed the *Charles Rowley Booth*. A new hull, cabin, and wheelhouse were provided. The old lifting-propeller equipment of the original Alligator was changed to a pair of stationary 34-inch propellers. The price for this rebuild was $3,795, f.o.b., Simcoe.

As Clarence F. Coons so aptly points out: "On the remote, wooded shores of Lake Nilgaut, in Quebec, the abandoned Alligator, *Joseph Taylor*, rests and rots, testimony to the Dean of Canadian Lumbermen, The Great John R. Booth."[2]

Timber Operations in Northwestern Ontario

Extensive white pine timberlands were to be found in the Rainy Lake and Lake of the Woods regions of Ontario. The Rainy Lake watershed represents about 14,500 square miles, including the American side. The major portion is in Ontario. The Atikokan Museum has an old capstan on display that was found on Turtle Lake and dates back to 1915 when the Shevlin-Clarke Company of Fort Frances, Ontario, was logging that area.[1]

The first order received by West & Peachey from northwestern Ontario came in 1894 from The Ontario and Western Lumber Company of Rat Portage (later named Kenora), Ontario. The order was for Alligator #22, named *Nimsongis*. In 1900, a second tug was ordered by R.L. McKey, who also gave his location as Rat Portage, Ontario. This was also for a paddlewheel tug, name unknown, shipped as Alligator #38. In 1904, the order for paddle-

Alligator #61, the *Beaver*, owned by the Rat Portage Lumber Company, portages through dense forest between Namakon and Rainy lakes.

Courtesy of the Clarence F. Coons Collection.

wheel Alligator #61, named the *Beaver*, was filled and shipped on April 6, 1904, to The Rat Portage Lumber Company.

The *Beaver* was later located north of Atikokan at White Otter. Nearby was the *Perley Holmes*, which had begun life as a twin-screw tug (Alligator #98), named the *Northern*. She was built in 1910 and shipped to Fort Frances on order from The Northern Construction Company of Winnipeg, Manitoba. In 1916, the *Northern* was purchased by the Shevlin-Clarke Company, and her name was changed to the *Perley Holmes*.

The following year the paddlewheel Alligator #71, named *The British Lion*, was shipped to James Harty of Fort Frances, Ontario. By October 29, 1906, this tug was owned by Reginald V. Keating, also of Fort Frances. And by March 25, 1907, the Alligator had changed ownership again, having been sold to the Rainy River Lumber Company of Rainy River, Ontario. Still later the *British Lion* was sold to Shevlin-Clarke Company Limited of Fort Frances.

The twin-screw Alligator #109, named *Champion*, and twin-screw Alligator #111, named *Amphibian*, were shipped May 4, 1911, and May 24, 1911, respectively, to Fort Frances for Shevlin-Clarke. In 1912, the twin-screw Alligator #116, named *Beaver*, was shipped to Banning, Ontario, also for Shevlin-Clarke. That same year, E.F. Kendall of Kenora ordered paddlewheel Alligator #118, named *Pierre Dubois*. She was shipped on April 5, 1912, to Kendall Siding of Kenora, Ontario. Twin-screw Alligator #119 and twin screw Alligator #120, whose names are unknown, were shipped from Simcoe on April 9, 1912, to Fort Frances for delivery to the International Lumber Company, located just across the river in International Falls, Minnesota. In each case the company had ordered the machinery only.

The *British Lion*, Alligator #71, was shipped to James Harty of Fort Frances in 1906. It is being readied to enter the water at Kettle Falls. Oliver and Tom Knox are in the foreground with a team of horses, "Prince" and "Fred."
Courtesy of the Clarence F. Coons Collection.

The steam Alligator tugs used in the logging of the Quetico area were all owned by the Shevlin-Clarke Company. Two were *The British Lion* and the *Quetico*. On the Namakon River, below Quetico, was the Alligator tug *Wake-Em-Up*, which was named after a local Native man, and the *Edwin Price*, named for a local captain who originally

The Alligator tug, *Wake-em-up,* was rebuilt from the old *Beaver* #116 after it was wrecked at Kettle Falls.

Courtesy of the Clarence F. Coons Collection.

had come from New Brunswick. J.A. Mathieu, a lumberman of some renown in the general Fort Frances area, is said to have operated gasoline-powered 'gators in Quetico.[2]

Some insights into methods of logging in the northwest can be gained from an interview in July 1972 with eighty-two-year-old Bill Bergman[3] at his cabin on Eva Lake, Quetico Park. Bill Bergman was born in 1907 in St. Paul, Minnesota. He had lumbered in Wisconsin, Minnesota, and followed the operations north to Montana and finally out to the west coast. He had lumbered both sides of the Olympic Mountains, Oregon; in the Gray's Harbour area of the southern part of Washington State; and on north into British Columbia. Returning to the east, Bill worked first as a lumberjack, then as a cruiser in Quetico Park for the Shevlin-Clarke Company, beginning in 1923. He maintains that there is not a place he has not been in the park either walking or by canoe. He said he knew of the famous pictographs and had told Selwyn Dewdney about them. Dewdney then located them and wrote their story.

He explained in detail the job a timber cruiser performed once a company got an option on an area. The area, which usually included several townships, was located on a map. A base camp was set up and the cruiser and his compass man would lay out a "base line," or compass course. They then operated from that line, estimating "lumberable capacity" and covering about a 2-mile square a day. The cruiser was guided by a rule and predetermined tables in making his estimates. Each evening he wrote up his journal and located all his findings on a map of the limits. Gradually, the complete map would evolve. Once completed, his map with his recommendations was sent to head office with copies to each lumber camp in the area to be harvested.

The cruiser crew would carry in enough food to last for the whole summer if needed. Fresh meat and fish were available on site. The crew packed in cornmeal, oatmeal, flour, dehydrated potatoes, raisins, prunes, dried fruits, salt, sugar, and spices. No bread or canned goods were included as the bread was too bulky and did not keep and canned goods were too heavy and froze in winter. Camp was moved every seven to ten days.

Bears were a problem at times, particularly if the cook was careless in storing the camp's meat or in disposing of scrap food. Once a bear got a taste for these free meals, it became a real problem, most often only to be solved with a bullet. In winter, a cook was added to the crew. He stayed at the base camp, cutting firewood and preparing hot meals for the men upon their return to camp. In winter, food was drawn in on Bergman's 14-foot toboggan, piled 4 feet high with tents and supplies all tightly wrapped and secured in a heavy tarpaulin. This was pulled by a dog team. Several pounds of tallow were carried for the dogs. An egg-sized piece of tallow mixed with two cups of cornmeal and water was boiled and fed to the dogs once a day.

Art Masden, later a park ranger in Quetico, also reminisced about early logging in the 1920s and 1930s in the park. He first logged on Pickerel Lake in 1926 for the Shevlin-Clarke Company out of a camp on the west end of the lake, later called Mosquito Point. The logs were sluiced through a ¾-mile long flume from Batchewan Lake to McAlpine Lake. Bob Halliday and Tom Quinn were rangers at that time. In 1927, Art commented: "I was engineer on a logging gate. We boomed logs on McAlpine, then on Ann Lake and towed them to Quetico Lake. From there on to Beaver House Lake, then Namigan and Rainy Lake and to the sawmill there at Fort Frances."[4] Art's account continues:

> Beaver House Lake had been logged before that time but was a headquarter camp that branched out of Quetico Lake to Jean Lake, then a road to Badwater, Wolsley, and finally in the 1930s over to Lac La Croix at the mouth of the Maligne River. In the 1920s, they [Shevlin-Clarke] had some 2,000 men and four hundred horses working in there. I drove truck in the winter, and it took three trucks and a tractor going day and night to keep up on supplies. Four hundred horses can sure eat a pile of hay.
>
> In the Badwater Lake area, there were great stands of Norway Spruce and White Pine. On forty acres some stands went five million to seven million board feet. The greatest raft of logs I ever saw came down Quetico Lake. Seven million board feet on one tow hauled by a steam gator, (which had powerful winches on that carried ¾ mile of ¾ inch cable). These log drives often took all summer

before the logs reached the mill at Fort Frances, where by running two shifts [they] could saw ¾ of a million board feet in a day.

In those days the Lumber Barons were Kings and no attempt was made to conserve timber for the future. They even cut the last tree to the lake shore. Had they been compelled to practice selective logging and say left all pine ten inches or under there would of been good stands of pine in there to this day, instead of miles of brush and bush. A big fire got going in that area long about 1936 and sure went to town in that old slash, burning, burning for some twenty-five miles, which sure did not help.

Later, about 1938–41, logging was extended to Sturgeon Lake, Pooh Baa Lake, and eventually on to Basswood Lake. However, on Basswood they were compelled to leave 500 feet of timber around the shore, so now from the lake it looks like it was never logged and so it should be, so our grandchildren will be able to see a few mature pine stands too. In the heyday of logging around Beaver House area they logged from forty to fifty million board feet a year.[5]

Lumbering of the pine in the Rainy Lake watershed began later than in the more southern timberlands of Ontario. Quetico Provincial Park was established in 1913, but it was so inaccessible and remote that for years only hardy canoeists penetrated its boundaries. As late as the 1940s, the central Sturgeon Lake area of Quetico was opened up to timber harvest. Even at that late date no attempt was made to conserve future timber reserves by leaving trees of smaller girth to grow and provide sustained yields of prime timber at a later date. Not until logging began still later in the Basswood Lake area, in the southern part of Quetico Park, was the leaving of a 500-foot buffer around lake shorelines even enforced.

Some Alligator Accidents Over the Years

19

The three main hazards in operating an Alligator Steam Warping Tug involved the potential of fire, boiler explosion, and sinking. Over the years there were many reports of an Alligator being destroyed by fire, often from sparks from their own smokestack. In some such cases, the machinery was recovered and the tug was rebuilt to work effectively for many more seasons. Sinkings, too, often resulted in the scow being salvaged and put back into service.

The first recorded accident of a serious nature involved Joseph Jackson's Alligator #1 on July 17, 1890. While the Alligator was ascending rapids in the French River, Walter Winter of Simcoe, who was working for Jackson, fell overboard and was swept downriver in the swift and turbulent current. He drowned before anyone could attempt to rescue him.

Almost five years later, on May 29, 1895, the same Alligator, now owned by the Hardy Lumber Company, was involved in another tragic accident, again on the French River.[1] The company was a consortium of lumbermen, Frank W. Gilchrist, Frank W. Fletcher, and George L. Burrows, all of Alpena, Michigan. The Alligator had left her winter quarters at Big Island to commence work at Chaudière in the headwaters of the French River, south of the west end of Lake Nipissing. She was towing her punt. Upon reaching the Persia Rapids, which were one of the most dangerous sets of rapids of the many they had to navigate on ascending the French, five of the crew were put ashore. Their task was to run out the steel warping cable and make it fast to a sturdy tree 2,000 feet ahead of the tug and at the top of the rapids.

Once the cable was anchored to a tree well above the rapids, Joseph Lavallie, the engineer, put the winch in gear and began slowly pulling the Alligator into the wildly churning water of the rapids. McEachern and Bossett, two members of the crew, were stationed on the bow of the tug to fend her off the rocky walls of the chasm as they made the ascent. The fourth crew member aboard was on the stern to keep the tug clear and be ready to help wherever needed.

Lavallie was tense, but confident as they moved into the heart of the rapids, having taken the Alligator through these same rapids on two other runs upriver. All went well until about halfway through the run when a tremendous swell rolled over the bow of the tug and swamped her. The hull of the tug, with its heavy machinery, was pulled farther under by the churning waters of the rapids, the deck was torn loose, and as the hull plunged to the bottom the extra strain on the cable tore the tree anchor from the rocky wall of the chasm as if it were a matchstick.

Engineer Lavallie and the sternman, realizing instantly that all was lost, rushed for the punt still bobbing astern and rode it to the foot of the rapids and safety. As the swell of water came over the bow, Bossett was swept overboard into the rapids. Being a strong swimmer, he survived the wild ride to the calmer waters at the base of the rapids and swam ashore. McEachern, a non-swimmer, was not so lucky. As the bow of the tug went under, he managed to reach the safety of the deck cabin and cling to it on the wild ride to the base of the rapids. Here, the structure was caught in a powerful whirlpool and sucked under.

The man on shore reached out to McEachern with a pike pole, which McEachern succeeded in grabbing, but he was unable to hang on to it. It proved too slippery and he lost his grip to fall back into the churning river. Hope for his survival was short-lived, as with the rest of the tug, the river took poor McEachern to a watery grave. To this day, the first Alligator Warping Tug, product of John West's unique engineering skills and fertile imagination, lies abandoned, but not forgotten, in 40 feet of black water below the Persia Rapids of the French River.

Between 1904 and 1913, five tugs bearing the name *St. Maurice* were built for the Department of Public Works, Ottawa, and delivered to Shawinigan, Quebec. Leased to the St. Maurice River Boom and Drive Company of Trois-Rivières in the 1920s, the *St. Maurice No. 1* blew up September 17, 1924. *St. Maurice No. 5*, shown in this photo taken circa 1961, is thought to be the last West & Peachey Alligator still operating in the fall of 1967.

Courtesy of John Corby.

Considering the dangerous nature of their work, the Alligator Warping Tugs were relatively free of serious accidents. With the passage of time many, of course, have been forgotten or the record of them has been lost. One of the last serious accidents to occur involving an Alligator was recorded in the Trois-Rivières newspaper, *Le Nouvelliste*, on September 18, 1942. The tug involved was Alligator #63, built in 1904 as the *St. Maurice No. 1*. She was built for and owned by the Federal Department of Public Works, Ottawa, and had been leased to the St. Maurice River Boom and Drive Company Limited on a long-term agreement in 1920. She was rebuilt in November of that year, before being put in service by her new owners on September 15, 1942.

Just before noon of September 17, 1942, four of the six-man crew left the tug where she lay at anchor close to shore at Grandes-Piles, Quebec. The mechanic, seventy-three-year-old Alphonse Doucet, and the fireman, fifty-one-year-old Maxime Boisvert, remained on board. Alphonse Doucet had worked for the Boom and Driving Company for the past twenty-five years.

The four crew members of the tug had no sooner reached shore at the nearby mill when the air was rent by a tremendous explosion as the boiler of the *St. Maurice* burst. Witnesses claimed that the sturdy little tug leapt a couple of feet out of the water as a result, instantly killing the two crew members still on board the doomed craft. Within two minutes the shattered tug sank in 40 feet of water. Pieces of the boiler were thrown some 100 feet. One piece hit a man named Gauthier and another hit an employee of the mill named Gagne, who suffered a serious cut on his face. The cause of the explosion was attributed to lack of water in the boiler.

When one thinks of the hazards the crews of the Alligator tugs were exposed to daily, it is remarkable that so few serious accidents occurred. It speaks well of the safety standards insisted upon by John West in the building of the warping tugs, as well as the rigorous training that he and his employees of the West & Peachey firm gave to inexperienced captains and firemen of newly built Alligator tugs.

Technical and Operational Details in the Construction of Alligator Tugs

The forests of Norfolk County supplied all the timber that went into the construction of the Alligator hulls, decks, and cabins. West & Peachey bought sawlogs for their on-site sawmill from local farmers, or occasionally they would buy a woodlot or standing timber to supply their needs. Signed agreements with landowners, detailing the number of trees and harvesting methods to be used, still exist in the Norfolk Historical Society's archives housed in the Eva Brook Donly Museum in Simcoe. Monroe Landon, who farmed south of Simcoe at the turn of the century, periodically recorded in his diary the sales to West & Peachey of white oak and pine logs from his woodlot in Charlotteville. At times he also mentioned bringing some of the sawn lumber from the sawmill on Union Street home for use on the farm.

THE HULL AND SUPERSTRUCTURE

James Peachey was responsible for all woodworking aspects of the Alligator tugs that were assembled in the yard during the winter months from prefabricated sections built in the nearby shop. He was meticulous in overseeing this important work and often seen working on the hulls himself. The Alligator was a no-frills work boat, designed in a scow form as a strong and rigid craft, well able to withstand the rough usage of portaging, often many miles, and then moving among the heavy logs as they were floated to the sawmills.

Planking for the bottom, bow, and stern was from 3-inch thick, white oak stock, planed and jointed with a caulking bevel filled with oakum. The 4-feet-deep sides were of dressed and jointed, 2-by-6-inch white pine laid flat on top of one another. Every foot a ⅝-inch diameter bolt was run through from top to bottom. Two 6-by-8-inch white oak timber runners, shod with ⅜-inch-thick steel, were laid the length of the bottom and spaced 6 feet apart. All of the bow and part of the bottom was covered with steel, boiler plate, adding both protection and strength to the craft.

A cabin covered the machinery, boiler, engine, winch, and the gearing. On top of this was a wheelhouse, the dimensions of which varied over the years. The entire super-structure was sheathed in tongue-and-groove white pine applied vertically. The roofs of the cabin and wheelhouse were felted, with walkways on the cabin roof. The hull size varied in accordance with buyers' specifications. Normally, a 37-by-10-foot boat was supplied with a larger model having a 45-by-11-foot hull.

The baby Alligator tugs produced in 1907 were either a 35-by-8-foot hull or one of 37 by 8 feet. By 1914, the standard Alligator had a hull length of 42 feet. Most of these tugs had a square, raked bow. A few were built with a pointed bow, the first being the large size, twin-screw Alligator #81, named the *Mississaga*. She was built in 1907, for the Eddy Brothers and Company of Blind River, Ontario. Another variation was Alligator #146, named the *Abitibi*, which had a 70-foot-long hull with a beam of 16 feet and sides 7 feet high. She was built in 1917 for the Abitibi Power and Paper Company Limited of Montreal, and was shipped to Low Bush, Ontario.

Not all Alligators were equipped with the white oak runners for portaging, so in a literal sense they were not true Alligators although they were certainly still warping tugs. Around 1902 the Alligator cabin was extended to provide for two bunks to be built behind the pilot. Later owners often extended the cabin even farther to provide a small galley and additional bunks.

The pointed-bow tug #81, the *Mississaga*, not having any oak runners, is being moved across Norfolk Street on trucks for testing in the Lynn River.

Courtesy of the Eva Brook Donly Museum, Norfolk Historical Society Archives, File 2 Neg. 17.

The hull life of Alligators was very much dependent on how much abuse they took during portaging. West & Peachey were often called upon to replace hulls, or supply the material for replacement within a year or two of a new tug being sold. For example, in 1897, they received a request for the replacement of the hull of Alligator #25, named *Baskatong*, and sold to Gilmour and Hughson in Hull in 1895. West &

Peachey replied with: "We will agree to send men and take machinery out of Baskatong Alligator and build new hull on Poigan Lake [Quebec] and replace machinery in new hull for the sum of $800.00."[1]

In addition, Gilmour and Hughson were required to pay the men's travel expenses and all freight charges, as well as team all materials from the railway terminus to the Alligator's location, which was frequently many miles distant.

The drum of an Alligator winch could hold up to one mile of ⅝-inch-diameter steel warping rope. It could warp up to sixty thousand sawlogs.
Courtesy of the Clarence F. Coons Collection.

THE WINCH AND CABLE-WINDING DEVICE

A big advantage of warping with the Alligators was the fact that a mile of cable, or warping rope, as it was called, could be used as opposed to the few hundred feet of manilla rope used on the cadge cribs. It was much stronger, too, allowing for much heavier payloads. It was essential that a mile of steel cable be wound properly onto the winch drum, however, or costly delays due to breakage would result. Initially, the winches often proved a problem in this regard.

Winches came with a standard drum 30 inches wide, or a smaller model 24 inches wide. The winch was driven off the main line shaft from the steam engine. The engineer could put it in gear by meshing the drive gear with the 45-inch diameter drum gear on the Alligator winch. Each winch was equipped with a brake band and lever to hold the cable if the winch was not in operation. It was of the utmost importance that the wire rope be wound on the drum evenly during warping. On early tugs, a carriage was placed in the bow with two sheave pulleys, which moved backward and forward across the bow, driven by a screw and drive chain controlled from inside by the engineer. When winding in, it required constant attention.

John West designed an automatic cable-winding device, first installed on Alligator #51, the *D. Lunam*, in November 1902. This device was supplied to owners of older tugs, if requested, for $50. In addition, four sheaves and plates were required for the bow at a cost of $10. The new device replaced

Technical and Operational Details in the Construction of Alligator Tugs

the manually operated screw with a left-hand and right-hand helix, having a length equal to the width of the cable drum.

In his application for patent rights, John West described the new automatic cable-winding device in technical terms, thus: "The carriage with its sheaves was traversed by a dog in a permanent engagement with the helices, the screw itself being driven by a flat link chain extending forward from a counter-shaft above the drum."[2] To the casual observer this meant that the cable now came in without fouling and was automatically laid evenly on the drum from one side to the other and back again until fully wound on. West's description continues: "This shaft, in turn, was driven from the drum gear by a plain disk, the latter being kept in contact with the gear by a pivoted weight. The drive could be disconnected in emergency by throwing the weighted arm upwards, while at the same time, since the disc and its shaft were free to move vertically, the arrangement would move to accept any irregularities in the periphery of the cast-winch gear."[3]

It seems that considerable slippage would be experienced in turning the cable drive by a friction gear, but it was not until 1918 that an improved version of the cable drive appeared. It was first installed in Alligator #147, the *Bustikogan*, built in 1918 for the Shevlin-Clarke Company Limited of Fort Frances, Ontario. The old friction drive was replaced with a stub-toothed gear, which now made rigid contact with the driving gear.

The weighted arm was eliminated and a cam arrangement was used for disconnecting the drive. The entire mechanism was moved inside the cabin and referred to as the inboard cable drive. The speed of rotation of the screw was reduced by interposing two machine-cut gears between the counter-shaft (a shaft turning in the opposite direction that turned the two gears, which reduced the speed of the screw) and the screw. These gears were enclosed in a gear case that also served as bearing for one end of the screw to which the larger of the two gears was keyed.

The sheaves guiding the incoming cable were mounted beneath a plate, the upper surface of which carried a pair of posts spaced by a tube whose internal diameter was just larger than the screw. The post adjacent to the gear case was extended on one side to provide a location for the dog (a spur on the gear case to lock the whole mechanism in place, when winding in cable such that as the screw was turned, the plate and its attachments were transversed laterally). The tube not only served as a support and guide for the screw, but also as a cover for it in the closed position.

Steel strips screwed to the deck maintained alignment and the cable was prevented from jumping out of the sheaves by an auxiliary roller fastened to the front of the carriage and moving with it. The whole assembly was rigid, compact, and far less prone to accidental damage than its predecessor. All Alligators built after its introduction were fitted with it. The inboard cable-winding device was not patented.

The Warping Rope, or Cable

The standard and large-sized Alligator were supplied with ½ to 1 mile of steel cable or warping rope that was ⅝ of an inch in diameter. The smaller Alligator tugs used lighter ½-inch diameter cable or rope, as it was usually called. In 1895, a mile of cable cost about $500. For many years West & Peachey were supplied with cable manufactured by the B. Greening Wire Company of Hamilton, Ontario.

The standard wire rope supplied for Alligator tugs was cast steel. If requested, a stronger plough steel rope was provided. It was not suitable for use in small pulleys or where small bends were experienced. Although it had a higher tensile strength, it forfeited pliability and toughness as a result. It was not recommended for use on Alligator tugs by its makers, but some owners preferred it. The wire rope was heavy, with a mile of ⅝-inch diameter rope weighing nearly 3,300 pounds. A half mile of ½-inch diameter rope, used in the smaller tugs, weighed 1,030 pounds. For proper maintenance of wire rope, West & Peachey recommended a special preparations of graphite grease both for lubrication while in use and for the prevention of rust when not in use.

Other competitors for the sale of replacement rope included the Dominion Wire Rope Company Limited of Montreal. Offering galvanized wire warping rope were Allan Whyte and Company of Glasgow, Scotland, through their Canadian agents, Drummond, McCall and Company Limited of Montreal.

It is obvious that both John West and James Peachey were continually striving to improve on the operations of their warping tugs that their product might provide the very best quality of material and efficiency of operation while in use in the remote areas of northern forest. West, for example, was constantly concerned with designing more rugged, trouble-free mechanisms that improved the warping tugs efficiency in the field. An example of this is shown by the changes he kept making to improve the smooth operation of the towing cable as it was brought into the tug, often under extreme tension, and rewound evenly onto the large cable drum.

21

The Alligator Warping Tug's Steam Engines

Almost all West & Peachey Alligator tugs were equipped with upright, single-cylinder steam engines manufactured in their Simcoe factory. They had been making this design of steam engine before the manufacture of Alligators for commercial use in sawmills, factories, and small steamboats. Their most popular steam engine had been a 5-inch bore and 5-inch stroke engine and was rated at 12 horsepower. All West & Peachey steam engines were equipped with a heavy 30-inch diameter flywheel about 6 inches in width. This ensured smooth, constant power from the engine. Should the cylinder stop on dead centre, the flywheel allowed the engineer to move it off and put the engine in motion again. Alligator engines turned over slowly, normally operating between 100 and 300 revolutions per minute.[1]

When the first Alligator Warping Tugs were built, they used a steam engine of identical design but with a 9-inch bore and stroke that was rated at 20 horsepower. The first larger steam engines with a 10-inch bore and stroke were offered in the Alligator tugs *Castor* and *Pollux* in 1907. These were also steel-hulled craft, 66 feet in length with a beam of 22 feet, supplied to the Upper Ottawa Improvement Company of Ottawa, the hull being built by the Canadian Ship Building Company of Toronto. In 1914, a large engine was placed in Alligator #130, named *P.B. and Company Ltd. No. 2*. She was 55 feet in length with a beam of 11 feet, and was shipped to Jonquière, Quebec, for Price Brothers of Chicoutimi.

Built the same year was Alligator #131, originally named the *Otter*, but later changed to the *Tommy Mathieu*. She was 60 feet long with a pointed bow and beam of 12 feet. West & Peachey installed twin 9-by-9-inch steam engines connected directly to 36-inch three-bladed propellers by a slip coupling. The propellers were made by the Kennedy Foundry of Owen Sound. The tug was built for Shevlin-Clarke of Fort Frances,

Ontario. In 1918, Shevlin-Clarke purchased Alligator #147, the *Bustikogan*, with twin 9-by-9-inch steam engines. She was also the first tug to have the inboard cable drive installed.

In 1908, the smaller steam engine with a 7-inch bore and stroke was developed, and they became the preferred power in the popular baby Alligator Warping Tugs. All West & Peachey Alligator steam engines were sturdy, simple, and contained a slide-type valve. They were non-condensing, exhausting the steam up the tall smoke stack. Each engine was equipped with a mechanical force feed oiler that supplied steam cylinder oil to the steam line from the boiler to the engine. The oiler, being operated by the engine, only pumped oil to lubricate the cylinder and valve when the engine was running.

Running a steam engine without cylinder oil would very quickly damage the cylinder wall, rings, and valve seat, so it was very important that the engineer be competent and always attentive to his duties in the maintenance and operation of the steam engine in his charge. He must also ensure that the cross-head and crankshaft bearings were properly adjusted and oiled or greased regularly. A well-maintained West & Peachey engine was almost indestructible, and many hulls built long after the turn of the century were being propelled and functioning most satisfactorily by engines manufactured in the 1890s.

This West & Peachey upright one-cylinder steam engine is shown as installed in the *St. Maurice No. 2* warping tug at Shawinigan Falls. Photo circa 1973.

Courtesy of the Clarence F. Coons Collection.

A steam chest of a West & Peachey steam engine shows the firm's identification as the maker of the engine.

Courtesy of the Eva Brook Donly Museum, Norfolk Historical Society Archives, F2 -1-1A.

BOILERS AND ACCESSORIES

Boilers for the West & Peachey Alligator Warping Tugs were manufactured at the Waterous Engine works in Brantford. They were regarded as one of the finest boiler works in the nation at that time. Shipping records for 1890 to 1905 indicate that all Alligator marine boilers were made by them. Although West & Peachey were equipped to make their own boilers, the Waterous Engine Works, a very large firm, could produce and supply them much more economically than West & Peachey could themselves.

A Waterous Clyde Marine dry-back, 3,200-pound boiler is shown as built for standard Alligator tug steam engines. Note screw jack for keeping the boiler level when portaging.

Courtesy of the Eva Brook Donly Museum, Norfolk Historical Society Archives, West & Peachey Collection.

Waterous marine boilers were all built under strict government inspection, beginning with an inspection of all boiler plate before use. Once all flanging and fitting was done and all holes drilled, the work was inspected again before a rivet was driven. Once finished, the boiler was again examined and tested. The inspector, if satisfied, then stamped it with the date tested, the serial number, maximum pressure allowed, and his initials. The Alligator tug boilers operated at pressures ranging from 85 to 135 psi (pounds per square inch). The pressure at which a particular boiler was operated was governed by their construction, age, and condition.

Almost all Alligator tug boilers were called Clyde, or Scotch, marine boilers. They were a return-flue type, containing a large central furnace flue and many small diameter return flues. In the Alligator the boilers were mounted on trunnions, projections on either side of a boiler allowing it to rest or hang on supports and to move up or down as required to keep it level, thus allowing the engineer to use a screw jack to keep them level when portaging. The Clyde return-flue boilers were very durable, compact, and efficient, with a long smoke path making for good combustion of wood gases. They had a low centre of gravity, as well, making them very suitable for marine use. The boiler plate used was ⁵⁄₁₆ inches thick, lap-seamed, and double-riveted.

Clyde marine boilers were supplied in two styles: water-back and dry-back. The water-back boiler circulated water around the back end of the boiler, thus exposing more heating surface and making it slightly more efficient. They were more expensive to build. The dry-back boiler was lighter in weight, about 10 percent cheaper to build, and easier to re-tube. Most Alligator tugs were equipped with dry-back boilers.

Several sizes of boilers were readily available from the factory. The standard and large-size Alligators were equipped with 48-inch diameter boilers, 72 inches long, containing a 23-inch furnace flue and sixty-four 2-inch diameter return flues. Each boiler weighed 3,200 pounds and developed 22 horsepower. If requested, water-back boilers 52 inches in diameter and 72 inches long were supplied. To further increase efficiency of operation, boilers could be insulated, if requested, to reduce heat loss.

Some very large boilers were built on special order. For example, Alligator #130, named *P.B. and Company, Ltd. No. 2*, and sold to the Price Brothers of Chicoutimi, had a 10-by-10-inch steam engine installed in an oversized hull with a large Clyde dry-back boiler, 60 inches in diameter and 74 inches long. This was the first Alligator tug to have West & Peachey's slide-throttle valve installed. It sold for $4,250.

Alligator #131, named the *Tommy Mathieu* and sold to the Shevlin-Clarke Company of Fort Frances was

Factory of the Waterous Engine Works Company Limited of Brantford, Ontario, as it appeared in an artist's rendition, circa 1895.

Courtesy of the Clarence F. Coons Collection.

fitted with a 9-by-9-inch steam engine and an even larger boiler. It was a Clyde water-back boiler, 66 inches in diameter and 84 inches in length. When the Baby Alligator

Warping Tugs were introduced in 1907, a smaller 40-inch diameter boiler, 60 inches in length, was installed in them.

The original Alligator tug was designed to burn wood cut in 3- or 4-foot lengths. In a 10-hour day an Alligator tug would burn ¾ of a standard cord of 4-foot wood. As they usually operated longer than a 10-hour day and often burned mill edgings, waste, and softwood, up to 2½ cords of wood might be burned in a single day's operation. Wood barges were often used to supply the large volumes of firewood required by a hard-working Alligator tug. By 1919, optional coal grates were available from West & Peachey. If a tug was operating near railway lines, coal — which was easier to move than wood, more compact to carry, and had a high calorific value — was often used as fuel.

ALLIGATOR BOILER ACCESSORIES

Alligator tug boilers were equipped with several accessories manufactured by other firms. Most had a Penberthy automatic injector, which could force water into a pressurized boiler from the lake or river and at the same time heat it with steam from the boiler. These were supplied from Detroit, Michigan. Before firing up a boiler, the engineer would check the water level by the direct-reading water glass. When the steam pressure reached 25 to 30 psi the injector could be activated, if required, to raise the level of water in the boiler. From a cold start it took about twenty minutes to raise sufficient steam pressure to put the tug in operation.

Since low water levels in the boiler could lead to its exploding, the role of the fireman in maintaining safe levels was critical. Operation of the injector was manual and required constant attention by the fireman whenever the engine was in operation. He could activate the injector at any time, leaving it on until the water glass indicated the water in the boiler was at a safe level.

Power to the steam engine was directly related to the steam pressure in the boiler and control of it by the throttle. The other important duty of the fireman was to keep a constant watch on the steam-pressure gauge and regulate his fire to keep the steam pressure just below the level that would activate the safety valves. Too little pressure led to loss of power, whereas too much resulted in wasting fuel and steam.

If a boiler operating at 100 psi had the pressure exceed that amount, the safety valve automatically released the excess steam into the air until the pressure fell back to its regulated safety level of 100 psi. Most Alligators were equipped with either one or two spring-loaded $1\frac{1}{4}$-inch safety valves. Later, specially designed twin safety valves were installed to protect the boiler from increased pressure to the point of explosion. Efficient firing of the boiler was an art learned only through attentive experience. Once maximum pressure was reached, it was controlled by the rate at which the fuel burned to produce steam. This was controlled, in turn, by the amount of wood in the firebox and the regulation of air admitted to the fire by the draft door.

Each tug boiler had a 14-inch diameter smokestack. A hard-working steam engine created a considerable draft in the boiler firebox, which caused burning wood and charcoal to be drawn up the stack. This created a serious hazard — especially when portaging — of fire, not only in the surrounding forest, but in the wooden Alligator tug itself. The burning of coal was much less hazardous. In 1894, to reduce the fire hazard, West & Peachey introduced a screen-spark arrestor that attached to the top of the smokestack and could be rotated in place by the fireman, if needed. This screen, on occasion, would clog with soot and interfere with the proper draft to the boiler. It had to be cleaned by hand when this happened.

By 1927 a much improved diamond-spark arrestor was provided, consisting of a cast-diamond ring fitted to the top of the smokestack. All sparks reaching the top of the stack fell into a trap located on one side of the ring. A cone-shaped wire screen set inside the stack allowed only the smoke to pass through. It was kept clean by the force of the steam escaping up the stack in the engine exhaust.

The early Alligator tugs were provided with a 2-inch gate throttle, which was adjusted by turning, and which controlled the flow of steam from the boiler to the engine. By 1914, West & Peachey had introduced a new slide valve that eliminated the slower turning method for throttle operation by the engineer. A steam-operated bilge siphon was supplied in many tugs, enabling the engineer to pump water from the tug's bilges if any should accumulate there. Last, but by no means least, was the provision of a whistle, normally located just ahead of the smokestack. In the often silent forest wilderness, the cheery echoing of an Alligator tug's whistle, which could be heard for miles around, brought a warm and welcoming feeling to the isolated loggers, skidders, and lumbermen of the logging camps. The cooks and shantymen often welcomed the friendly whistle of the Alligator also, as it was the signal that much-needed winter supplies were arriving before the fall freeze-up.

OTHER ALLIGATOR WARPING TUG EQUIPMENT

Lighting equipment was requested infrequently by Alligator customers. The first to request searchlights was Gilmour and Company of Trenton in 1893–94. Of the six Alligator tugs ordered, four were equipped with searchlights, which were mounted high above the wheelhouse. The current for these carbon-arc-type lights was generated by a dynamo and carried by copper wires to the light. The dynamo was turned by a small West & Peachey steam engine. The light was produced by two carbon pencils, their points mounted close together, so that when current flowed between them, a brilliant, white arc of light was produced. The intense heat slowly burned the carbon tips away, but they were kept a constant distance apart by the action of the current on a magnet. This lighting equipment was manufactured by the Brush Electric Company of Cleveland, Ohio. The rare sighting of a Gilmour tug and its brilliant searchlight working in the dark of night on the forested lake and river country of the Trent must have created a feeling of surprise and awe among the shantymen and settlers alike, when seen for the first time. One Gilmour tug was provided with a calcium-carbide light, similar to those used on the steam locomotives of the railways.

Douglas Stalker, grandson of John West, while home on winter break from university, in 1919, installed special lighting on Alligator #152, named the *James R.* She was built for the Schroeder Mills and Timber Company Limited of Pakesley Station, Ontario, and had many special features built into her, including coal grates, an insulated boiler, and her hull sheathed with 16-gauge galvanized plate. The selling price was $5,957.25. Doug Stalker installed a 1-kilowatt turbo generator, a searchlight, and five interior lamps in the *James R.*, all of which were incandescent.

Each Alligator warping tug came with a 500-pound cast anchor of malleable iron. As West & Peachey did not work in malleable iron, they were believed to be supplied by the William Hamilton Works of Peterborough, Ontario. Heavier anchors could be supplied if requested, and the Baby Alligators carried a standard anchor of 250 pounds. Replacement anchors were always available as they were sometimes lost in deep water.

When West & Peachey began building Alligator tugs with twin-screw propellers, the propellers were supplied in diameters from 28 inches to 34 inches and with three or four blades. These were all cast for the firm by the Kennedy Foundry in Owen Sound as the West & Peachey's foundry was equipped to cast only iron, brass, and bronze. Therefore, if cast-steel gearing was ordered for an Alligator tug, it had to be farmed out to a foundry in Montreal. For example, the Gilmour and Hughson Alligator tug

Baskatong, built in 1895, was equipped with cast-steel gears because they were stronger and less subject to breakage. There was an extra charge of $50 for this.

About 1900, William Kennedy and Sons in Owen Sound built a special plant and moulding shop for the production of steel castings. It was the only firm in Canada, west of Montreal, making steel castings at that time. From then on West & Peachey purchased all cast-steel gears from the Kennedy Foundry, and did all the machine work required in their Simcoe plant. The first twenty-four tugs built prior to this had only cast-iron gears. Those that followed, according to orders received, had one or the other, or a mix of both.

The Kennedy Foundry in Owen Sound where all propellers and cast-steel gearing for West & Peachey Alligators were made. Photo circa 1903.

Courtesy of the Ministry of Natural Resources, from *The Canadian Lumberman and Woodworker*, R4-19A.

22 The End of a Dynasty

In January 1917, John West became quite ill and remained in poor health for a considerable period of time. In early July 1918, it was reported that he had been ailing again for some time and had been confined to his bed. Finally on July 20, the sad news reached the townspeople that one of Simcoe's most favoured and honoured citizens had passed away at the age of seventy-three. His obituary in the July 25, 1918, edition of the *Simcoe Reformer* read in part:

> The Late John West
>
> John Ceburn West passed to the great silence at noon of Saturday last. He was within a month of completing his 74th year … Something like forty years ago, he formed a partnership with Mr. James Peachey, to engage in foundry work and machinery repairs. That connection, then formed, lasted until the day before his death, the older man grasped his partner's hand and in his last conscious utterance, whispered, "Good-bye, old boy!"

Mr. Peachey's testimony to his deceased associate, given to the *Reformer*, was that he had lived and worked with John West for forty years, and the first strained word had still to be exchanged between them. The paper went on to point out that:

> [A]s everyone here is aware, the original business has grown very greatly and has become one of the valued assets of the town's industrial life. One of the principal articles of manufacture, the so-called alligator boats or warping tugs, have an international fame and have done much to solve the difficulties of lumbering in new country.

No one at all familiar with the business and municipal life of Simcoe for years past need to be told how greatly our community is indebted to John West for laborious tasks undertaken and accomplished for the town; kind and generous deeds done for friends and neighbours; for valued advice freely given whenever sought. In all the town's many problems involving machinery or construction work, he has been the court of final resort. Our admirable waterworks and comprehensive sewer system are monuments to his capacity and skill.

Mr. West was in politics a Conservative; in religion an Anglican. In the activities of his church, he always took a useful part and served the congregation of Trinity Church as Warden for some years. His life partner, who before her marriage was Miss Margaret Elliott, of Simcoe, survives. Of their union, seven children were born, of whom four survive; John and Charles, and Mrs. J.H. Stalker, of Simcoe, and Mrs. William Cope, of Toronto. Two grandsons, Charles and Jack, sons of Mr. John S. West, are at the war in France.

The funeral was in charge of the Master and members of Norfolk Lodge, No. 10. A.F. & A.M. of which he was a Past Master. It took place on Monday afternoon from Trinity Anglican Church with burial in Oakwood Cemetery. Mayor Sihler, in recognition of the loss of one of the town's leading citizens, invited the Council and all civic officials to attend the funeral. The business men of the town responded by drawing down all their blinds in their places of business, during the hour of his funeral service.

WEST & PEACHEY: A FAMILY BUSINESS

During the entire production of the Alligator Warping Tugs, the West & Peachey firm continued as a family business. John West and James Peachey each had seven children. Although not all became employees or partners over the years, several did. Three generations of Wests and two generations of Peacheys were involved in the firm's operation and ownership.

John Stalker, whose family had settled in Port Ryerse upon arrival from Scotland, had married Mary Jane West, known to all as Minnie. John worked at the West & Peachey factory from 1888 to 1903. John West's son, Charles T. West, worked there for a few years around the turn of the century. Both these men left in April 1903, and moved to Revelstoke, British Columbia, where they were employed by the Canadian Pacific Railway. John Stalker, however, returned to Simcoe in 1904 to buy the Steinhoff

Foundry, which had originally been built as the Kent Brewery located on Colborne Street North. It was now a machine shop where Mr. Steinhoff had been busy making windmills. Naming it the Stalker Engineering Company, John did away with the foundry and began making dies for Canadian Canners, located in Simcoe on the corner of Head and Robinson streets. During the First World War the company turned out wheel-boxes for gun carriages.

By the time of the Second World War, they were turning out crankshafts for Corvettes for the Navy. Most factories, before the advent of hydroelectric power, were run by gas engines. John Stalker both sold and maintained gas engines at his shop. Colonel Douglas Stalker was involved with his father in managing the Stalker Engineering Company, and, after his father's death, took charge of the firm until his own passing.

Around the time that John Stalker left the firm of West & Peachey, Arthur Peachey, eldest son of James Peachey, took employment at the Waterous Engine Works in Brantford. James Peachey's only daughter, Evelyn, joined the company for a few years, helping her father with administrative duties and acting as his secretary.

In the fall of 1908, Simon John "Jack" West and Arthur Peachey, eldest sons of the founders, joined the firm as machinists. They obviously met all their father's expectations as good employees, for on October 1, 1913, the partners' name was officially changed to West, Peachey & Sons. Jack West remained active with the firm until his death in 1939. Two other sons of James Peachey, Harry and Ted, were employed for a few years by the firm, as well. After the death of his father in 1918, Charles T. West, who in his earlier days was a well-known bass soloist, returned to the firm and remained an active member until a year prior to his own death in 1944.

As a young man, Simon John "Jack" West's son, Charles E. West had first gone to work as an apprentice for his uncle, John M. Stalker, of the Stalker Engineering Company. After finishing his four-year apprenticeship there in 1915, Charles E. joined the army. He went overseas with the Motor Transport Service, where he served in France until the war ended three-and-a-half years later, allowing him to return home to Simcoe. He immediately took a job with the firm and remained with West, Peachey & Sons until 1923, when he took charge as manager of the J.B. Jackson Limited Garage on Union Street in Simcoe. Charles E. later opened his own garage in Delhi and operated it successfully until 1933.

Charles E. West married Eva Gilbertson, daughter of Mr. and Mrs. J. Gilbertson. Their union produced a son, Captain W.J. West, a veteran of the Second World War, and a daughter, Jeanette, who married John Murray of Toronto. Charles E. served as a member of the Simcoe School Board, and as a town councillor for many years. He later was appointed to the Simcoe Public Utilities Commission, and was also a member and past master of Norfolk Lodge No. 10, A.F. & A.M.

Upon the retirement of James Peachey in 1932, the Wests bought out the Peacheys' interests and the firm became simply West's Company. After the death of James Peachey in 1933, Charles E. West returned to the family firm to become the last of the West family dynasty to own the family company. In 1939, following the death of Simon John "Jack" West, the name was again changed to West Machinery Limited.

The firm built another fifty-nine Alligator Warping Tugs, following the death of John West in 1918. The majority of these were of the twin-screw type. One reason for this may have been due to the fact that many of the Alligator tug owners were now using them to move large quantities of pulpwood rather than sawlogs. The factory staff were very busy indeed for the next three years, taking orders for six tugs in 1919, seven in 1920, and fourteen in 1921. There was only one order for a tug in 1922, but in the three years that followed, orders picked up again, with six being ordered in 1923, four in 1924, and seven tugs in 1925.

In 1926, the Driving Boom Company took delivery of an Alligator at Sturgeon River. This was a consortium of seven different logging companies on and around the Sturgeon River. These company logs were all stamped to identify the different owners, and, on reaching the mouth of the river, they were sorted and towed to their respective mills by the various steam tugs operating in the area. For about eighteen years the Alligator tug *Woodchuck* moved millions of logs off Cedar Lake, Island Lake, and others, as well as off Temagami and Sturgeon rivers. During the war years, the *Woodchuck* was replaced by a steel-hulled Alligator and was left to rot on one of the limits. But there was more to come for the *Woodchuck*.

John B. Smith came to Toronto from Scotland and he set up a retail lumber business in 1851 and ran it successfully until his death in 1894. Their sawmills in Frank's Bay and Callander supplied the retail outlets directly as well as their window and door factory. The John B. Smith & Sons Lumber Company was a unique operation in that its leadership and control remained in the same family throughout the 116 years of its existence. John B's son, W.J. Smith, was in control of the mill until his death in 1925, when his brother Robert took charge. He was followed by W.J.'s son Jaffray Smith and then Jaffray's brother Christie. In the early years, John B's sons, John M. and James H., ran the Callander mill.

The J.B. Smith & Sons Lumber Company used their Patterson Township limits for fifty years before moving to Temagami and later to Marten River. They used many types of owned and leased vessels in moving their logs. The 55-foot *Sparrow* was their first tug, one of the many types of vessels used before acquiring an Alligator. The first West & Peachey tug delivered to the J.B. Smith & Sons Company was the *Tillicum*, shipped to Kenney, Ontario, in 1925.

When shortages due to the war made it impossible for the J.B. Smith & Sons Lumber Company to buy a new Alligator, they sought out the abandoned *Woodchuck*, bought her for very little money, loaded her on a raft, and floated her out to Sturgeon Falls and from there to Callander Bay. She was restored in a shortened hull and her restored steam engine converted to burn coal. Victor Darling, a long-time employee of J.B. Smith & Sons, took command of the *Woodchuck* as captain, and ran her until his retirement in 1953. Michael "Mac" Masson, Darling's second in command on J.B. Smith vessels, then took charge.[1] Both served as captains of the large, company, work tug, *Seagull (II)*, which brought the booms of logs from Sturgeon Falls and chained them to Smith Island. The *Woodchuck* brought the smaller booms of logs from Smith Island to the J.B. Smith mill in Callander. Finally, the *Woodchuck*'s need for hull repairs was so extensive that the crew demolished her in 1953. This marked the end of an era on Lake Nipissing as the diesel-powered, steel-hulled *Siskin* took over her towing duties. The *Woodchuck* was the last steam Alligator Warping Tug to operate on Lake Nipissing.

Many Alligator tugs had plied the waters of Lake Nipissing and its tributaries over the years. The Gordon Lumber Company of Cache Bay had operated there from 1900 to 1965, during which time they owned and operated the *Castor*, the *Mafeking*, the

These units are indispensable to you!

LAND or WATER WORKERS

Instal this up-to-date and powerful equipment and save labor costs. These remarkably efficient workers will tow a boom of 60,000 logs to the mill, climb overland to another lake, and skid heavy logs with its powerful winch and mile of cable. Buyers in increasing numbers testify to their capability and notable economy. List sent on request.

WEST PEACHY & SONS
SIMCOE, ONTARIO

An advertisement for West, Peachey & Sons as it appeared in the *Canadian Lumberman and Woodworker* in 1924.

Courtesy of the Eva Brook Donly Museum, Norfolk Historical Society Archives, File 4, Neg. 17A-18.

Grasshopper, the *Nighthawk*, and the *Temagami*. In 1892, they owned the *Turtle I*, followed by the *Turtle II*, which was still moving logs into the 1920s. Not all of their boats were West & Peachey tugs, however. As early as 1908, the Gordon Company asked Fred Clarke, a well-known boat builder of Sturgeon Falls, to build them an Alligator-type boat they named the *Veuve*. She served them well for a decade when, in 1918, she was replaced by the Clarke-built *Whitney*. The *Whitney*, in turn, lasted for twice that time, being replaced in 1938 by the *Whitney II*. She ran until 1955. The Russel Brothers of Fort Frances had taken over the building of Alligator-type boats by the time Clarke built the *Whitney II*. When it was replaced in 1945 by the *Whitney III*, the builder for the Gordon Lumber Company was Russel Brothers, who were now well-established in Owen Sound.

The last all-new Alligator #204, *Amos*, built by West & Peachey for Frank Blais & Sons of Amos, Quebec, winches herself aboard a railcar at the Lake Erie and Northern station in Simcoe, April 1929.

Courtesy of the Eva Brook Donly Museum, Norfolk Historical Society Archives, File 4, Neg. 10.

J.R. Booth, though a good customer of the West & Peachey firm, having used many of their Alligator tugs over the years, had, in 1909, ordered a boat from Fred Clarke, modelled after the famous Alligator Warping Tugs and named the *Wisawasa*. Fred Clarke went on to produce several Alligator-type warping tugs, as well as many standard-type steamboats. Over the years other boat builders attempted to emulate and compete with West & Peachey in these endeavours.

By 1920 the West & Peachey management was aware of the fact that competition was growing from the Russel Brothers and their light steel, gasoline- or diesel-powered warping tugs. Although orders for steam-powered tugs had remained strong, West & Peachey's usual clients were becoming aware also of the new tugs being offered out of Fort Frances. Orders dropped to four warping tugs in 1926, two in 1927, and only two again in 1928. The handwriting, as they say, was on the wall and in spite of orders for three tugs in 1929, the day of the sturdy, steam-powered "Work Horse of the Woods" was over. The last, all-new, Alligator Warping Tug built by the firm was Tug #204, named the *Amos*. She was shipped on April 23, 1929, to Frank Blais & Sons, Limited of Amos, Quebec. The *Amos* sold for $5411 f.o.b., Simcoe, Ontario. This year, 1929, was also the year of the stock-market crash and the beginning of the Great Depression. Tough times were in store for everyone.

The Russel Brothers' Gasoline-Powered Warping Tugs

John Ceburn West's brilliantly designed Alligator Steam Warping Tugs had reigned supreme in the forests of Ontario, Quebec, and beyond from 1889 to the mid-1920s. By the spring of 1927 Alligator #200 had been built at the West & Peachey Factory in Simcoe, Ontario, and shipped on April 28, 1927, to the Lake Superior Paper Company Limited in Sault Ste. Marie.

Colin and Robert Jardine Russel, in the early years of the twentieth century, were working as machinists in the Grand Trunk Railway shops in Winnipeg, Manitoba, but they had been born and raised in Ottawa. Having both ambition and faith in the future of Canada, much like John West and James Peachey, who decided to go into business on their own in 1878. As young men, the Russel brothers went to Fort Frances in 1907. Here, they rented a shed from an L. Christie and opened up a machine shop for the repair of engines, boats, and general machine-shop work. At that time there were no more than a few miles of roads out of Fort Frances. There were, however, a number of sawmills and both work and pleasure boats were plentiful on the Rainy River and the adjacent Rainy Lake. In 1909, they moved their operation up river to the corner of Armit and Front streets and built their own shop.

A challenge to West & Peachey's supremacy in the supply of warping tugs was launched around 1912 when the Russel brothers designed a gasoline-powered competitor to the steam-powered Alligator Warping Tug. They placed their craft on the market, referring to it as "The Shaw Motor-Headworks" or the "Gasoline Warping Tug."[1]

By the mid-1920s, Russel Brothers tugs and winch boats had become West & Peachey's main competitor in the warping-boat market. As in so many other areas, steam power was giving way to the simplicity and convenience of the gasoline engine. The days of the steam engine, despite its advantages as a power source, were obviously numbered.

The Russel Brothers' first gasoline wooden-hulled warping tugs were very similar in design to the West & Peachey Alligators, but they were smaller and lighter. They were driven by a 30-horsepower, Campbell gasoline engine, manufactured by the Campbell Motor Company of Wazatta, Minnesota. The barge-like hull was constructed of white pine, oak, and tamarack. The sides were 4-inch-thick pine, the bottoms and ends were of 2-inch oak, sheeted forward with steel. The boat was 30 feet in length, with a beam of 7 feet. Two 4-by-6-inch steel-shod runners of tamarack extended from bow to stern to carry the boat when portaging. The warping winch carried 2,000 feet of half-inch wire rope. A 250-pound warping anchor was also supplied.

This Russel tug, the *R.J. Beaumont*, was built in Owen Sound in 1958. The photo, taken in 1980, illustrates the front-winch roller used to raise and lower "the piece," a squared log used to push or bulldoze other logs into place around chutes or dams. Here the tug is backing up to the pier in Beaumont, Quebec.

Courtesy of Dr. Steve Briggs. Yves Cloutier, photographer.

The Russel Brothers pointed out the following advantages of their boat over the steam Alligator tug: it required less stores, needed no wood barge, and as a result no time was lost in cutting and supplying wood or in getting up steam. When it came to portages, their boat was lighter and could be transported, in many cases, on a tote sleigh. A typical crew while warping consisted of four men, an engineer, two logmen, and a cook.

By 1923 the Russel Brothers firm was marketing lighter winch boats capable of warping a million board feet of logs or 1,000 cords of pulpwood. These boats carried 1,500 feet of wire rope and a 200-pound warping anchor. They were 25 feet in length and powered by a 14-horsepower Campbell marine engine. In 1923, the Russel

Brothers purchased the rights to manufacture Campbell gasoline engines from the Campbell Engine Company of Wazatta, Minnesota, and transferred the whole operation to their own factory in Fort Frances. They renamed the engines the "Russel," and began manufacturing the marine engines they required. They were soon building marine engines for all purposes, ranging in size from 5 horsepower to 60 horsepower.

Up until this time the Russel gasoline-powered warping tugs and winch boats had a minimal competitive effect on the sale of Alligators as they had been produced in small numbers. By the end of 1924, however, Russel Brothers had sold twenty winch boats, fifteen single-drum warping tugs, and eight double-drum warping tugs. Interest in the gasoline-powered tugs and the resultant sales were increasing annually. The demand for the Russel boat forced the brothers to seek more capital, and, in 1924, they became incorporated as a joint-stock company under the name of Russel Brothers Limited with a capital stock of $100,000.

West & Peachey had sold 195 steam-powered Alligator tugs by the end of 1924, but sales were dropping and only three tugs were ordered in 1926. That same year the Russel Brothers had installed the first marine diesel-powered engine in a logging boat. These engines had a crankshaft that extended from the frame both fore and aft. The after end was fitted with a friction clutch and a reverse gear that would allow the propeller to turn in either direction, or to stay still when the winch was being used. The forward end of the crankshaft was fitted with a friction clutch only to either drive the winch or stay neutral.

In 1927, the first Russel welded-steel hull was completed. It was likely the boat named the *Dorothea M. Geary*. The Russel Brothers are touted as being the first firm in North America to have commercially built electric-welded steel-hull boats. The company also purchased the rights, though they never used them, to manufacture the Hill Diesel Company's diesel engine in Canada, which up to this point had only been produced in the United States. By the next year the Russel Brothers had developed larger, more powerful models of their diesel-powered tug. That year they built a 56-foot-long tug of the double drum type, carrying 7,000 feet of wire-warping rope and an 800-pound warping anchor for the Fort Frances Pulp and Paper Company. The tug was powered by two of their 60-horsepower gasoline engines. It was equipped with a galley and sleeping quarters for eight men. This powerful warping tug could handle a boom of 5 million board feet of logs with ease. This new efficiency and the technology embodied in the Russel warping boats were catching the attention of the lumbermen and the pulp and paper companies, and was about to spell the demise of the West & Peachey steam-powered Alligator Warping Tug.

In 1936, realizing that their chances for growth in Fort Frances were limited, Russel Brothers began to consider a more central location for their expanding business. Most of their raw material and components came from eastern Canada and most of their boats were being shipped east. In 1937, they moved their whole operation to a large property with a good building on a channel leading to the harbour in Owen Sound. Their operations proved successful there and many firsts were attributed to Russel vessels, still being built under the name of "Steelcraft." In 1938, they gained the Ontario distributorship for engines built by Cummins Diesel, a well known firm located in Columbus, Indiana. On D-day, June 6, 1944, many Russel-built landing craft, owing their design in part to John West's original Alligator tug, took part in the Allied landing in Europe. By 1953 the thousandth Steelcraft vessel was completed. They built two of the *Maid of the Mist* boats for use in the Niagara River, and from 1974 to 1989, the Russel boats, the *Ancaster* and the *Missinaibi*, graced the Canadian dollar bill.

24

The End of the Alligator Era

The year 1930 passed with no orders crossing the desk of West, Peachey & Sons in Simcoe and only one was received for 1931. The uncertainty of the markets and the after effects of the stock-market crash were being felt around the world as the economies went into depression mode.

The single 1931 order to West, Peachey & Sons was not for a new Alligator tug, but rather the rebuilding of an earlier tug delivered to the J.R. Booth operation on the Ottawa River. It was registered as Twin Screw Alligator #206 when completed. The order called for a new hull, cabin, and wheelhouse, new cable installed, and the old lifting propellers to be converted to 34-inch diameter, stationary propellers. She was delivered April 7, 1931, to Kipawa, Quebec, for J.R. Booth Limited, Ottawa, and was renamed the *Charles Rowley Booth*.

The rebuilt Alligator #106, *Charles Rowley Booth*, was the second-last warping tug to leave the West & Peachey shop, seen in the background. It was shipped by rail to Kipawa, Quebec, on April 7, 1931.

Courtesy of Library and Archives Canada, #PA 72-2516.

JAMES PEACHEY, THE OTHER HALF OF THE PARTNERSHIP

After the death, in 1918, of John West, his lifelong partner, James Peachey continued to work in his same dedicated manner in the firm they had established some thirty-nine years before. He had helped to build the first Alligator Warping Tug from John West's design and had made a significant contribution to the construction of every one of them since.

James Peachey's interest and major skills lay with the construction of Alligator tug hulls, cabins, and decks. Over the years he was to be found out in the assembly yard of the firm in all kinds of weather. There behind the factory building, where the lawn-bowling greens stand today, he supervised and took part in the careful construction of each new Alligator. Of even more importance to the smooth running of the extensive West & Peachey business were the managerial and bookkeeping skills that James Peachey possessed. These abilities were of prime importance to the success of their many enterprises, for without good administration and prompt attention to orders, pricing, and collections, even the best of enterprises will eventually fail.

In addition to the enormous responsibility James Peachey held for so many years in the West & Peachey firm, he was also very much involved in his community's affairs. James Peachey was a lifetime member of the First Baptist Church in Simcoe, active in the choir, and latterly the choir's honourary president. Like his partner John West, he gave freely and unstintingly of his time and many talents. Peachey served for twelve years, 1901 to 1913, as a member of the Board of Education. He was chairman of the Board of Licence Commissioners of North Norfolk, from 1907 to 1915. A lifetime interest for him was in the maintenance and beautification of Simcoe's Oakwood Cemetery, where he served as president and an active member of the cemetery board for thirty-five years.

In 1909, James Peachey and his family moved into a new home on Wilson Avenue, within view of the West & Peachey firm, and directly across the street from the local high school. The home still stands today, although no longer occupied by the Peachey family. James Peachey built the first cottage to be constructed on the beach of Port Ryerse and his partner John West built a cottage next door. For many years both families enjoyed their summers in this quiet, popular summer resort.

When interest was first shown for the building of a hospital, James Peachey was at the forefront as a promoter of the idea. He provided valuable service in the construction of the Norfolk General Hospital in Simcoe in 1925 and sat on the hospital's board from its inception until 1931. James Peachey served on the War Memorial Committee, and was also an exuberant hockey fan who took a keen delight in attending all the local hockey games. The Peacheys had a family of two daughters: Evelyn (Mrs. E.W. Depew) and Mary (Mrs. Bruce Cameron), and four sons: Harry M. Peachey and Edward Peachey of Simcoe, Arthur J. Peachey of Delhi, and William G. Peachey, of Vermillion, Alberta.

On January 8, 1928, James Peachey sponsored a banquet for all employees of the firm to celebrate the fiftieth anniversary of the founding of the West & Peachey firm.

Thirty-four guests assembled in the Melbourne House, a popular hotel on Robinson Sreet in Simcoe. James Peachey's son-in-law, Bruce Cameron, was the master of ceremonies for the evening. George Purcel, a senior member of the employees in the firm, presented Mr. Peachey with a gold-headed cane on behalf of the firm's employees.[1] Following a sumptuous banquet and the formal part of the evening, cards and music were enjoyed by those present. James Peachey retired from the firm in 1932 at the advanced age of seventy-six years, and following a year of poor health, he died in 1933.

It would appear that the last Alligator tug #207 to be shipped from the West's Company on April 20, 1934, was the rebuilt Alligator #122, first shipped as a new tug on September 21, 1912. It still retained its name as the *St. Maurice No. 4*. It was rebuilt and its equipment upgraded, including installation of 34-inch-diameter twin stationary propellers. The original Boiler No. 2073 was replaced with a new Boiler No. 3257. The cost to the St. Maurice River Boom and Driving Company Limited of Trois-Rivières, Quebec, for this upgrade was $4,250 f.o.b., Simcoe, Ontario. The tug was shipped to Grandes-Piles, Quebec.

Thomas White of Simcoe, who apprenticed to the firm of West Company in 1934, has fond memories of working on the reconstruction of Alligator #207, the last warping tug to leave that famous establishment. Tom White and his family had come from Ireland in 1925, and his father worked for Perry Sowden of Evergreen Hill Farm on the southern border of Simcoe. Tom became a talented woodworker and musician, and has been a member of several local orchestras, where he played violins made in his own shop.

Tom White became very familiar with the Alligators as for several years after the last one was shipped from the factory, orders kept coming in for parts to repair tugs still in operation throughout Ontario and Quebec. In the late 1970s, he and Tom Drayson undertook a project to build a half-size replica of the famous Alligator Warping Tug. Once completed, it was launched in Lake George and floated there for many years as a reminder to the residents of Norfolk County of their lumbering heritage. Regrettably, it sank in the early 1990s.[2]

The regular meeting of the Norfolk Historical Society, held in the Eva Brook Donly Museum on Thursday, November 15, 1979, was one of special interest to all Alligator Warping Tug buffs, as the guest speaker was Clarence Coons of Kemptville, Ontario, who was researching the history of the famous scows that were built right in Simcoe. Mr. Coons was introduced as a regional forestry specialist with the Ontario Ministry of Natural Resources and a writer for *Your Forests*.[3] He had amassed an impressive amount of detailed information on these workhorses of our northern forests.

The Alligator Warping Tug was invented to make it easier for the great timber barons and lumbermen of our northern forests to harvest the virgin timber found throughout that enormous tract of land, all contained within the boundaries of Ontario, Quebec, and the Maritimes, within Canada. It had brought relief to thousands of loggers from the cold, monotonous, back-breaking drudgery of cadge cribs and capstans, and to the owners it brought astounding savings in costs of operation and therefore an increase in profits.

The disappearance of the steam Alligator tugs from these once-forested lands paralleled the disappearance of the last proud stands of virgin pine that once grew there. Today, no West & Peachey steam Alligator Warping Tugs are known to be working in forest tracts anywhere. The last operational Alligator known was the *St. Maurice No. 2*, still working on the St. Maurice River in Quebec in 1965.

A sunken paddlewheel Alligator is visible in the French River, just above the Dallas Rapids.

Courtesy of Clarence F. Coons Collection.

The *Algonquin*, Alligator #59, was abandoned on the shore of Burntroot Lake in Algonquin Park. Photo circa 1959.

Courtesy of the Clarence F. Coons Collection.

RECOGNITION BY THE ONTARIO HERITAGE FOUNDATION

On Sunday, October 24, 1982, the Norfolk Historical Society sponsored the installation and dedication of an Archaeological and Historic Sites Board of Ontario plaque as a tribute to the West & Peachey Alligator Steam Warping Tug. The plaque was erected on the site of the foundry in which they were built. John Wallace, president of the Norfolk Historical Society, was master of ceremonies. Greetings were brought by James Earl, mayor of Simcoe, and Bob Causyn, for the chairman of the Regional Municipality of Haldimand-Norfolk. Remarks followed from John White, chairman of the Ontario Heritage Foundation. Colonel W.D. Stalker, past president of the Norfolk Historical Society, and also a grandson of John West, inventor of the Alligator Warping Tug, provided some historical background. Further historical information was provided by Harry B. Barrett, past president and chairman of historic sites, Norfolk Historical Society, who was the liaison with the Ontario Heritage Foundation for the plaque. The unveiling was carried out by Colonel W.D. Stalker

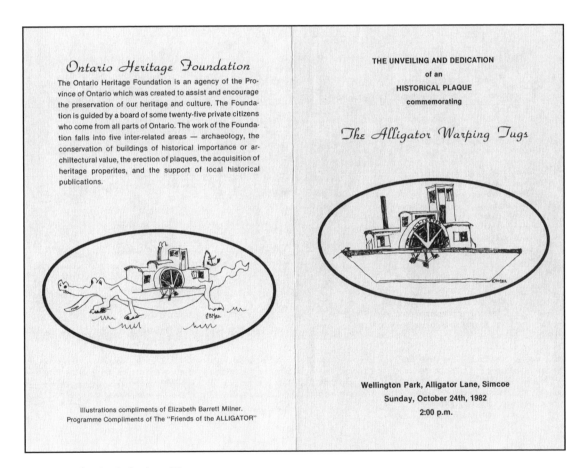

Ontario Heritage Foundation

The Ontario Heritage Foundation is an agency of the Province of Ontario which was created to assist and encourage the preservation of our heritage and culture. The Foundation is guided by a board of some twenty-five private citizens who come from all parts of Ontario. The work of the Foundation falls into five inter-related areas — archaeology, the conservation of buildings of historical importance or architectural value, the erection of plaques, the acquisition of heritage properites, and the support of local historical publications.

Illustrations compliments of Elizabeth Barrett Milner.
Programme Compliments of The "Friends of the ALLIGATOR"

THE UNVEILING AND DEDICATION
of an
HISTORICAL PLAQUE
commemorating

The Alligator Warping Tugs

Wellington Park, Alligator Lane, Simcoe
Sunday, October 24th, 1982
2:00 p.m.

Programme for the dedication of the historic plaque.
Illustrations by Elizabeth Barrett Milner.
Courtesy of the Norfolk Historical Society.

and Dr. John Peachey and his brother, Mr. James Peachey, grandsons of James Peachey. The plaque was then dedicated by Canon Harvey L. Parker, rector of Trinity Anglican Church. A reception and refreshments followed at the Eva Brook Donly Museum.

The unveiling ceremonies of the Archaeological and Historic Sites Board of Ontario's plaque to the West & Peachey steam-warping tug took place beside Alligator Lane, on the site of the West & Peachey foundry on October 24, 1982. The dignitaries included (l–r): James Earl, mayor; Robert Causyn, representing the regional chair of Haldimand-Norfolk; John Wallace, president, Norfolk Historical Society; Harry B. Barrett, Historic Sites, chair, Norfolk Historical Society; Dr. John Peachey, grandson of James Peachey; Colonel Douglas Stalker, grandson of John West; John White, chair of Ontario Heritage Foundation; and Canon Harvey Parker.

Courtesy of Norfolk Historical Society.

The text of the plaque follows:

THE "ALLIGATOR" TUG

By the late 19th century, lumbering in Ontario had retreated from easily accessible waterways and the movement of logs became difficult and expensive. An imaginative solution to this problem, the amphibious steam warping (or winching) tug, was developed in 1888–89 by an inventive local entrepreneur, John Ceburn West. His remarkable vessel, commonly called the "Alligator," was driven by paddle wheels and housed a powerful winch that enabled the scow to tow large log booms cheaply and efficiently and to pull itself over land from lake to lake. West's iron foundry, West & Peachey of Simcoe, quickly became the major producer of "Alligators," supplying the North American lumbering industry with some 200 tugs by 1932. Although considerably modified, the "Alligator" is still in use today.[4]

As a further memorial to the production, on this site, of the famous Alligator Steam Warping Tugs by West & Peachey, the Town Council of Simcoe named the short street, north of the post office where the West & Peachey factory, once stood, Alligator Lane. Some residents expressed disappointment that the name of the street was not designated "Alligator Alley," which some felt had a more pleasant ring to it.

As Clarence F. Coons points out, this, to many citizens of Simcoe, was an acknowledgment that: "West & Peachey, owners of a small foundry and machine shop in southwestern Ontario had by their timely invention of the Alligator steam warping tug brought prosperity to the town of Simcoe and themselves. Furthermore, they had served a major role in the development of our forest industry … a remarkable Canadian invention contributing to a great Canadian industry."[5]

Donations to the Norfolk Historical Society, by Patricia Campbell, daughter of William Kirkwood,[6] a talented machinist who had worked for John Stalker for many years, and her son, Ray W. Campbell, are further reminders of the legacy left to Norfolk County by the West & Peachey establishment and the Stalker Engineering Works. The donations are tiny working models: one a replica of the vertical steam engine that powered the Alligator Warping Tugs and the other a replica of the horizontal steam engine that powered the machinery used in the Stalker Engineering Company from about 1900 to 1925. Kirkwood had built the detailed model steam engines in 1969 and 1970 for his daughter and grandson, who, upon moving to British Columbia, felt the models should return "home."

25

Aftermath

As the virgin forests disappeared and new technologies developed, the steam-operated Alligator tugs became a part of our forest history. Upon the completion of their last harvest, many of these sturdy, reliable warping tugs were abandoned where last they served their owners. In many remote areas, the cost of bringing them out again far surpassed their value, even for salvage, and they were abandoned on the shore of some forgotten lake or left to sink at a disintegrating dock or anchorage.

In other more accessible locations the Alligator tugs were destroyed, their salvageable metal components going to the scrapyard, while the hulls and upper works were burned. Bush pilots, hunters, and fishermen often report sightings of those that were abandoned across our north country, when they stumble on their eroding remains, overgrown by the reviving forests that have sprung to life around them.

ALGONQUIN PARK ALLIGATOR TUG *WILLIAM M.*

A visitor to Algonquin Park can receive an excellent reminder of the logging of the virgin pine forests of northern Ontario by visiting the Algonquin Logging Museum, which illustrates all aspects of that historic era. The museum was established by the Ontario Ministry of Natural Resources with the co-operation of the Algonquin Forestry Authority and the Friends of Algonquin Park. While walking a ¾-mile loop trail, as part of the museum exhibit, one is able to visit a replica log Camboose camp that would sleep fifty loggers, then a horse stable of logs from the same period. As one proceeds, the tools, sleighs, and methods are illustrated for the visitor. Further stops are at the Alligator tug *William M.* and a pointer boat. A reconstructed dam and log chute are on Mud Creek. The Alligator Warping Tug on view here began life as the *Max* or Alligator

#73, built in 1905, and sold to the Beck Manufacturing Company of Penetanguishene for $2875, intended for use north of the French River.

Lumberman Carl Beck had built a sawmill in Penetanguishene in 1872, which burned in 1880. It was replaced by a new and larger mill known far and wide as "The Big Mill." In 1887, he purchased the nearby Keene Mill. The extensive Beck timber limits were scattered around Georgian Bay and through the Algoma, Nipissing, and Parry Sound districts, which meant that the moving of logs was a huge job. The Alligator *Max* joined the other tugs, the *C.W. Chamberlain* and the *Wahnapitae*, in moving the company's logs to their mills.

Max's ownership changed over the years, and in 1921 she was returned to West & Peachey to be rebuilt and renumbered as Alligator #171, and was named the *William M.*, for the Schroeder Mills and Timber Company of Pakesley, Ontario. In 1927, Schroeder sold its sawmill at Lost Channel on the Pickerel River and some of their Pakesley timber limits to Gillies Brothers of Braeside, near Arnprior, Ontario. They acquired the Alligator *William M.* in the deal.

The *William M.* was winched ashore at Brent, on Cedar Lake in Algonquin Park, and abandoned in 1946. According to Bud Doering, before leaving the warping tug the crew held "a sort of a party" on the deck to celebrate her retirement.
Courtesy of the Clarence F. Coons Collection.

The Gillies brothers were well-established lumbermen operating on the Ottawa River; in 1873 they had purchased a sawmill at Braeside, a town on the Ottawa River, about 5 miles north of Arnprior. They ran their milling business until 1963 when the company was taken over by the Consolidated Paper Corporation, now Consolidated Bathurst Incorporated. The Gillies Brothers had previously purchased Alligator #47, the *Coulonge*, in 1901, and Alligator #121, the *Matabitchuan*, in 1912.

By 1935, the *William M.* was working for the Gillies Brothers in their limits in Algonquin Park. She steamed around Cedar Lake on the north side of the park until she hauled herself out of the water at Brent for the last time in 1946. Here she lay in lonely isolation until 1959 when she was hauled down to the Algonquin Park Logging Museum, near the east gate of the park and the village of Whitney. The *William M.* was rebuilt on location for display purposes during the winter of 1972–73.

The refurbished *William M.*, proudly representing West & Peachey warping tugs, is on display at the Algonquin Logging Museum located near the east entrance to the park.

Courtesy of the Clarence F. Coons Collection.

WAKAMI LAKE PROVINCIAL PARK ALLIGATOR

Another fine display of a reconstructed Alligator Warping Tug is to be found at the Wakami Lake Provincial Park near Chapleau, Ontario. She was rebuilt from parts of two abandoned Alligators in the area. The original Alligators used were Alligator #54, the *John McLean*, and Alligator #132, the *Fairy Blonde*.

The paddlewheel Alligator Warping Tug *John McLean* was purchased in 1903 by Cook and Brothers Lumber Company of Spragge, Ontario. In 1883, Cook and Brothers built one of the first important sawmills on the north shore of Lake Huron. By 1902 this mill was cutting 23 million board feet of lumber and 5 million lath annually. The company owned extensive timber limits on the Serpent, Spanish, Blind, and Mississaga rivers. Eventually, the tug *John McLean* was abandoned on the north shore of Spanish Lake in Abney Township, District of Sudbury.

The twin-screw Alligator tug *Fairy Blonde* was purchased in 1914 by the Devon Lumber Company of Ottawa and Devon, Ontario. They had just put a new sawmill 4 miles east of Chapleau into operation on the main line of the Canadian Pacific Railway. This mill could saw 125 thousand board feet a day of white, red, and Jack pine. In 1928, the *Fairy Blonde* was transported from Devon to Wakami Lake and rebuilt by Joe

Lepine, an employee of the McNaughton Lumber Company of Wakami, Ontario. By October 1936, the tug was owned by the Wakami Lumber Company Limited of Sultan, Ontario. Logging stopped on Wakami Lake in the early 1950s and the *Fairy Blonde* was abandoned on the shore of the lake. Around 1965 the steam engine was removed from this Alligator and the derelict boat was burned.

In 1970, the boiler, engine, paddlewheels, and other useful parts of the *John Mclean* were combined with remaining parts of the burned *Fairy Blonde* to reconstruct an Alligator Warping Tug to be displayed at the Wakami Park Museum.

ATTEMPTS TO RETURN AN ALLIGATOR WARPING TUG TO NORFOLK COUNTY

While serving as president of the Norfolk Historical Society in the early 1970s, I was encouraged by the membership to try and locate an abandoned Alligator tug that could be returned to its birthplace and displayed in the vicinity of the West & Peachey Foundry. Enquiries were made along with a request for assistance from the Honourable James N. Allan, treasurer for Ontario and MPP for Haldimand-Norfolk. Eventually the derelict remains of an Alligator Warping Tug were located deep in the interior of Algonquin Park. Through Jim Allan it was arranged that the Ministry of Natural Resources would provide a pilot and a Twin Otter aircraft to fly a crew of local enthusiasts in to the site to view it and, it was hoped, to recover the engine at least for display in Lynnwood Park in Simcoe.

Late Friday afternoon of the appointed March weekend, I, with Bob Carson and William Andrew in one car and George Cruise with two friends in the other, drove independently to a motel near the park entrance. The intent was to rendezvous with the Otter and its pilot next morning. During the night it turned unusually mild, foggy, and began to rain. The plane was delayed and by noon cancelled for that day as the weather was not improving. The ministry would try again early on Sunday to take the men in to the site.

After lunch we drove to Kinmount, to visit my mother's sister, Aunt Phyll, and her husband, Tom McGrath. Tom had served, by age fifteen, as an assistant cook in the lumber camps of the Haliburton Highlands and had been, by the time of his retirement, the head sawyer of the big Austin sawmill in Kinmount. He regaled us with tall tales of Alligators, log drives, and scrappy Irish lumbermen of his acquaintance over the years.

Sunday morning dawned with a heavy overcast and a drizzle of rain. The ministry contact called to inform them that the mild weather and rain had made the ice of the lake the plane was to land on unsafe for the Otter's skis. Regrettably, the flight plan was aborted. The forecast was freezing rain. Around noon, the group left for home, a very disappointed gang.

The car was behaving so erratically by the time we reached Barrie that I stopped to check out the problem. I no sooner stepped onto the pavement than I landed flat on my back. The road was a slick glare of black ice. We all decided that the car had done very well to get us that far safely. As we finished a refreshing snack and coffee, the radio blared a warning to all drivers on Highway 400 of a twenty-car pileup south of Barrie and closure of the road south indefinitely. We crept home cautiously by a different route over less-travelled, mostly gravel, roads. Further efforts to retrieve that Alligator were for naught, as well.

GLADYS PIETTE SCHULTZ AND LOIS PIETTE CHURCHILL REMEMBER

One spring day in 1993, Bill Yeager, curator of the Eva Brook Donly Museum, was fascinated by a visit from two sisters, the Piette girls, Gladys and Lois, aged ninety-one and eighty, respectively. Sister Evelyn could not come. They were bubbling over with reminiscences of their youth and great times enjoyed in the big West & Peachey foundry. Their grandfather John Piette had begun working for Mr. West as a millwright even before Mr. Peachey joined the firm. According to Gladys, "He was very young and just grew up with the job." John Piette spent his whole working life with the firm and died at eighty-eight years of age. When John's son, Archie, was old enough, he, too, apprenticed as a millwright and joined the West & Peachey firm. Both father and son enjoyed their work.

"They made one Alligator boat at a time, taking about a month to do it. It was just matter of course that they made them, it was not unusual." said Gladys. "It was great to go in the factory, but [there was] lots of dirt and grease."[1] Both sisters talked of how much they enjoyed riding on the Alligator tugs when they were tested on the river. They also enjoyed swimming in "The Dingle," boys and tomboys together, and then coming home to put salt on all the bloodsuckers that were attached to their legs. The Piette girls used to live on McCall Street and would go to the factory every day after school. The men did not mind them being in the shops.

Their father, Archie Piette, worked at the factory before the First World War, but when the war started he and his friend, Captain Hilton Paulin, enlisted. The day before Archie was to leave, while loading an Alligator on a railcar, it tipped and smashed his leg. "I didn't want that to happen," their father is reputed to have said.

The sisters described how, later, their father and one engineer used to take boats to northern Quebec and all over, then reassemble them there. They would be gone about a month, just the two of them from Simcoe and a whole crew of French Canadians to help them there. Their father told them about a crew of loggers who were working in the woods with them, when they heard sleigh bells. The Frenchmen all jumped down and knelt in the snow. The local priest, "Father," they called him, was driving by in his cutter. Archie refused to follow their example, exclaiming, "He's not my father!"

They also told how whenever their father, Archie Piette, had been in the north woods assembling an Alligator tug, he had to "get out of every inch of his clothes" and get in the bathtub before their mother would let him back in the house. She was worried about bugs. Archie went to work at 7:00 a.m. and worked to 6:00 at night. The pay was good. "He educated three girls," said Lois.

Archie Piette left the firm and went to the United States for a time, where he and his father bought up three grocery stores jointly. "They also tried it in Calgary, but did not like the thin air," said Gladys, "so they came back to his old job at West & Peachey. Dad still had an office at West & Peachey's firm when he died at eighty years of age."

PAINTING OF A DEAD ALLIGATOR

In 1986, two professional foresters traded a bit of banter over a "painting" they thought should interest "the Alligator Man," Clarence Coons. However, it would seem that the idea of giving the painting as a gift to Clarence never materialized. In October 1996, at their annual general meeting in Thunder Bay, the Canadian Institute of Forestry awarded this painting to Chris Lee upon his retirement as its executive director.[2] The letter follows:

> 485 Maple Lane, Ottawa
> 22nd September, 1986
>
> To: Philip Anslow, RPF
>
> Enclosed is a slide. It is of a painting I have just completed of a Dead Alligator. I took a picture of it in 1952 when it had been dead for only 20 years. I took the alligator man in to look at it 30 years later. By that time it was very ripe. So I painted it as it looked in 1952.

I am conceited enough to think it [the painting] would amuse the alligator man as a gift at an appropriate time, if he ever finishes his book, or maybe it would serve as a frontispiece in the volume of alligator lore. The painting I would donate. Someone else might be sweet talked into producing a suitable frame. What do you think?

Yours in fellowship in that place between
The hard rock … the hard place.

(Signed) Ewan
Ewan R. Caldwell ING F, RPF[3]

Although the steam-powered workhorses of the woods are no more, we still have many reminders of the essential part they played in the harvest of the majestic, virgin pine forests of the Great Lakes, St. Lawrence River watershed. Hunters and trappers in our northern forests still report stumbling on the abandoned remnants of a West & Peachey Alligator Warping Tug, often when least expecting to do so. Museums throughout the forested country in which they once so proudly worked tell their story, or, display them, to visitors and descendants of the lumbermen who once operated them. In the town of Simcoe, which gave them birth, a replica, the *W.D. Stalker*, still periodically builds a head of steam and chuffs up and down the Lynn River in the heart of town to remind the townsfolk of their early and intriguing heritage.

26 The *W.D. Stalker*: An Alligator Reborn

Interest in returning an Alligator to Norfolk County still simmered beneath the surface in Simcoe and beyond. It surfaced again in 1989 when Bob Ramsey of the Simcoe Kinsmen Club began talking of building a replica Alligator tug and contacted the Ministry of Natural Resources with the idea. It came to the attention of Peter Gill, in the Simcoe office of the ministry at the time, who promoted the idea within the Simcoe Rotary Club and through ministry contacts across the province.

Interest was growing, and by 1991 "The Great Alligator Hunt" was launched by the recently formed Alligator Restoration Committee of Simcoe. In due course, letters and articles in the press spread the word across Ontario and Quebec for information on any abandoned scows that might be available. Reports of derelict Alligators were received and volunteers checked them out, but none quite qualified. Then came word of an Alligator tug quite readily accessible on Clearwater West Lake, north of Atikokan (north of Thunder Bay).

The committee travelled to the site to inspect the find, which was on Crown land and therefore came under Ministry of Natural Resources control. Negotiations began at once to return the

The Norfolk crew retrieve their abandoned and derelict Alligator Warping Tug, *Beaver*. They are (l–r): Peter Gill, piper; Wilf Cox, Ludwig Transport; Charlie Judd, Ron Judd, Michael Wright, Don Budd, Tom Trinder, and Dave Dallaway. The remains of the Alligator are loaded on the transport in rear of photo.

Courtesy Norfolk Historical Society. Don Budd, photographer.

"Alligator tug remains" to Simcoe. The good news caused a surge of enthusiasm and excitement among members of the Norfolk Historical Society, who acted as owner of the tug, members of all local service clubs, and the citizenry of Norfolk County in general.

In early September, a group of Norfolk County residents, including Ron Judd and Mike Wright, a great-grandson of James Peachey, in Ron's farm truck, and Charlie Judd, Don Budd, Dave Dallaway, and Tom Trinder in Tom's van, drove to the site north of Atikokan. They were closely followed by Peter Gill and Wilf Cox in a flatbed truck from Ludwig's Transport. The men worked feverishly to prepare the "Alligator remains," with the aid of an Atikokan contractor, for hoisting on the flatbed. The available crane, however, was not up to the job. A frantic search by Peter Gill for a replacement proved fruitless at first, but finally on the fourth call, a crane, plus a well-equipped hydro crew from Atikokan, arrived to load the beast. By Wednesday evening the site was cleaned up and the tug thought to be the Shevlin-Clarke Company *Beaver* was ready to travel.

The 2,400-mile round trip was successful in returning the disintegrating hull and machinery of the West & Peachey–built tug to the Norfolk County Fairgrounds in time to display it during the current fall fair. More and more volunteers responded to the calls for help as the tug sat in storage. Finally, in 1993, the tug was removed to Ed Chandler's barn, four miles east of town, where, as project manager, he took charge of rebuilding it with the dedicated help of many skilled and enthusiastic volunteer workers. Among them were Ken Spiers, Ron and Fred Judd, Julius Wychopen, Donald Budd, Albert Potts, Bob Wingrove, Tom Trinder, Mike Wright, and many others. The men encountered many problems and setbacks in the process, but slowly the tug began to take shape.

More trips north were required. On one, Ed Chandler, in his Crocodile Dundee–style hat, headed for Sioux Lookout and Ignace with truck and trailer to collect propellers, rollers, and other pieces of machinery. Approaching American customs (the most direct route is through Michigan) in a jovial mood at the International Falls–Fort Frances border crossing, Ed answered as to the purpose of his trip with: "Just huntin' Alligators." Customs were not amused. They tore Ed's truck and trailer apart while he and his crew fumed, but to no avail.

A serviceable steam engine was still needed. Tom Backus came to the rescue by helping to locate a 9-by-9-inch West & Peachey steam engine in a Port Rowan barn, an engine that a Mr. Chamberlain, himself a boat builder, had acquired from the Norfolk Knitting Mills in Port Dover when they closed. Ed Plyley, owner of a machine shop in

Simcoe, renovated the boiler; Jack Maytham, Port Dover's marine architect helped with boiler and boat certifications. Dave Townsend of Townsend Lumber, Tillsonburg, and Rick Lambert, a local forestry consultant, supplied lumber. The list of names was endless. When Albert Potts, a retired teacher in Simcoe, compiled a list of volunteers to invite to a celebration of the final completion of the *W.D. Stalker* Alligator Warping Tug, he had in excess of 120 names.

Under the auspices of the Norfolk Historical Society's ownership from 1991 to 1998, donations and employment grants were accessed to finance the acquisition of the tug and the material costs of rebuilding. This amounted to $45,000. As Ron Judd, who was now the project manager, pointed out, if the value of volunteer labour were added, the total cost would be more than doubled.

The finished tug, which the Norfolk Historical Society requested be named after one of their most respected historians and past president, Colonel W. Douglas Stalker, was finally complete. The naming of the tug could not have been more appropriate as Colonel Stalker, who was also a grandson of the designer of the original tug, John West, had followed the acquisition of the *W.D. Stalker* with great interest, but unfortunately passed away before its launch.

Finally it was launch day, the time that everyone had been looking forward to for the past four years — Friday, June 13, 1997. An excited and expectant crowd of two thousand supporters were milling around on both sides of the Lynn River. As on that day in 1889, at the launch of the first tug just upriver, the schoolchildren of Simcoe had been granted a holiday. The *W.D. Stalker* had been towed by Fred Judd's and Tom Trinder's four-wheel-drive farm tractors to the bank of the river.

By 1:00 p.m. Wayne and Chuck Thompson of Woodhouse had cables from their truck winches across the river attached to the 25-ton Alligator. The rollers were in place, the cables took the strain and the tug crawled slowly over the edge of the bank. Then, with a loud crack, a cable snapped. Friday the 13th was playing its role with the superstitious. Old sailors and fishermen would never sail or start a new project on a Friday, let alone on Friday the 13th. However, the break was quickly repaired and the tug rolled toward the water. The schoolkids began to chant in rhythm: "Pull! Pull! Pull!"

As the tug neared the water's edge, Ron Judd led Shirley Stalker, daughter of the tug's namesake, to the tug's bow where the proverbial christening with a bottle of champagne was to take place. Several lusty swings by Shirley failed to bring results. Ron grabbed the bottle and hurled it at the hull. It was Friday, the 13th — same result. On his second mighty effort the result brought a prolonged cheer, as Ron helped Shirley climb back up the bank. By 2:05 p.m. the tug dipped her blunt nose into the river and soon after was safely afloat, to the resounding cheers of all present.

In 1998, the Town of Simcoe assumed ownership of the *W.D. Stalker* and, with the Simcoe Rotary Club and The Friends of the Alligator, collaborated to create a park funded by the Rotary Club. A secure dock and steps were provided as a permanent location for the Alligator below the Argyle Street Bridge, financed through the Simcoe Foundation and the William and Christie Jackson Fund. The *W.D. Stalker* Alligator Warping Tug and her machinery had passed all inspections and was fired up for the first time to travel the river under its own steam power.

On September 27, 1999, Lynne Hagen, resident of Port Dover and president of the Norfolk Historical Society, was responsible for an exhibit at Queen's Park in Toronto, featuring a scale model of the Alligator tug and its intriguing history. This was a part of the "Ontario in a New Century" exhibit, which was featured until January 24, 2000.

Shirley Stalker, great-granddaughter of John West, beams following the successful launch of the rebuilt Alligator warping tug, *W.D. Stalker*, named in honour of her father, Colonel Douglas Stalker.
Courtesy of Norfolk Historical Society.

NORFOLK COUNTY IS FOREST CAPITAL OF CANADA FOR 2008

On steam-up day in May 2008, as a part of the county-wide celebrations over Norfolk County's designation as "The Forest Capital of Canada," the *W.D. Stalker* Alligator Warping Tug gained its own special exhibit. With the aid of a government grant and the dedicated work of James Christison of Booth's Harbour, Norfolk County, and Brad Rawlings of Windham Centre, Norfolk County, a permanent Interpretive Centre dedicated to the Alligators and to the firm of West & Peachey was opened in an abandoned telegraph building on the grounds of the old Lake Erie and Northern Radial Car Station, just east of the *W.D. Stalker* dock. Here video screens, photos, and other Alligator memorabilia tell the amazing history of these incredible amphibious craft. It was a gala day and part of a larger festival on the site to celebrate the heritage and the era when the Alligator Warping Tugs were "Kings of the Woods."

On July 12, 2008, the hundredth anniversary of the founding of the St. Williams Forestry Station was celebrated with displays and a monster picnic at the Forestry Interpretive Centre on the Forestry Station grounds north of St. Williams, Ontario —

James Christison, Ruth Fleming Sommerville, in an alligator costume she designed and made for the occasion, and Brad Rawlings pose with a model Alligator tug in the Alligator Interpretive Centre in Simcoe on opening day, May 15, 2008.

Courtesy of the Norfolk Historical Society.

all a major part of the celebration of having been named "The Forest Capital of Canada," by the Canadian Forestry Association. A history of the St. Williams Forestry Station, founded in 1908, was written by myself, and the book, *They Had a Dream*, was launched as part of the event.

A beautifully carved wooden plaque, created by Delbert "Dub" Juby of Castleford, Ontario, was presented to Norfolk County Council and the Forest Capital of Canada Committee. Dub's father had worked on an Alligator tug on the Ottawa River for the Gillies Lumber Company in the Arnprior area. Dub would often regale Dave Lemkay with tales of his father's experiences. When Dub was about five years old he remembered his mother anxiously scanning the river daily to see which way the smoke was coming from. In this way she would know which wharf her husband's smoke-belching Alligator would be tying up to at the end of the day. He and his mother would then climb in the family Model A Ford to either chug up, or down the River Road "to get Dad."

Another double celebration took place on the Ottawa River in time for Canada Day, July 1, 2008, when Tom Stephenson,[1] using timber donated by the Shaw Lumber Company of Pembroke, built a 30-tonne replica timber crib, 24½ feet wide by 32 feet long. Once completed at the mouth of the Bonnechére River, enthusiasts navigated it downriver to the Museum of Civilization to celebrate the hundredth anniversary of the last square-timber rafting to take place on the Ottawa River in 1908. The raft was also a part of the celebration, at a waterfront park, of the City of Pembroke's 180th anniversary of the arrival of the area's first settlers.

As the year 2008 was ending, plans were forming for an extended celebration into 2009 of the Forest Capital designation in Norfolk County, under chairmanship of John DeWitt. The *W.D. Stalker* and her regular steam-up days, would continue to play an important part in the 2009 celebrations under the present Alligator committee consisting of Fred Judd, chair; Albert Potts, treasurer; and directors, Ron Judd, Bob

Wingrove, George Freeman, Dave Woods, and Cheri Emerson. With Norfolk officially named Forest Capital in 2009, celebrations of our lumbering heritage in general, and the celebration of the Alligator Warping Tugs and their creator, West & Peachey of Simcoe, Ontario, will continue.

Meanwhile, under the capable care of Ron Judd and his son, Fred, the present chairman of the Alligator Committee, the *W.D. Stalker* continues her regular "steam-up days," when she builds a head of steam in her boiler and then chuffs majestically up and down her special preserve on the river. More recently, Cheri Emerson, who has

taken over command of the *W.D. Stalker*, proudly puts her through her paces on these occasions. As spectators watch in awe along the riverbank, more than one is heard to murmur "Isn't she a beauty!" Beauty, in this case, being in the eye of the beholder. Granted she is not of the Rita Hayworth style of beauty, but more the solid, red-hair-and-freckles style of the plain, but cheery farm girl in straw hat, denim coveralls, and rubber boots. But to Ron Judd and the host of volunteers who provided the brains and brawn to put the *W.D. Stalker* back in our hearts in Norfolk, she is "a thing of beauty and a joy forever!"

Those attending the opening ceremonies for the Alligator Warping Tug's Interpretive Centre included (l–r): security officer, Royal Canadian Mounted Police; the Honourable Dianne Finley, MP for Norfolk; Mayor Dennis Travale, County of Norfolk; Murray McKnight, piper; Toby Barrett, as a lumberman complete with his cant hook, MPP for Haldimand-Norfolk; Dave Lemkay, general manager, Canadian Forestry Association; and John de Witt, chair, Forest Capital Committee. Included were two pseudo alligators, Ruth Fleming Sommerville and James Bell.
Courtesy of Norfolk Historical Society.

Volunteer workers relax once all is ready on the day of the opening ceremonies (l–r): Fred Judd, captain/engineer of the *W.D. Stalker* Alligator; Steve Buehner, vice-president, Norfolk Woodlot Owners Association; Steve Shier, Cemetery & Forestry Department, Norfolk; Wendy Kemp, Norfolk County staff; Ron Judd, project chair; Albert Potts, treasurer; Margaret Dryden, manager, Culture and Heritage Department for Norfolk; Mark Sommerville, president, Norfolk Woodlot Owners Association; and in front, Ruth Fleming Sommerville, alligator.
Courtesy of the Norfolk Historical Society.

Appendix A
Two Alligator Tales

This interesting account of the role of four Alligator tugs in saving a town during a forest fire was printed in the *Detroit News-Tribune* on October 20, 1901, under the banner of "Millionaire's Ingenuity Saves Canadian Town from Ruin: How Saint Genevieve was plucked from a Forest fire and came to be known as Little Venice."

On the shore of Skeengwauk Lake in Northern Ontario there is a village of half a hundred whitewashed houses not much bigger than dovecotes, and a stuccoed church not big enough by many cubic feet to contain the people of the parish. Behind the village stands some gray, rain-scoured rampikes, branded with black scars — ghostly in the moon glare and depressing at any time — all that the fire left of a vast and ancient forest of pine.

The name of the village was Saint Genevieve for fifty years, but since the amazing thing that happened to the place four years ago they have called it Little Venice. Canadian author Marstyn Pollough-Pogue tells here what that little thing was and how it came about.

Saving Of Saint Genevieve by Marstyn Pollough-Pogue

For four weeks no rain had fallen and now wind had stirred the air, and the scorching heat of the flaring sun was baking and blistering north Ontario. The worst forest fire within the memory of the oldest lumbermen was flaying the French River country. It ravened night and day; it devoured square miles of standing timber every hour; it ate a village every round of the sun: avidly it reached out dumb, flickering tongues across settlers' clearings, futilely plowed to retain it, and licked up houses and barns; it had caught even two steamboats and a railway train and had disturbed traffic over a great transcontinental railroad for a week. It had bared all the width of land between two parallels of latitude. Blaring and roaring, it leaped and bounded southward, blanking the map of north Ontario, a visitation worse than war. And it took toll in human lives, too — the lives of men, women and children. And the wild birds and beasts that lived in the trees and under them rushed before the red Terror in flocks and herds, and the hindmost were caught and eaten.

Just then you could have bought the big timber limit from its owners at your own price; but it would have been a foolish investment, though the rampikes which would be left might be worth something. But no man in Bowchink would have given as much as a ten dollar bill for the little kalsomined village of Saint Genevieve, including the very little rough-cast church, within which the good Father Fallance was praying for the preservation of the village.

Waiting for News

It was twelve of the clock; midnight, and many men were sitting around the open door of the little shanty where the telegraph office was, but they smoked in silence, and only the instrument in the suffocating, dimly-lit room was talking. Langdon, the telegrapher, sat beside his table chewing an unlit cigar. All his raiment was a pair of white drill trousers and canvas shoes, and his broad chest and his forehead were streaming. He seemed to be listening with strained intentness. But to me the tapping of the machine sounded as loud as tack-hammering. Presently Langdon leaned forward and scraped about forty words on the pad in front of him with a wet and slippery pencil.

The president of the Bowchink Lumber Company, which owned the limit that already lay under the black shadow of doom in the shape of a fat smoke cloud from the burning cedar swamp, and owned other limits besides, and the big mills at Bowchink and other mills elsewhere, lived in Ottawa, for he was a cabinet minister of the Canadian Government, as well as a five-fold millionaire. For three days, ever since the fire had threatened the company's property, the telegraph had kept him well informed about the march of the land-waster. At intervals he had replied, telling everyone concerned to cheer up. The message Langdon had just written down was from him. The operator spoke up in his deep voice and read this message to us. It ran:

"Raleigh, Brownie, Fisher, Boyd et al:

Instruct engineers of four "Alligators" raise steam without unnecessary delay. Tell Saint Genevieve cheer up, for I am coming. I wish to behold the bonfire, being a boy. Also I have little scheme. Special with Ogemah will arrive 1:15."

CALLING OUT THE ALLIGATORS

The sleepy-eyed men who pulled at their pipes were impressed by this telegram. The Ogemah was his private car; Raleigh, Brown and Fisher were mill foremen, and sat with Boyd and myself on the doorstep. Boyd was manager of all the mills. He rose to go down to the wharf where all the "Alligators" lay, when the telegraph mechanism was again actuated by the key under the finger of the operator at Ottawa. Langdon said "Wait" and his nervous pencil point slid wriggling across the yellow pad again, while the instrument kettle-drummed. A minute later he read aloud the president's second message, which was more incomprehensible than the first. It was to Boyd, and said: "Instruct foremen to have one hundred picked men with hand spikes on board 'Alligators' ready to start Saint Genevieve when I arrive. Also all available green skids."

Boyd turned to the foreman with a puzzled look. "I haven't the least idea what the old man intends. But we have to obey orders." Then he went away.

You must know that of all the craft, little and big, that have moved under sail or steam upon the face of the waters of all the world since this globe began to turn in the lathe of Time, the "Alligator" warping tugboat is the most wonderful and strange. For she also moves over the face of the land under her own steam, crawling on her belly like a beetle, and performs miracles in the way of dragging things of weight. The engineers were playing poker when Maynard's siren whistle screamed like a soul in torment. Maynard was the night engineer of the electric plant. It was part of his duty to blow a siren loud enough to call up the dead from their graves when a fire broke out in the town at night. The poker players jumped when they heard, and ten minutes afterward smoke was pouring from the short, fat, lead-coloured funnels, and mixing with the other smoke in the atmosphere.

Within a short time the grizzled, bull-necked French-Canadians who had been picked by the foremen from several hundred mill hands and villagers arrived on the wharf, and the foremen told them to collect hand spikes and skids, and they collected them in wonderment. Then they sat on the decks of the "Alligators" conjecturing while the steam gauge fingers crawled around their dials to the 200-pound mark.

The president's special swayed into Bowchink from the south a few minutes after 1 o'clock, howling like a banshee. The old man stepped from his private car.

The Alligators Purred

The dynamos of the "Alligators" were purring, and from the brass drums of their search-lamps streams of white luminance jetted, slanting to the wharf and playing upon the president and Boyd like water from a hose. The great bull whistles blared a greeting to the old man. "We are going across to St. Genevieve as fast as these old tubs can walk," he said. "We are going to put skids under the village and pull it off the shore into the water to save it from the fire."

As he made this statement he skipped nimbly on board the Alligator *Musquash*. Instantly the mooring lines were let go; the gongs clanged in the engine rooms; the paddles spanked the water, and the little fleet pawed itself from the wharf, the four search rays stabbing the deep gloom ahead, and moving to right and left like long white antennae feeling nervously for something in the dark. In a few minutes the flotilla reached the village.

"Where's the fire?" Asked Boyd.

"She's comin' hell-a-whoopin'; she'll be here afore noon tomorrow," answered the English-speaking men of St. Genevieve. Then both French and English turned to help with the skidding.

The president and I observed what followed, and it was an interesting spectacle. Ours were the only idle hands; everyone else worked with cheerful energy. The round, pink face of the president, framed in the silver of his hair and beard, lit with joy as the work progressed. This is how the feat was done, with the search rays fed by the human dynamos to aid.

With shoutings the men lifted the twelve by fifteen foot cottages, which had no foundations except the red sand, and slipped round skids under them. This was easy and the shouting made it easier for the French-Canucks. The cottages were about two hundred feet from the water's edge. Therefore not much more than two hundred feet of each of the wire hawsers, which all the Alligators used for warping and portaging, and which were reeled on the drums of the steam winches, were unreeled.

Whimpering, groaning and shuddering, the cottages rolled on their skids when the winches snicked and each cable strained taut with a whine. When the cottages had been pulled up against the scow noses of the "Alligators," the cables were un-snubbed, a swarm of men aided the pawing paddles to back the boats off the sand, while other men pushed the houses into deep water with pike poles; and four men in a punt towed each cottage some distance from the shore and anchored it with a large stone, to which a short rope had been made fast.

Then the warping tugs crept like huge crawfish up into other positions opposite other cottages, and the same skidding and winch work was done over again with assorted whoops and the "Hoy'yoe" of men heaving all together with bending hand spikes, many arms and backs always assisting the winding winches. So the work went on, and twelve of the cottages were anchored in a row two hundred yards from land before the dawn came stealing over the round-flanked Laurentian hills on the eastern land line.

It was in this hour that the fire, having devoured the cedar swamp, reached out its red fangs and took hold of the dark, still pine forest, and bit into it. Afterwards, with a deep roaring and crackling and smashing sounds loud and sharp, the fire rolled toward Sheengwauk Lake, a tidal wave of flame engulfing the woods. And billows of fat, black smoke tossed and shouldered above the fire. And through the smoke blazing brands and embers and sparks were spewed and spat upward, and fell in a continuous red rain.

Moving of St. Genevieve buildings into Skeengwauk Lake.
Courtesy of L.A. Dool, artist.

The workers at Saint Genevieve did not behold the fire until two hours after sunrise, but they smelt it while it was yet a long way off. Near seven of the clock those whose business it was to anchor the houses off shore, enjoyed a view of the fire, sulphur-yellow and damask-red, all along the sky above the woods. They shouted to the busy men on shore, but these did not work any harder or faster, because they could not. Neither steam nor human energy was capable of higher pressure. There was two hundred pounds in the boilers, and the men heaved and pushed mightily, and the sweat ran into their eyes. But the work was almost finished.

All but four of the cottages floated in safety off shore, and the power of all the chattering winches together had torn the church, which was a wooden building, plastered on the outside, off the four cedar posts it rested upon. It was what builders call a rough-cast edifice, and much more heavily framed than the houses, and it was impossible to get skids under it. So the boats took position abreast opposite it, and all four cables were made fast and with the four hundred indicated horse-power available they dragged the church down to the water, while the men, having cut away the base boards with axes, pried with long poles to ease the building over the lumps and roughnesses in its path.

With cheering that went far up through the smoke bank that was heaping down and folding them around, they got the church afloat, and Father Fallance, who had done good work with a handspike that night, said that God had ordered it all.

Then more smoke was un-rolled over the tops of the tall pines and dropped like a pall and hid everything, and the men with the handspikes groped for the four cottages that were left. They found them, for they stood behind the church yard, in which the bones of many coureur de bois lay disintegrating, and the cottages were dragged over the graves, which was a desecration, but the living men were in haste. It was their last hour of time; they could hear the roar of the flames, and it was like the bellowing of a thousand mad bulls.

In the Deep Smoke

The brown drapery of the smoke was so thick that the engineers of the warping tugs started their dynamos again. But the search rays would not penetrate the smudge. The much enduring workers could not see, and the wood smoke was choking them, but they finished their job just as a shower of blazing chunks descended through the smoke upon the town-site of Saint Genevieve.

Ten minutes afterward the Alligator tugs were steaming at speed toward Bowchink, crowded with weary men whose most pressing need was breakfast. After breakfast they would require much sleep. They talked in French and English and mentioned a strange thing that had happened after the smoke had closed around them during that last hour. They had seen nothing in the smoke, but they had heard sounds that were very unlike any sounds that were ever issued from human throats, or sounds made by the complaining cottages, or the straining cables, or the clinging winches or the trampling engines. There was no need to explain, for everyone knew that an unknown number of bears and deer, refugees from the burning woods had blundered among the men in the smoke.

One of the tugs towed a scow in which the women of Saint Genevieve were huddled with their children and house furniture. They met many canoes crossing over from Bowchink being paddled by citizens of Bowchink, who wished to enjoy a near view of the fire, which was spectacular. When these people beheld Saint

Genevieve, a little water-logged, but floating nicely, and neatly arranged in two streets out in the lake, they were much surprised.

And the village which was pulled back on shore again when the fire had burned itself out, has been called Little Venice ever since, and the stranger always asks the native why. Then doth the stranger hear this story, not told plainly, as I have told it, but with frills and embroidery.

This next story appeared in the January 1905 edition of *The Canadian Lumberman and Woodworker*. It refers to the Alligator Warping Tugs in a humorous way. It has been somewhat condensed:

Three Men in the Woods by James Barr

"This is the region of the big-game shooters," declaimed Peters. "No other can compare with it. In the air eagles, wild geese and ducks galore; in the woods moose as big as horses, bear, caribou, deer; in the waters muskinonge, alligators, sturgeon …"

"Alligators?" queried McWhinnie.

"Yes, alligators," repeated Peters.

"In these waters?" inquired McWhinnie, sceptically, sweeping his hand toward Quinze Lake.

"Certainly, in these waters. There is no catch, McWhinnie, I tell you that in this lake are alligators," said Peters, "real, big, bustling alligators—"

"You're crazy!" was all McWhinnie would say.

"I tell you I saw one this morning," continued Peters, emphatically. "It lay close inshore kicking up a deuce of a fuss in the water. It was in plain view for ten minutes, or more, floundering about, lashing the water, and seemed to take refuge at last down there beside those logs on the far side of the storehouse. I never saw such a big alligator as this one in all my days, believe me, I was as much surprised as you are disbelieving, which is saying a bit."

"You're crazy!"

McWhinnie polished away at a twenty-two-bore rifle. We brought it to secure rabbits and partridge, but found it varied a good three feet at a twenty-yard range. The worst was that it seldom varied in the same direction. McWhinnie did not know this yet and polished industriously.

"It's all very fine for you to sit there and parrot 'You're crazy,' but I tell you I saw an alligator with my own eyes."

"You're crazy!"

"But, McWhinnie," I put in, "there are alligators in these waters."

"You're crazy!"

So I shut up. Silence for a time. Then McWhinnie broke in, "Yesterday's trying walk and driving rain has turned your heads. You're both crazy!"

The three of us sat on the front porch of the log house on Douglas Farm, Quinze Lake, Quebec. Our 5:30 a.m. breakfast, at that weird hour, for fat, fried pork and apple pie, was such a jar to our systems that we were now trying to recover by taking it easy. Our two guides were busy with the canoes, testing each suspicious spot in the birch bark by putting his lips to it and sucking with all his might. If air came through, it was patched with steaming pine resin.

[The] Douglas farm is a patch of vivid green, ringed by a giant wall of woods. Before the log house stretches Quinze Lake, in shape almost circular; indeed, a mighty amphitheatre in the wooded highlands. The Douglas farm supplies fodder to the lumbermen's camps in the district. Douglas farm is the farthest outpost of the bustling world that stands in that part of the globe, so far outside, that the marching and counter marching of nations are heard of only at long intervals. For city-weary eyes no place could be more refreshing — the silent waters, the ghostly woods and the ineffable sweep of the sky. A sceptical soul must ever be horribly out of place in such a green sanctuary as Douglas farm. Yet there one sat polishing a twenty-two rifle.

Suddenly round the corner came the mistress of the house, a kindly, intelligent woman, busy with the onerous duties of the farm. Peters leaped to his feet. "Excuse me," he said, "but was not that an alligator I saw this morning in the lake the other side of the storehouse?"

"Oh, yes," she answered pleasantly.

Peters waited for McWhinnie to say "You're crazy!" but, instead, the rifle polisher sat gazing in wonderment at the woman.

"Do you think it is there now?" asked Peters.

"I am sure it is," she replied.

"Thank you. I think we better photograph it." Mrs. Johnson entered the house.

"You don't mean to tell me—" stammered McWhinnie.

"Of course I do, that is exactly what I mean. There is a Canadian freshwater alligator lying in the water behind that storehouse, or, at least, there was earlier this morning."

McWhinnie, now vividly interested, dived into the house and reappeared with his camera.

"Steady on!" cautioned Peters. "We must not burst upon the thing or we might stampede it. I am particularly anxious to secure a first-class photo of it to take back to London. Try to imagine yourself a Red Indian on the scout. We'll go down Indian file; you first, chronicler next and I'll bring up the rear."

McWhinnie, nervously fingering his camera, asked, "What range should I set for it? I must have a good shot of the brute!"

"One hundred feet should do nicely," Peters advised, in a hoarse whisper. "Make your way as silent as a stalking cat, step out quickly, the sun is right and the view will be clear."

A small wharf surrounded the storehouse and the three crept toward it, McWhinnie hugging his camera to his chest, ready to detect their prey at the first possible instant. We stole down the grassy slope, gingerly placing moccasined feet on the rough planks. McWhinnie braced himself and at the moment he raised his foot to step up on the wharf, Peters tripped over a loose plank, uttered an unearthly yell and fell flat on the wharf.

Without even looking around McWhinnie sprang out into the sunshine and swept the foreshore of the lake in a lightning-like, comprehensive glance. "There's no alligator here," he barked. "Your bawling has frightened the beast away, confound you!" Peters was by his side like a flash.

"Not at all. There it is. Quick!"

"I don't see it! Where?"

"There — there — where I point. Can't you see it plain as a patch on —"

"I only see that rickety, old steamboat."

Peters tone was contemptuous. "Steamboat! — that's no steamboat — that's an Alligator!"

McWhinnie dropped the body of his camera, maintaining a strong hold on the strap. He whirled on Peters and swung the camera in one mighty sweep straight for the foreman's head. Peters, prepared and skilled in rugby tactics, tackled him sudden and strong. Down the two went while I, throwing myself on the infuriated McWhinnie's feet, held on with the hug of a bear, at the same time calling with might and main for the guides.

McWhinnie was barking: "Let me up and I'll do for the two of you," all the while fighting and heaving into mighty contortions, and Peters, every time he could get enough breath to articulate, interpolated: "I'll explain all, McWhinnie, when you are calm, I'll explain all."

"I don't want your explanations!"

"Help us hold him for a minute; he's had a fit," said Peters to the guides. They joined in the melee, and we soon had McWhinnie spreadeagled on the wharf. Peters sat on his chest and began. "Now, McWhinnie, you've flown off the handle again. That is an alligator. You adopted too narrow-minded a course. You set your mind on one sort of alligator only, and that the common insect one. Here I have shown you a unique creation only to be met with in this part of the world—"

"Let me up and I'll talk to you!"

"There rides the most wonderful steamer you have ever seen, and the name of its class is Alligator. There are quite a number of them in this vast region of bush, and they are all Alligators. They are the Canadian fresh-water alligators. Can you guess why they are so named?"

"Get off me and I'll—"

"They are called Alligators because they can run on water or land indiscriminately. They are used to tow rafts of logs down these wilderness streams. The waterways here are rich in falls and chutes, up which, or down which, no craft can go. So when one of these falls is reached the tow steamer takes to the land and passes by the turbulent waters, entering the stream again when the rapids are passed. Isn't that ingenious and interesting?"

"I'd be more entertained if you would kindly get off my chest."

Then Peters stood up. McWhinnie slowly rolled over until his legs hung down from the wharf and his moccasins touched the water. There he sat and gazed at the Alligator.

"Now, sir," said Peters, at last, "are you not glad you came? Will you take a photograph of an Alligator now?"

McWhinnie shook his head. "Not today," he said. "I'll wait 'til I come back. I don't feel like snapping the thing now. Let's get away."

It befell, however, that at the very first portage we came to there was an Alligator high and dry, snorting and scrambling its way overland. We saw it do the last hundred yards and enter the water at the foot of wild rapids. McWhinnie condescended to photograph it for us.

Appendix B
Original Patent Application for
Alligator Warping Scow

To all whom it may concern:

Be it known that I, John Ceburn West, of the town of Simcoe, in the County of Norfolk, in the Province of Ontario, Canada, Machinist, have invented a certain new and Improved Steam Warping Scow of which the following is a specification.

The object of the invention is to design a scow which may be propelled in water and on land, and provide with steam-driven mechanism for propelling it in water, hauling it over the land, and warping or hauling logs and rafts; and it consists, essentially, of a scow provided with steel-covered runners and contains an engine and boiler connected to a mechanism which with slight adjustment may be directed to operate a pair of paddle wheels or a cable-winding drum, the boiler being carried in suitable trunnions and provided with adjusting mechanism by which the angle of the boiler may be readily altered; the whole mechanism being arranged substantially as hereinafter more particularly explained.

Figure 1, is a perspective view of my improved warping scow, one of the paddle-wheels being removed for the purpose of exposing the operating mechanism contained in the scow.

Figure 2, is a cross-section of the scow without the mechanism.

In the drawing A, is the scow, on the bottom of which two steel-covered runners, B, are placed. C, is the boiler supported at its centre in suitable trunnion bearings, B. E, is a heavy arm securely riveted to the boiler, C, and designed to hold a nut, F, through which the adjusting screw, G, passes. The bottom end of the screw, G, is pivoted in and secured to the strap, H, which is fastened to the bottom of the scow. The steam pipe, I, is jointed, the said joint being made on a line with the centre of the trunnion, D, so that the

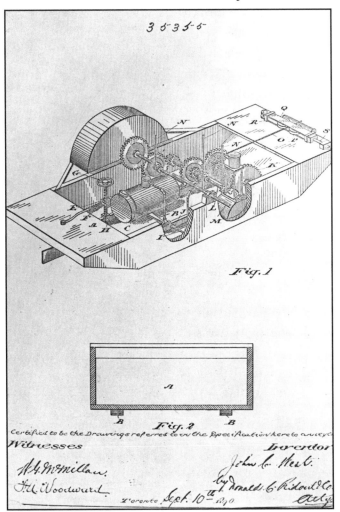

Drawing of John West's application for patent of steam-warping tug, September 10, 1890.

boiler, C, may be rocked on its trunnions without affecting the steam pipe. By arranging the boiler in this way it may always be kept level, no matter how steep the hill the scow may be passing over. K, is a cable-winding drum, suitably geared as indicated to the engine-shaft, L. M, is a paddle-wheel shaft which is also geared, as indicated, to the shaft, L. Shifting handles, N, are provided, so that either the drum, K, or the paddle-wheel shaft, M, may be connected to or disconnected from the driving-shaft, L.

I do not claim anything particular in the operating gearing, as it may be changed to suit the taste of the constructing engineer. The only point to be observed is that the gearing must be strong in its construction. O, is a cable attached to the cable-winding drum, K, which I connect to the raft, and after anchoring or snubbing the scow, A, I throw the mechanism into operation to wind the drum, K. This cable, it will be observed, passes between two friction pulleys, P, suitably journaled in the frame, Q, which is secured to the scow, A, by two staples, R. This frame may be adjusted longitudinally, or, in other words across the bow, of the scow. An adjusting screw, S, may be substituted.

WHAT I CLAIM as my invention is:

1. A scow, A, provided with steel-covered runners, B, substantially as and for the purpose specified.
2. A boiler, C, pivoted in a scow, on suitable trunnion bearings, D, a jointed steam pipe, I, in combination with an arm, E, nut, F, and screw, G, substantially as and for the purpose specified.
3. A drum, K, having a cable, O, connected to it, and connected by suitable adjustable driving mechanism to the engine-shaft, L, substantially as and for the purpose specified.
4. A scow provided with paddles, in combination with adjustable driving mechanism arranged to connect the paddle-shaft, M, with the driving-shaft, L, substantially as and for the purpose specified.
5. A cable, O, connected to a cable drum, K. and passing between the friction pulleys, P, suitably journalled in the frame, Q, which is adjustably held to the scow, A, substantially as and for the purpose specified.

Signed: John C. West.
Toronto, September 10th, 1890

Signed in the presence of:
Charles C. Baldwin
J.A. Woodward

Appendix C
Patent Application for Cable-Winding Mechanism

To all whom it may concern:

Be it known that I, John Ceburn West, of the town of Simcoe, in the County of Norfolk, Province of Ontario, Canada, have invented certain new and useful improvements in steam warping scows, of which the following is a specification:

My invention relates to a steam warping scow known as an "Alligator" which forms the subject matter of Canadian Patent No. 35, 355 dated November 5th, 1890.

In that patent is shewn an engine which may be put in gear with a paddle wheel shaft or with a cable winding drum. The cable from the drum passes through a transversely moveable guide operated by a screw to cause the cable to wind evenly on a drum. In the original invention the scow was operated by hand requiring the constant attention of one man when the "Alligator" was warping. I overcame this objection by operating the screw by suitable gearing from the drum and provided for the automatic reversal of the direction of motion of the slide by forming a right and left thread on the screw connecting at each end, the threads being engaged by a pivoted dog in the nut of the slide which automatically shifts from one thread to the other at each end of the screw, substantially as hereinafter more specifically described and then definitely claimed.

Figure 1. is a slide elevation of a warping scow provided with my improvements.

Figure 2. is a plan view of the front portion of a scow showing my improvements.

Figure 3. is a perspective detail of the adjustable bearing of the friction disk.

Figure 4. is an enlarged sectional elevation shewing the right and left hand threaded screw and swivel dog.

Drawings of John West's application for patent of automatic cable-winding device, September 20, 1902.

Figure 5. is a plan view of one end of the right and left hand threaded screw.

Figure 6. is a perspective detail of the friction disk.

Figure 7. is a perspective detail of the bands used to enlarge the diameter of the disk.

In the drawings like letters of reference indicate corresponding parts in the differential figures.

In addition I have used as far as possible the same letters used in the original patent referred to, to indicate the corresponding parts illustrated and described in the present application.

In Figs. 1 and 2, L indicates a driving shaft driven directly by the engine T.

K is a cable winding drum suitably geared as indicated to the shaft L, the gearing being provided with shifters N by means of which the drum may be put into and out of gear with the driving shaft.

From the drum the cable O passes over the roller U at the bow of the scow. Between the drum and the roller is located a cable guide Q preferably formed of a suitable frame within which the guide pulleys P are journaled. This cable guide is adapted to slide transversely in the guides R.

The parts just described, with some slight differences in the details of construction, are substantially the same as shewn and described in my prior patent. In my prior patent a screw S having a bearing on the scow and working in a nut on the cable guide was employed to give this guide the transverse motion necessary to wind an endless right and left hand thread a running into one another at each end as indicated in Fig. 5. The screw has a bearing b on the scow within which it rotates freely but is held from endwise motion. It also passes through the nut c formed on or secure to the guide Q. In this nut is swivelled a dog d working in the thread a. From the construction described it follows that if the screw be rotated continuously the dog working in the endless in the right and left hand screw thread will constantly reciprocate the guide causing the cable to be wound on the drum alternately from one end to the other as desired.

While this screw may be turned by hand as was done with the screw shewn in my original patent, I prefer to operate it from the drum itself. To this end I journal adjacent to the drum a shaft e one bearing f fixed to the side of the scow and the other bearing g made vertically moveable on the standard adjacent to the end of the drum.

As shewn in Fig. 3 I permit of this vertical motion of the bearing by forming slots h therein through which the bolts i securing it to the standard may pass. This standard is shewn in section in Fig. 2.

Within a recess in the back of the bearing slides a small block j on which is pivoted one end of the short crank arm I secured to the crank shaft m journaled in the standard. The other end of this crank shaft is provided with a weighted arm n which thus tends constantly to pressing the bearing g downwards.

On the shaft e close to this bearing is secured the friction disk o which through the action of the weighted arm n is thus maintained in driving connection with the periphery of the gear formed at one end of the drum. While I deem it most convenient to allow the friction disk to contact with the gear I might if I deemed it desirable form a special friction disk on the end of the drum with which it might engage.

The arrangement for maintaining the friction disk in contact with the drum permits of its raising to any inequalities in the gear without breaking the driving connection, the fixed bearing f being made sufficiently loose to permit of the slight rocking motion of the shaft. It is also evident that by pulling up the weighted arm o the friction disk may be drawn out of contact with the drum and the rotation of the shaft e thus stopped.

A sprocket wheel p on the shaft e is connected by a sprocket chain with the sprocket wheel k on the end of the screw S so that a driving connection is thus formed between the drum and the screw. The disk and the sprocket wheels are so proportioned as to properly time the movements of the cable guide.

As cables after being used for a certain length of time stretch and become a little thinner it becomes necessary to vary the movements of the cable guide to keep it in proper time with the rotation of the drum. I accomplish this by providing a series of rings q progressively increasing in size. When I find that the stretch of the cable has thrown out the time of the movements of the guide I slip on the smallest ring q and screw it to the disk, suitable holes being provided in both the disk and the ring for that purpose. After the cable has stretched further I slip on the second ring, and so on adding ring after ring until the cable has stretched its limit. It will be seen that these rings are of such a size as to exactly fit one over the other from the smallest to the largest, the smallest exactly fitting the disk.

CLAIM:

1. In a warping scow a cable winding drum and a transversely moveable cable guide in combination with a screw journaled on the scow and provided with endless right and left hand threads, a nut on the guide adapted to receive the screw, a swivelled dog carried by the nut and engaging the threads of the screw, a shaft journaled adjacent to the drum, a friction disc fast on the shaft and engaging a circular part of the drum, substantially as described.

2. In a warping scow a cable winding drum and a transversely moveable cable guide in combination with a screw journaled on the scow and provided with endless right and left hand threads, a nut on the guide adapted to receive a screw, a swivelled dog carried by the nut and engaging the threads of the screw; a moveable journaled friction disk; means for moving the friction disk into or out of contact with the drum; and means for conveying rotary motion from the disk to the screw, substantially as described.

3. In a warping scow a cable-winding drum on a transversely moveable cable guide in combination with a screw journaled on the scow and provided with endless right and left hand threads, a nut on the guide adapted to receive the screw; a swivel dog carried by the nut and engaging the threads of the screw; a moveable journaled friction disk means for moving the friction disk in to or out of contact with the drum; one or more rings adapted to be progressively secured about the periphery of the disk; and means for conveying rotary motion from the disk to the screw, substantially as described.

4. In a warping scow a cable-winding drum; and a transversely moveable cable guide, in combination with a screw journaled on the scow and provided with endless right and left hand threads; a nut on the guide adapted to receive the screw; a swivel dog carried by the nut and engaging the threads of the screw; a shaft adjacent to the drum; a fixed slightly loose bearing for the end of the shaft furthest from the drum; a vertical moveable bearing for the shaft adjacent to the drum having a recess formed therein; a suitably journaled crank shaft having a short crank engaging said recess; a weighted arm secured to the crank shaft and tending to press the bearing downward; a friction disk secured to the shaft and adapted to engage a circular part of the drum; and a means for conveying rotary motion from the disk to the screw, substantially as described.

Appendix D
Alligator Warping Tugs
Production Records

The following information lists every known Alligator warping tug, or, scow manufactured by West & Peachey, including machinery manufactured by the firm for tugs that were completed by the buyers.

Most of the information was compiled from actual records of the firm of West & Peachey and are the only comprehensive ones known to have survived. There are more details for tugs built after 1913. These records begin with Alligator #16, named *Hunter*. Information on Alligators numbered 1 to 15 and 35 to 39 was compiled from newspapers, journals, and Canadian Shipping Registers. Buyers' addresses came chiefly from West & Peachey records. In some cases these are head office addresses, in others, for the same company, they are field office addresses.

It should also be noted that some buyers' names changed over the years as partnerships were formed or dissolved and as corporations evolved from the operations of the timber barons and lumbermen.

Abbreviations:

PW: Paddlewheel Alligator
TS: Twin-Screw Alligator

The Alligator Warping Tug

1889
PW #1: *Alligator*   Shipped April 14 to Joseph Jackson of Simcoe, Ontario. Later owned by Hardy Lumber Co., Trout Creek, Ontario. On May 29, 1895, it sank in the French River.

1890

PW #2: Name unknown   Shipped March 18 to Moore Lumber Co., Detroit, Michigan.

PW #3: *H. Trudel*   Shipped March 20 to R.H. Klock and Company, Klock's Mills, Ontario.

Trudel II: In 1904, a set of machinery, less boiler and engine for a standard-sized tug, was ordered with a $3^{15}/_{16}$-inch diameter paddlewheel shaft and hubs and gears of $3^{15}/_{16}$-inch diameter. The tug was rebuilt at Douglas Farm, Quinze Lake, Quebec, for R.H. Klock & Company, Klock's Mills, Ontario. By June 1924, it was owned by Rochester & McKegg of North Témiscamingue, Quebec. In April 1927, the tug was changed to twin-screw, 30-inch diameter, stationary propellers.

1891

PW #4: *Saginaw*   Shipped March, to J.W. Howry, Saginaw, Michigan.

1892

PW #5: *Lorne*   Shipped March 31, to Saginaw Salt & Lumber Company, Saginaw, Michigan.

PW #6: *Madawaska*   Shipped to McLachlin Bros., Arnprior, Ontario. Assembled at Arnprior.

PW #7: *Bonnechére*   Shipped to McLachlin Bros., Arnprior, Ontario.

PW #8: *Amable du Fond*   Shipped to McLachlin Bros., Arnprior, Ontario. Rebuilt in 1894.

1893

PW #9: *Ballantyne*   Shipped to McLachlin Bros., Arnprior, Ontario.

PW #10: *North River*   Standard-size tug. Shipped, knocked down, to Shepard & Morse Lumber Company, Ottawa, Ontario. Delivered to Lake Octaboning, Quebec. May 1898, owned by McLachlin Bros., Arnprior.

PW #11: *Beaver*   Shipped to Alex Lumsden, Lumsden Mills, Quebec.

PW #12: *Samson*   Shipped to Upper Ottawa Improvement Company, Ottawa, Ontario.

PW #13: *Alligator*   Shipped May. Thought to be to Gilmour & Company, Trenton, Ontario.

PW #14: *Trent*   Shipped to Gilmour & Company, Trenton.

PW #15: *Muskoka*   Shipped to Gilmour & Company, Trenton.

1894

PW #16: *Hunter*   Water-back boiler No. 481. Shipped to Gilmour & Company, Trenton, Ontario. Later owned by Ontario Lumber Co. and J.R. Booth, Ottawa.

PW #17: *Peck*   Standard-size, tug 25 hp. Water-back Boiler No. 479. Equipped with electric searchlight. Shipped to Gilmour & Company, Trenton.

PW #18: *Nipissing* Water-back boiler No. 480. Shipped to Gilmour & Co., Trenton, Ontario, February 1921. Next owned by St. Maurice Paper Co., Montreal, Quebec. Named *Lac Oureau.*

PW #19: *C.S. Read* Boiler No. 478. Paddlewheel shaft 3⅜-inch diameter. Shipped to Buell, Hurdman & Company (Hull Lumber Company), Hull, Quebec.

PW #20: *Joseph Taylor* Standard-size tug. Boiler No. 484. 9-by-9-inch engine. Rebuilt in 1906. Karton Injector. New steel gear and large sheave shaft. Line shaft 2⁷⁄₁₆-inch diameter. Paddlewheel shaft 3⅛-inch diameter. Shipped to J.R. Booth, Ottawa. This Alligator is abandoned on the shores of Lake Nilgaut, Quebec.

PW #21: *Spanish Ranger* Boiler No. 487. Shipped to Robert Booth, Pembroke, Ontario.

PW #22: *Nimsongis* Boiler No. 486. Large size. Paddlewheel shaft 3⅜-inch diameter. Shipped to the Ontario & Western Lumber Company. Rat Portage (Kenora), Ontario.

PW #23: *Hamilton H* Boiler No. 485. Shipped April 30, 1894, to J.W. Howry & Sons, Saginaw, Michigan. Used to supply their mill at Fenelon Falls, Ontario.

1895

PW #24: *Victoria* Boiler No. 488. Standard-size tug. Paddlewheel shaft 3³⁄₁₆-inch diameter. Hubs 3³⁄₁₆-inch diameter. Shipped June 8 to Hardy Lumber Company, Trout Creek, Ontario. She replaced Alligator #1, which sank in the French River May 29, 1895.

PW #25: *Baskatong* Boiler No. 532. Standard-size tug. Penberthy injector. Shipped March 4, 1895, knocked down, to Messrs. Gilmour & Hughson, Hull, Quebec. Delivered to Lake Baskatong, Quebec. By 1927, it was owned by the Canadian International Paper Company.

PW #26: *Weslemkoon* Boiler #534. Standard-size tug. Penberthy injector. Shipped March 8 to John Ferguson, Renfrew, Ontario. By 1927, the *Weslemkoon* was owned by the Canadian International Paper Company.

PW #27: *Otter* Water-back boiler No. 538. Penberthy injector. Shipped to Alex Lumsden, Ottawa, Ontario. By 1923, it was owned by Riordan Pulp Corporation and stationed at Témiscamingue, Quebec.

PW #28: *Lorne Hale* Boiler #561. Shipped August 3, 1895, to Hale and Booth, Pembroke, Ontario. Delivered to Serpent River, Ontario.

1896

PW #29: *Ohio* Large 66-by-84 inch dry-back marine boiler No. 575. Oversize hull, 55 feet long, 11-foot beam, powered by twin duplex steam engines, rated 40 hp. Shipped November 12, knocked down, to Barney & Stevens, Dayton, Ohio. Delivered to Barrinquilla, Colombia, South America.

PW #30: *F.W. Avery* Standard-size tug. Boiler No. 292. Shipped February 17, knocked down, to Buell, Hurdman & Company (Hull Lumber Company) Hull, Quebec. Delivered to Sunnyside, Quebec. February 1919, converted to twin-lifting screws. Owned by Riordan Pulp Corporation.

PW #31: *St. Anthony No. 1* Standard-size tug. Penberthy injector. Boiler No. 564. Shipped to St. Anthony Lumber Company, Whitney, Ontario.

PW #32: *Hardy*   Standard-size tug. Shipped to Hardy Lumber Company, Trout Creek, Ontario.

PW #33: *Mink*   Water-back boiler No. 590. Machinery only supplied with this order. Shipped to Alex Lumsden, Ottawa, Ontario.

1897

PW #34: *Kegebongo*   Standard-size tug. Boiler No. 593. Shipped, knocked down, on March 3 to Gilmour & Hughson, Hull, Quebec. Delivered to Bark Lake, Quebec, February 9, 1921. Owned by Gatineau Company, a subsidiary of Riordan Pulp & Paper Corporation Ltd.

1899

PW #35: Name unknown Machinery for standard-size Alligator shipped in April to W.C. Edwards, New Edinburgh, (Ottawa), Ontario.

PW #36: Name unknown Shipped to Wallace, McCormack & Sheppard, Orillia, Ontario.

1900

PW #37: *Emma*   Shipped March, knocked down, to McLaurin & McLaren, East Templeton Lumber Co., East Templeton, Quebec. Delivered to Pembroke, Ontario. By 1910 it was owned by Gilmour & Hughson, Hull, Quebec.

PW #38: Name unknown Shipped to R.L. Mackey, Rat Portage (Kenora), Ontario.

PW #39: *W.T. White*   Standard-size tug. Shipped to Buell, Hurdman & Company (Hull Lumber Company) Hull, Quebec.

PW #40: *Annie*   Large-size tug. Water-back boiler No. 976. Cast-steel gearing. Shipped August, knocked down, to Lewis Miller, Millertown, Newfoundland. Delivered to Red Indian Lake, Newfoundland.

1901

PW #41: *E.B. Eddy*   Standard-size tug. Boiler No. 1044. Large sheave gear $4\frac{7}{16}$-inch diameter. Line shaft $2\frac{1}{4}$-inch diameter. Penberthy injector. Shipped February 25 to E.B. Eddy & Company, Hull, Quebec.

PW #42: *Hercules*   Water-back boiler No. 1037. Machinery supplied only. Engine 9-by-9 inch diameter, paddle-wheel shaft $4\frac{7}{16}$-inch diameter by 14 feet long. Line shaft $2\frac{7}{16}$-inch diameter, large sheave. Penberthy injector. Shipped February 18 to Upper Ottawa Improvement Company, Ottawa, Ontario.

PW #43: *Holland and Graves*   Standard-size tug, large sheave 4⁷⁄₁₆-inch diameter. Line shaft 2¼-inch diameter. Penberthy injector. Boiler No. 1052. Shipped March to Holland and Graves, Buffalo, New York.

PW#44: *Sweepstake*   Standard-size tug, large sheave gear 4⁷⁄₁₆-inch diameter. Line shaft 2¼-inch diameter. Penberthy injector. Boiler No. 1045. Shipped March 4, 1901, to Turner Lumber Company, Midland, Ontario.

PW #45: *Traveller*   Standard-size tug, large sheave. Boiler No. 1053. Shipped March 4, 1901, to Turner Lumber Company, Midland, Ontario.

PW #46: *Victoria*   Large-size tug. Paddlewheel shaft 3½-inch diameter. Turned to 3⅜-inch diameter. Large sheave 4⁷⁄₁₆-inch diameter. Line shaft 2¼-inch diameter. Boiler No.1064. Shipped May 1, 1901, to Victoria Harbour Lumber Company, Toronto, Ontario.

On December 4, 1922, machinery was shipped to the Victoria Harbour Lumber Company Limited, Whitefish, Ontario. A West & Peachey crew was dispatched to convert the *Victoria*'s paddlewheel drive to a twin-screw drive.

PW #47: *Coulonge*   Large-size tug. Penberthy injector. Line shaft 2¼-inch diameter. Water-back boiler No. 1070. Shipped August 1901 to Gillies Brothers, Braeside, Ontario.

PW #48: *Beaver*   Standard-size tug. Penberthy injector. Boiler No. 1071. Shipped August 1901 to The Georgian Bay Lumber Company, Waubaushene, Ontario. By 1919, owned by Caswell Lumber Company, Limited, Sudbury, Ontario.

1902

PW #49: *Hazlitt*   Standard-size tug. Boiler No. 1083. Shipped April 28, 1902, to Dickson Lumber Company, Peterborough, Ontario. Delivered to Lakefield, Ontario. By September 12, 1907, owned by Cavendish Lumber Company, Lakefield, Ontario. By April 7, 1911, owned by Munn Lumber Company, Orillia, Ontario.

PW #50: *James Thompson*   Standard-size tug. Boiler No.1136. Shipped June 4, 1902, to Robert Hurdman, Ottawa, Ontario. By March 4, 1920, owned by J.R. Booth. New hull, cabin, and wheelhouse supplied and shipped to Kipawa, Quebec, and converted to twin-screw propellers at that time. By March 1925, owned by Lindsay & Larochelle, Bearn, Quebec.

PW #51: *D. Lunam*   Standard-size tug. Boiler No.1149. First tug equipped with automatic cable-winding device and split-paddlewheel gear. First tug equipped with engine with short crankshaft and bow carriage. Shipped November 1902 to Hawkesbury Lumber Company, Ottawa, Ontario.

1903

PW #52: *Wawaskesh*   Standard-size tug. Dry-back Boiler No. 1208. Split-paddlewheel gear. Automatic cable-winding device. Paddlewheel shaft 3⅜-inch diameter. Line shaft 2⁷⁄₁₆-inch diameter. Shipped March 1903 to Holland and Graves, Buffalo, New York.

PW #53: *Pontiac*   Standard-size tug. Dry-back Boiler No. 1227. Paddlewheel shaft 2⁷⁄₁₆-inch diameter. Split-paddlewheel shaft, short crankcase, automatic cable-winding device. Shipped April 1903 to Shepard & Morse Lumber Company, Ottawa, Ontario. By June 24, 1921, new hull, cabin, and wheelhouse supplied and a West & Peachey crew were dispatched to assemble it and to convert it to a twin-screw operated tug at Kipawa, Quebec.

PW #54: *John McLean*   Standard-size tug. Boiler No. 1235. Automatic cable-winding device. Shipped August 1903 to Cook and Bros. Lumber Company, Spragge, Ontario.

PW #55: *R.B. Eddy*   Standard-size tug. Boiler No. 1236. Automatic cable-winding device. Shipped October 7, 1903, to Eddy Bros. & Company, Blind River, Ontario.

PW #56: *Cook and Brothers*   Standard-size tug. Boiler No. 1258. Shipped November 13, 1903, to Cook and Bros. Lumber Company, Spragge, Ontario.

1904

PW #57: *Wabassee*   Standard-size tug. Boiler No. 1269. Shipped January 20, 1904, to James McLaren Company, Limited, Buckingham, Quebec.

PW #58: *J.W. Hennesy*   Standard-size tug. Boiler No. 1275. Paddlewheel shaft 3⁷⁄₁₆-inch diameter. Gears and hubs 3⁷⁄₁₆-inch diameter. First Alligator with the paddlewheel shaft not turned down. Shipped February 4, 1904, to J.R. Booth, Ottawa, Ontario. To be delivered to Eau Claire Station, Ontario.

PW #59: *Algonquin*   Standard-size tug. Boiler No. 1290. Paddlewheel shaft 3⁷⁄₁₆-inch diameter. Steel gears. Shipped February 18, 1904, to McLachlin Bros., Arnprior, Ontario. To be delivered to Brule Lake Station, Ontario.

PW #60: Name unknown.   Only machinery supplied for standard size-tug. Boiler No. 1291. Shipped April 1904 to W.C. Edwards, Rockland, Ontario.

PW #61: *Beaver*   Standard-size tug. Boiler No. 1298. Cast-steel gears. First Alligator with two large sheaves bored to 1½-inch diameter hole in sheaves. Shipped April 6, 1904, to Rat Portage Lumber Company, Rat Portage, Ontario.

PW #62: *St. Anthony No. 2*   Large-size tug. Steel gears, large sheaves bored to 1½-inch diameter. Shipped May 1, 1904, to St. Anthony Lumber Company, Ottawa, Ontario. To be delivered to Whitney, Ontario. On June 11, 1920, a new hull was shipped for Alligator #62, owned by the Colonial Lumber Company, Limited. Pembroke, Ontario, and delivered to Kipawa, Quebec.

PW #63: *St. Maurice No. 1* Standard-size tug. Boiler No. 1307. Steel gears, paddlewheel-gear split shaft 3$\frac{7}{16}$-inch diameter. Large sheaves bored to 1$\frac{1}{2}$-inch diameter. Shipped July 9, 1904, to Department of Public Works, Ottawa, Ontario. In November 1920, transferred on lease to the St. Maurice River Boom and Drive Company. Rebuilt that same year. Destroyed by boiler explosion on September 17, 1942, at Grandes-Piles, Quebec.

1905

PW #64: *Gordon* Standard-size tug. Boiler No. 1358. Steel gears, paddlewheel gears, split shaft 3$\frac{7}{16}$-inch diameter. Large sheaves bored 1$\frac{1}{2}$-inch diameter. Shipped February 7, 1905, to George Gordon and Company, Cache Bay, Ontario. To be delivered to Markstay, Ontario.

PW #65: *Alligator* Standard-size tug. Boiler No. 1366. Steel gears, automatic cable-winding device. Shipped, knocked down, on March 3, 1905, to the Norwood Manufacturing Company, Tupper Lake, New York. To be delivered to Long Lake West, New York.

PW #66: *St. Maurice No. 2* Standard-size tug. Boiler No. 1373. Steel gears, paddlewheel shafts 3$\frac{7}{16}$-inch diameter. Sheaves bored 1$\frac{1}{2}$-inch diameter. Shipped to Department of Public Works, Ottawa, Ontario. To be delivered to Shawinigan. Quebec. In June 1927, transferred on lease to the St. Maurice River Boom and Driving Company, Trois-Rivières, Quebec. Broken up and replaced by twin-screw tug of same name in 1929. Some of the original machinery used in the rebuild.

TS #67: *St. Maurice No. 3* This was the first twin-screw Alligator tug manufactured, completed in 1904. Boiler No. 1297. Shipped April 10, 1905, to Department of Public Works, Ottawa, Ontario. To be delivered to Trois-Rivières, Quebec. Destroyed by fire at Trois-Rivières on October 12, 1912. Salvaged and rebuilt on site in 1914. Rebuilt again at Trois-Rivières in 1925. Broken up in 1941.

PW #68: *Holland & Graves No. 3* Standard-size tug. Paddlewheel shaft 3$\frac{7}{16}$-inch diameter. Large sheaves bored 1$\frac{1}{2}$-inch diameter. Shipped April 12, 1905, to Holland and Graves, Buffalo, New York. To be delivered to Wanapitei, Ontario.

PW #69: *Holland & Graves No. 4* Standard-size tug. Boiler No. 1381. Shipped April 22, 1905, to Holland & Graves, Buffalo, New York. To be delivered to Callander, Ontario. By October 1920, owned by the Sable & Spanish Boom Company, Limited, Algoma.

PW #70: *La Belgique* Standard-size tug. Boiler No. 1393. Shipped May 9, 1905, to the Belgo Pulp and Paper Company, Limited, Shawinigan Falls, Quebec. To be delivered to Van Bruyssel Siding, Quebec. By March 25, 1929, owned by Canada Power and Paper Company Corporation, Shawinigan Falls, Quebec. (Head Office, Montreal.)

PW #71: *British Lion* Standard-size tug. Boiler No. 1398. Shipped May 27, 1905 to James Harty Esquire, Fort Frances, Ontario. By October 29, 1906, owned by Reginald V. Keating, Fort Frances. By

March 25, 1907, owned by Rainy River Lumber Company, Limited., Rainy River, Ontario. Later sold to Shevlin-Clarke Company Ltd., Fort Frances, Ontario.

PW #72: *Marjorie*   Standard-size tug. Boiler No. 1404. Shipped July 19, 1905, to the Northern Lumber Company, Sudbury, Ontario. To be delivered to Warren, Ontario. By August 21, 1920, owned by Spanish River Pulp and Paper Mills Limited and converted to lifting-type twin screws. By January 20, 1925, owned by Canadian Timber Company, Limited, Toronto, Ontario. (See #188) Rebuilt in Simcoe.

PW #73: *Max*   Standard-size tug. Boiler No. 1409. First Alligator tug to have the steam pipe installed in the top of the steam chest of the engine. Shipped August 24, 1905, to C. Beck Manufacturing Company, Penetanguishene, Ontario. To be delivered to Wanapitei, Ontario. By April 1921, owned by Schroeder Mills and Timber Company, Limited. (See #171) Rebuilt and renumbered #171. Renamed the *William M.*

1906

PW #74: *Temagami*   Standard-size tug. Boiler No. unknown. Shipped April 17, 1906, to Temagami Lumber Company, Orillia, Ontario. To be delivered to Cache Bay, Ontario. By December 1924, owned by Hope Lumber Company, Sault Ste. Marie, Ontario.

On February 18, 1925, materials for a new hull and decks were supplied for Alligator #74. Two new steel rudders and tillers were also supplied and a West & Peachey crew was dispatched to assemble the new fixtures in Ruel, Ontario.

PW #75: *John W. Wells*   Standard-size tug. Boiler No. unknown. Shipped May 1906 to White Pine Lumber Company, Webbwood, Ontario.

1907

PW #76: *Albert*   Large-size tug. Boiler No. 1500. Shipped February 1907 to Victoria Harbour Lumber Company, Toronto, Ontario.

PW #77: *Chapleau*   This was the first small-size, 8-by-37-foot Alligator tug. Dry-back Boiler No. 1447. Cast-iron gearing, shafts $1^{15}/_{16}$-inch diameter, small sheave $3^3/_8$-inch diameter, paddlewheel shaft $2^{15}/_{16}$-inch diameter. Shipped March 1907 to The Mageau Le Blanc Lumber Company, Chapleau, Ontario. By March 12, 1919, owned by Arnold and Bell, Massey, Ontario. By April 11, 1927, owned by the Spanish River Lumber Company, Massey, Ontario.

PW #78: *Kealy*   Boiler No. 1554. Shipped March 1907, to East Templeton Lumber Company, East Templeton, Quebec. To be delivered to Maniwaki, Quebec. By March 1910, owned by Gilmour and Hughson, Hull, Quebec.

PW #79: *Castor* Only the machinery supplied with this order. The first large-size steam engine, 10 by 10 inch, supplied by the firm of West & Peachey. Boiler No. 1553. All shafting $2^{15}/_{16}$-inch diameter. Paddlewheel shaft $5\frac{1}{2}$ inch by 18 feet. All cast-steel gearing. Easy injector No. 15. The large steel hull, 22 by 66 feet, was supplied by the Canadian Ship Building Company, Toronto, Ontario. Shipped April 1907 to the Upper Ottawa Improvement Company, Ottawa, Ontario. To be delivered to Pembroke, Ontario.

PW #80: *Pollux* Only the machinery supplied with this order, which was identical to that of the *Castor* #79, above. Shipped April 1907 to the Upper Ottawa Improvement Company, Ottawa, for delivery to Pembroke, Ontario. She was reported to have burned in the Ottawa River, near Pembroke, date unknown.

TS #81: *Mississaga* Large-size tug. First Alligator to be manufactured with a stem post and pointed bow. Boiler No. 1548. Easy injector No. 12. Shipped April 1907 to Eddy Bros. and Company, Blind River, Ontario. Later owned by the Mississaga River Improvement Company Limited.

PW #82: *V.R.B. Co. Ltd. No. 2* Standard-size tug. Boiler No. 1556. Penberthy injector. Shipped May 1907 to the Vermilion River Boom Company, Limited, Wanapitei, Ontario. To be delivered to Larchwood, Ontario.

TS #83: *H.H. Bishop* Standard-size tug. Boiler No. 1592. Shipped June 1907 to the Thessalon Lumber Company, Thessalon, Ontario. By June 1923, owned by Lake Superior Paper Company Limited, Sault Ste. Marie, Ontario.

TS #84: *Nellie* Standard-size tug. Boiler No. 1593. Shipped August 1907 to the Shuswap Lumber Company, Shuswap, British Columbia.

TS #85: *Laurentide Paper Company, Ltd.* Standard-size tug. Boiler No. unknown. Shipped September 1907 to Laurentide Paper Company, Ltd., Grand-Mère, Quebec.

1908

TS #86: Name unknown Machinery only supplied. Engine 7 by 7 inch. Boiler No. 1658. Shipped February 15, 1908, to The Laurentide Paper Company, Ltd. Grand-Mère, Quebec. To be delivered to St. Felix de Valois, Quebec.

TS #87: Name unknown Machinery only supplied. Boiler No. 1659. Engine 7 by 7 inch. Shipped February 15, 1908, to the Laurentide Paper Company, Ltd., Grand-Mère, Quebec. To be delivered to St. Felix de Valois, Quebec.

PW #88: *Eunice* Large-size tug. Boiler No. 1656. Shipped February 26, 1908, to the Spanish River Pulp and Paper Company, Sudbury, Ontario. To be delivered to Bannerman Siding, Ontario. Rebuilt in 1925, and renamed *Margaret*. By 1934, owned by Abitibi Pulp and Paper Company.

PW #89: Name unknown — Standard-size tug. Boiler No. unknown. Shipped March 11, 1908, to Waldie Bros. Ltd., Toronto, Ontario. To be delivered to Spragge, Ontario. By February 1920, owned by Graham and Shannon.

PW #90: *Fisher* — Large-size tug. Boiler No. unknown. Shipped April 27, 1908, to the Upper Ottawa Improvement Company, Ottawa, Ontario. To be delivered to Témiscamingue, Quebec. She was rebuilt in 1919 at Témiscamingue and renamed the *Muskrat*. Her size was 10 feet 4 inches by 48 feet.

TS #91: *Gordon Mac* — Large-size tug. Boiler No. unknown. Shipped May 4, 1908, to International Lumber Company, International Falls, Ontario. By March 31, 1909, owned by Keewatin Lumber Company Ltd. Keewatin, Ontario.

1909

TS #92 : *Bay City* — Large-size tug. Boiler No. unknown. Shipped April 9, 1909, to Eddy Bros. & Company, Blind River, Ontario. By June 1919, owned by Hope Lumber Company, Thessalon, Ontario, and located at Dean Lake. By May 1929, owned by Carpenter-Hixon Company Limited, Blind River, Ontario.

PW #93: *Wawa* — Large-size tug. Boiler No. unknown. Paddlewheel 11-foot diameter. Shipped to Bonser & Miller, Latchford, Ontario. By March 18, 1920, owned by J.R. Booth, Elk Lake. Renamed *A. Ferguson*.

TS #94 : *W.J. Bell* — Standard-size tug. Boiler No. unknown. Shipped August 10, 1909, to Spanish River Lumber Company, Massey, Ontario. To be delivered to Spanish River Station, Ontario.

1910

PW #95: *Reginald* — A knocked-down hull and a vertical boiler only was supplied. A vertical boiler was unusual, but no further details are available. Boiler No unknown. Shipped to Spanish River Pulp and Paper Company, Sudbury, Ontario. To be delivered to Bannerman Siding, Ontario.

TS #96: *R. Jackson* — Standard-size tug. Boiler No. 1806. Shipped to Waldie Bros. Ltd. Toronto, Ontario. To be delivered to Blind River, Ontario.

PW #97 *Metabachuan* — Standard-size tug. Boiler No. 1882. Shipped to Shepard & Morse Lumber Company, Ottawa, Ontario. To be delivered to Temagami, Ontario.

TS #98 *Northern* — Standard-size tug. Boiler No. 1820. Shipped to the Northern Construction Company, Winnipeg, Manitoba. To be delivered to Fort Frances, Ontario. By 1916, owned by Shevlin-Clarke Company Ltd., Fort Frances, Ontario. Renamed *Perley Holmes*.

PW #99: *Osaquaw* — Standard-size tug. Boiler No. 1686. Shipped to D.L. Mather, Kenora, Ontario. To be delivered to Ignace, Ontario. By May 1923, owned by Indian Lake Lumber Company.

PW #100: *Dominion* Small-size tug, built in 1908. Boiler No. 1607. Shipped to Munday Lumber Company, Bradford, Pennsylvania. To be delivered to Three Valley, British Columbia.

PW #101: *Bersimis* An oversized tug with stem post and pointed bow, assembled at Port Ryerse on Lake Erie. Boiler No. 1848. Selling price $7,000. Delivered by water to Montreal, Quebec, to Howard & Craig, Sherbrooke, Quebec.

TS #102: *Saguenay* Large-size tug. Boiler No. 1871. Shipped August 1910 to Department of Public Works, Ottawa, Ontario. To be delivered to Chicoutimi, Quebec.

TS #103: *Beaver* Standard-size tug. Boiler No. 1872. Shipped November 8, 1910, to Herman H. Hettler Lumber Company, Callander, Ontario.

1911

PW #104: *Durocher* Standard-size tug. Boiler No. 1870. Shipped, knocked down, to Frasers and Bryson, Ottawa, Ontario. To be delivered to Haileybury, Ontario. By May 6, 1919, owned by Kipiwa Fibre Company Limited, Montreal, Quebec. By 1926, owned by Riordan Pulp Corporation and converted to twin screw. By July 1929, owned by Canadian International Paper Company. Renamed *C.I.P. No. 9*.

PW #105: *McKinnon* Standard-size tug. Boiler No. 1909. Shipped February 16, 1911, knocked down, to Frasers & Bryson, Ottawa, Ontario. To be delivered to Brule Lake, Ontario.

TS #106: *The Cleveland* Standard-size tug. Boiler No. 1912. Shipped February 16, 1911, to the Cleveland-Sarnia and Sawmills Company, Sarnia, Ontario. To be delivered, knocked down, to Nairn Centre, Ontario. Later owned by the Spanish River Pulp and Paper Mills, Limited. By December 1924, owned by the Canadian Timber Company Limited, Toronto, Ontario.

TS #107: *John McLean* Boiler No. 1910. Shipped, knocked down, on March 1, 1911, to Eddy Bros. & Company, Blind River, Ontario. To be delivered to Thessalon, Ontario. By July 1919, owned by McFadden & Mallory, Blind River, Ontario. On April 9, 1923, material for a new hull, cabin, and wheelhouse was shipped to Dean Lake, Ontario, for Alligator #107, owned by J.J. McFadden Limited, Blind River. By May 1929, owned by Carpenter-Hixon Company Limited. Blind River, Ontario.

PW #108: *Dreadnought* Small-size tug. Boiler No. 1829. Shipped April 7, 1911, to D.L. Mather, Fort Rouge (Winnipeg), Manitoba. To be delivered to Ignace, Ontario.

TS #109: *Champion* Standard-size tug. Boiler No. 1873. Shipped April 3, 1911, to Shevlin-Clarke Company Limited, Fort Frances, Ontario.

TS #110: *W.H. Carter* Large-size tug. Boiler No. 1908. Shipped May 4, 1911, to Keewatin Lumber Company, Keewatin, Ontario.

TS #111: *Amphibian* Standard-size tug. Boiler No. 1911. Shipped May 24, 1911, to Shevlin-Clarke Company Limited, Fort Frances, Ontario.

TS #112: *St. Maurice Hydraulic Company* Standard-size tug. Boiler No. 1960. Shipped July 21, 1911, to St. Maurice Hydraulic Company, Montreal, Quebec. To be delivered to Harvey's Junction, Quebec. By December 21, 1921, owned by Abitibi Power and Paper Corporation and renamed the *J.J. McCarthy*.

TS #113: *George McPherson* Large-size tug. Boiler No. 1959. Shipped to the Keewatin Lumber Company, Keewatin, Ontario.

1912

PW #114: *Samson* Oversized tug, 16 by 50 feet. Boiler No. 2029. Machinery only supplied. Paddlewheel shaft 5½-inch diameter. All shafting 2^{15}⁄₁₆-inch diameter. Hull built by the Collingwood Shipbuilding Company Limited, Collingwood, Ontario. Shipped January 31, 1912, to the Upper Ottawa Improvement Company, Ottawa, Ontario.

TS #115: *P.B. & Company Limited, No. 5* Large-size tug. Boiler No. 1991. Shipped to Price Bros. & Company Limited., Chicoutimi, Quebec.

TS #116: *Beaver* Standard-size tug. Boiler No. 1992. Shipped to Shevlin-Clarke Company Limited, Fort Frances, Ontario. To be delivered to Banning, Ontario.

PW #117: *Kenogami* Large-size tug. Boiler No. 1988. Shipped March 26, 1912, to La Compagnie de Pulpe de Chicoutimi, Chicoutimi, Quebec.

PW #118: *Pierre Dubois* Small-size tug. Boiler No. 1916. Shipped April 5, 1912, to E.F. Kendall, Kenora, Ontario. To be delivered to Kendall's Siding, Kenora, Ontario.

TS #119: Name unknown Machinery only. Boiler No. 1993. Shipped April 9, 1912, to International Lumber Company, International Falls, Minnesota. To be delivered to Fort Frances, Ontario.

TS #120: Name unknown Machinery only. Boiler No. 1990. Shipped April 9, 1912, to International Lumber Company, International Falls, Minnesota. To be delivered to Fort Frances, Ontario.

TS #121: *Matabitchuan* Large-size tug. Boiler No. 1989. Shipped May 4, 1912, to Gillies Brothers, Braeside, Ontario. To be delivered to Rib Lake Siding, Ontario. By June 1922, owned by J.R. Booth Limited, Ottawa, Ontario.

March 26, 1924, Alligator #121 was rebuilt in Simcoe. A new hull, cabin, and wheelhouse were constructed. The engine, boiler, and gearing were repaired. The drive was changed from lifting propellers to stationary-type screws. The tug was renamed *J.R. Booth No. 5* and shipped to Kipawa, Quebec.

TS #122: *St. Maurice No. 4* Standard-size tug. Boiler No. 2073. Shipped September 21, 1912, to the Department of Public Works, Ottawa, Ontario. To be delivered to Grandes-Piles, Quebec. In November 1920, transferred on lease to the St. Maurice River Boom & Driving Company, Trois-Rivières, Quebec. (See #207.)

1913

PW #123: *Eddy*	Standard-size tug. Boiler No. 2077. Cable not included. Later fitted with new boiler No. 2712. Shipped January 25, 1913, knocked down, to E.B. Eddy Company Limited, Hull, Quebec. To be delivered to Moor Lake, Ontario.
TS #124: *St. Maurice No. 5.*	Large-size tug. Boiler No. 2075. Selling price, f.o.b. Simcoe $3,450. Shipped March 25, 1913, to Department of Public Works, Ottawa, Ontario. To be delivered to Trois-Rivières, Quebec. By November 1920, transferred on lease to St. Maurice River Boom & Driving Company, Trois-Rivières, Quebec.
PW #125: *S.R.L. Co.*	Small-size tug. Boiler No. 2059. Shipped March 27, 1913, to Spanish River Lumber Company, Massey, Ontario. To be delivered to Walford, Ontario. By May 1924, owned by Graham & Wilkieson, Spanish, Ontario.
TS #126: *Virginia*	Large size, 11 by 48 feet. Boiler and cable not included. Shipped April 12, 1913, to Virginia and Rainy Lake Company, Virginia, Minnesota. To be delivered to Cusson, Minnesota.
PW #127: *O.F.P*	Large-size tug. Boiler No. 2076. Shipped April 18, 1913, to the Ouiatchouan Falls Paper Company, Chicoutimi, Quebec. To be delivered to Lac Bouchette, Quebec.
PW #128: *Windermere*	Small-size tug. Boiler No. 2164. Shipped April 30, 1913, to Austin & Nicholson, Chapleau, Ontario. To be delivered to Nicholson Siding, Chapleau, Ontario.
TS #129: *Jessie*	Standard-size tug. Boiler No. 2074. Shipped May 3, 1913, to A.T. Mackie and Company, 506 Standard Bank Building, Toronto, Ontario. To be delivered to Bannerman Siding, Ontario. Later owned by Tomiko Lumber Company, Smokey Falls, Ontario. By April 1923, owned by the Canadian Timber Company Ltd.

1914

TS #130: *P.B. and Co. Ltd. No. 2*	Large-size tug. Dry-back Boiler No. 2229, 60 by 74 inches. Oversized hull, 11-foot beam by 55 feet in length. Engine 10 by 10 inches. Large steel gear with 5-inch face. Drum braces forward of drum, bevel gearing. Cookhouse installed. The first Alligator tug to have the West & Peachey slide-throttle installed in her. Selling price was $4,250. Shipped, knocked down, March 5, 1914, to Price Brothers and Company Limited, Chicoutimi, Quebec. To be delivered to Jonquière.
TS #131: *Otter*	Name later changed to *Tommy Mathieu*. Large-size tug. Water-back Boiler No. 2234, 66 by 84 inches. Oversized hull. 12-foot beam by 60 feet in length, with a pointed bow. This tug was different in that it had twin upright 9-by-9-inch engines installed. They were directly

connected to the screws by slip couples. The port engine drove the ⅝-inch cable drum through bevel gears, while the starboard engine drove the ⅜-inch cable through bevel gears. She had twin three-blade propellers, 36 inches in diameter, made by Kennedy's Foundry, Owen Sound, Ontario. She was shipped, knocked down, on March 28, 1914, to Shevlin-Clarke Company Ltd., Fort Frances, Ontario.

TS #132: *Fairy Blonde*   Standard-size tug. Boiler No. 2179. Shipped April 29, 1914, to Devon Lumber Company, Limited, Ottawa, Ontario. To be delivered to Devon, Ontario. By April 1929, owned by McNaughton Lumber Company Limited. By October 1936, owned by Wakami Lumber Company Limited, Sultan, Ontario.

1915

PW #133: *Lac Ha! Ha!*   Large-size tug. Boiler No. 2177. Shipped February 1, 1915, knocked down, to La Compagnie de Pulpe de Chicoutimi, Chicoutimi, Quebec. To be delivered to Ha! Ha! Bay Junction, Quebec. Now owned by Canadian International Paper Company, Montreal. She still lies near the shoreline of Lac Ha! Ha! in Quebec.

TS #134: *S.R.L. Co. No. 4*   Standard-size tug, equipped with twin 4-blade propellers, 28 inches in diameter. Boiler No. 2178. Shipped February 15, 1915, to Spanish River Lumber Company Limited, Massey, Ontario.

PW #135: *H.B. Shepard*   Standard-size tug, 10 by 37 feet. Boiler No. 2281. Shipped, knocked down, March 1, 1915, to Shepard & Morse Lumber Company, Ottawa, Ontario. To be delivered to New Liskeard, Ontario. By March 15, 1923, owned by J.R. Booth Limited. Ottawa, Ontario.

TS #136: *P.B. Co. Ltd. No. 3*   Boiler No. 2280. Equipped with twin three-blade propellers, 30 inches in diameter. Cookhouse installed, runway along sides, boat guard on stern. Shipped, knocked down, on March 10, 1915, to Price Brothers and Company Ltd. in Chicoutimi, Quebec. To be delivered to Metabetchouan, Quebec.

PW #137: *Chandler*   Large-size Alligator, 11 by 45 feet. Boiler No. 2279. Shipped April 12, 1915, to La Compagnie de Pulpe de Chicoutimi, Chicoutimi, Quebec. To be delivered to Chandler, Gaspé County, Quebec.

TS #138: *Manitou*   Standard-size tug, 10 by 42 feet. Boiler No. 2072. Shipped April 15, 1917, to Gulf Pulp and Paper Company, Quebec.

PW #139: Name unknown   Small size tug, 8 by 35 feet. Boiler No. 2233. Engine 7 by 7 inches. Cast-steel gears. Stay rods on wall-block and paddle-shaft bearings. Shipped April 22, 1915, to J.D. McArthur Company, Winnipeg, Manitoba. To be delivered to Lac du Bonnet, Manitoba.

1916

PW #140: *W.J. Patterson* Small-size tug, 8 by 35 feet. Dry-back Boiler No. 2324, 40 by 58 inches. 3500 feet of ½-inch steel cable. Cast-iron gears with a duplicate set of gears supplied. Stay rods on wall box and paddlewheel boxes. Shipped, knocked down, on March 23, 1916, to Little Current Lumber Company, Bay City, Michigan. To be delivered to Little Current, Ontario. By September 1921, owned by the C. Beck Manufacturing Company, Limited, Penetanguishene, Ontario.

TS #141: *Edith Hope* Large-size tug with pointed bow. Dry-back Boiler No. 2289, 48 by 72 inches. Anchor with 5-foot shank, centre to centre. Shipped March 24, 1916, to Hope Lumber Company, Thessalon, Ontario. By March 1930, owned by J.J. McFadden Limited, Spragge, Ontario. By September 1932, owned by Crane Lumber Company, Limited, Thessalon, Ontario.

PW #142: Name unknown Machinery only supplied with the order. Dry-back Boiler No. 2325, 40 by 58 feet. Engine 7 by 7 inches. 3500 feet of ½-inch cable. Anchor, steering gear sheaves, cable guide, chain, etc. Twin three-blade propellers, 29-inch diameter. Shipped March 14, 1916, to Laurentide Company Limited, Grand-Mère, Quebec. To be delivered to Grandes-Piles, Quebec.

1917

TS #143: *Mastigouche* Standard-size tug. Boiler No. 2350. Twin three-blade propellers — 30-inch diameter. No cable supplied. This Alligator was not erected until April 1918. Shipped, knocked down, on March 13, 1917, to St. Maurice Paper Company Limited, Montreal. To be delivered to St. Gabriel de Brandon, Quebec.

PW #144: Name unknown Large-size tug. Machinery only supplied. No boiler, cable, or hull material supplied. Equipment that was supplied: 9-by-9-inch engine, cast-steel gearing, steering gear, automatic cable guide, deck fittings, with all blocks and anchor bolts. Shipped March 17, 1917, to Frank Blais, St. Theele Station, Quebec.

TS #145: *Col. White* Large-size tug. Boiler No. 2337. No cable anchor, portage equipment, or external runners were supplied. Shipped April 14, 1917, to the Riordan Pulp and Paper Company Limited., Montreal. To be delivered to Hawkesbury, Ontario.

PW #146: *Abitibi* Oversized tug with 16-foot beam, 70-foot length, and 7-foot sides. Standard 9-by-9-inch engine. Abitibi supplied the boiler and main engine to drive the paddlewheels. Shipped to Abitibi Power and Paper Company, Limited., Montreal. To be delivered to Low Bush, Ontario.

1918

TS #147: *Bustikogan* Oversized tug, 11-foot beam, 55 feet in length, sides 4 feet, 9 inches deep. Equipped with two 9-by-9-inch engines directly connected to the screws through slip couplings. The first

Alligator tug equipped with an inboard-cable drive with a short carriage. Shipped, knocked down, on April 24, 1918, to Shevlin-Clarke Company Limited, Fort Frances, Ontario.

PW #148: *Madawaska* Small-size tug, 8 by 35 inches. Dry-back Boiler No. 2353, 40 by 58 inches. Engine 7 by 7 inches. 3500 feet of ½-inch steel cable. Stay rods on wall box and paddlewheel boxes. Cast-iron paddlewheel gear, other gears are cast steel. Shipped May 4, 1918, to Ferguson and Findlay, Renfrew, Ontario. To be delivered to Barry's Bay Station, Ontario.

PW #149: Name unknown Small-size tug. Boiler No. 2354. 7-by-7-inch engine, 3500 feet of ½-inch steel cable, cast-iron paddlewheel gear, other gears cast steel. Shipped June 3, 1918, to Dryden Timber & Power Company Limited, Dryden, Ontario. On May 15, 1920, equipment shipped to change Alligator #149 to twin-screw operation. (Cost was $525.20 f.o.b., Simcoe.)

1919

TS #150: *National* Small-size tug, 8 by 35 feet. Dry-back Boiler No. 2382, 40 by 58 inches. Equipped with 7-by-7-inch engine, 3500 feet of ½-inch cable, cast-iron drum and bevel gears, other gears made of cast-steel. Twin four-blade propellers — 28-inch diameter. She was the first small-sized Alligator to be equipped with an automatic cable guide. Shipped April 8, 1919, via Canadian National Railways to Laforest & Cochrane, Sudbury, Ontario. To be delivered to Gogama, Ontario.

TS #151: *Marshay* Small-size tug, 8 by 35 feet. Dry-back Boiler No. 2381, 40 by 58 inches. Equipped with 7-by-7 inch engine, 3500 feet of ½-inch cable, cast-iron drum and bevel gears. Other gears cast-steel. Automatic cable guide. Twin 4-blade propellers — 28-inch diameter. Shipped April 8, 1919, via CNR to the Marshay Lumber Company, Sudbury, Ontario. To be delivered to Thor Lake, Ontario.

TS #152: *James R.* Standard-size tug, 10 by 42 feet. Dry-back Boiler No. 2290, 48 by 72 inches. Equipped with standard 9-by-9-inch engine, 5,000 feet of ⅝-inch steel cable, cast-iron drum and bevel gears. Other gears made of cast steel. New inboard cable guide. Coal grates supplied. Boiler insulated. The hull was sheathed in 16-gauge galvanized plate. Twin three-blade propellers, 30-inch diameter. The cabin roofs were felt-covered and false-decked. This tug was equipped with a turbo generator, a searchlight and five lamps. The selling price was $5,957.25. Shipped April 22, 1919, to Schroeder Mills and Timber Company, Limited, Pakesley Station, Ontario. To be delivered to Pickerel Station, Ontario.

TS #153: *Beaver* Small-size tug, 8 by 35 feet. Boiler No. 2383. Engine 7 by 7 inches. 3500 feet of ½-inch cable. Cast iron drum and bevel gears, other gears made of cast steel. Automatic cable guide. Twin four-blade propellers, 28-inch diameter. Selling price — $3700 f.o.b., Simcoe. Shipped May 21, 1919, to W.H & M.J. Poupore & Company, Stackpool, Ontario.

TS #154: *T.J. Stevenson*   Large-size tug, 11 by 45 feet. Boiler No. 2288. Dry-back Boiler, 48 by 72 inches, set facing forward. Standard 9-by-9-inch engine. 5,000 feet of ⅝-inch steel cable. Cast-iron drum and bevel gears. Other gears made of cast steel. Automatic cable guide, inboard drive. Twin three-blade propellers — 34-inch diameter. Selling price — $5950 f.o.b., Simcoe. Shipped November 14, 1919, knocked down, to Kipawa Company Limited., Montreal. To be delivered to Ville-Marie, Quebec. Later owned by Canadian International Paper Company, Montreal, and renamed *C.I.P. No. 1*.

TS #155: *J. Gwyne*   Large-size tug, 11 by 45 feet. Dry-back boiler No. 2397, 48 by 72 inches, set facing forward. Engine, standard 9 by 9 inches. 5,000 feet of ⅝-inch steel cable. Cast-iron drum and bevel gears. Other gears cast steel. Automatic cable guide, inboard drive. Twin three-blade propellers — 34-inch diameter. Selling price — $5950 f.o.b., Simcoe. Shipped knocked down, November 14, 1919, to Kipawa Company Limited, Montreal. To be delivered to Ville-Marie, Quebec. Later owned by Canadian International Paper Company, Montreal, and renamed the *C.I.P. No. 2*.

1920

TS #156: *St. Donat*   Standard-size tug, 10 by 42 feet. Dry-back Boiler No. 2396, 48 by 72 inches. Standard 9-by-9-inch engine. 5,000 feet of ⅝-inch cable supplied for additional cost of $644. Cast-iron drum and bevel gears. Other gears made of cast steel. Automatic cable guide, inboard drive. Twin three-blade propellers — 34-inch diameter. Selling price $5120 f.o.b., Simcoe. Shipped January 24, 1920, knocked down, to St. Maurice Paper Company, Montreal. To be delivered to Ste-Agathe-des-Monts, Quebec.

TS #157; Name unknown   Equipment only supplied for standard-size tug, no hull. Boiler No. 2440. Cast-iron drum and bevel gears. Other gears cast steel. Automatic cable guide, inboard drive. Twin three-blade propellers — 30-inch diameter. Selling price $4,475 f.o.b., Simcoe. Shipped March 1, 1920, to W.C. Edwards & Company, Limited, Ottawa. To be delivered to Plaisance, Quebec.

TS #158: *W.A. Christie*   Small-size tug, 8 by 35 feet. Dry-back Boiler No. 2442, 40 by 58 inches. Engine 7 by 7 inches. 3,500 feet of ½-inch cable. Cast-iron drum and bevel gears. Other gears cast-steel. Automatic cable guide, inboard drive. Twin three-blade propellers — 30-inch diameter. Selling price — $3,800 f.o.b., Simcoe. Shipped to Lewis Miller & Company Limited, Ingramport, Nova Scotia. To be delivered to Newport Station, Nova Scotia.

TS #159: *Como*   Small-size tug, 8 by 35 feet. Boiler No. 2446. Engine 7 by 7 inches. 3,500 feet of ⅝-inch cable. Cast-iron drum and bevel gears, other gears cast-steel. Automatic cable guide, inboard drive. Twin 3-blade propellers — 30-inch diameter. Selling price — $3,850.00

f.o.b., Simcoe. Shipped May 14, 1920, to Austin & Nicholson, Chapleau, Ontario. To be delivered to Nicholson, Ontario.

TS #160: *Lion* Small-size tug, 8 by 35 feet. Dry-back Boiler No. 2441, 40 by 58 inches. Engine 7 by 7 inches. 3,500 feet of ½-inch cable. Cast-steel gears. Automatic cable guide, inboard drive. Twin three-blade propellers, 30-inch diameter. Selling price — $3885.00 f.o.b., Simcoe. Shipped April 21, 1920, to the Poupore Lumber Company, Ottawa. To be delivered to Mile 71, Ruel Division of the CNR, via Sudbury, Ontario.

TS #161: *Sioux* Large-size tug, 11 by 45 feet. Dry-back Boiler No. 2439, 48 by 72 inches. Standard 9-by-9-inch engine. 5,000 feet of ⅝-inch cable. Cast-iron drum and bevel gears, other gears made of cast steel. Automatic cable guide, inboard drive. Twin three-blade propellers, 30-inch diameter. Whistle pipe installed through stack hood and whistle valve installed below deck. Wheelhouse made in upper and lower sections in order to take it down. Smokestack hinged. Selling price — $5,850 f.o.b., Simcoe. Shipped May 5, 1920, to G.E. Farlinger, Sioux Lookout, Ontario.

TS #162: *James G.L.* Small-size tug, 8 by feet. Dry-back Boiler No. 2447, 40 by 58 inches. Engine 7 by 7 inches. 3,500 feet of ½-inch cable. Cast-iron drum and bevel gear, other gears made of cast steel. Automatic cable guide, inboard drive. Twin three-blade propellers, 30-inch diameter. Selling price — $3,750 f.o.b., Simcoe. Shipped May 31, 1920, to New Ontario Contracting Company, Limited, Port Arthur, Ontario. To be delivered to Smith, Ontario. By 1938, owned by C.W. Cox Limited, Hudson, Ontario.

1921

TS #163: *G.H. Millen* Large-size tug, 11 by 45 feet. Dry-back Boiler No. 2500, 48 by 72 inches. Engine 9 by 9 inches. 5,000 feet of ⅝-inch cable. Cast-iron drum and bevel gears, other gears made of cast steel. Automatic cable guide, inboard drive. Cabin roof — felt-covered, false-decked. Morrison-throttle valve. Twin three-blade propellers, 34-inch diameter.

Selling price — $7050 f.o.b., Simcoe. Shipped January 14, 1921, to E.B. Eddy Company, Limited, Hull, Quebec. To be delivered to New Liskeard, Ontario.By April 1926, owned by Edwards Lumber & Pulp Limited, Pembroke, Ontario. Renamed *E.L.& P. No. 2.*

TS #164: *J.R. Booth No. 1* Standard-size tug, 10 by 42 feet. Dry-back Boiler No. 2509, 48 by 72 inches. Engine 9 by 9 inches. 5,000 feet of ⅝-inch cable. Cast-iron drum and bevel gears, other gears made of cast steel. Automatic cable guide, inboard drive. Two-inch Powell-gate throttle valve. Twin three-blade propellers, 30-inch diameter. Cabin roofs, felt-covered, false-decked. Selling price — $6,600, f.o.b., Simcoe. Shipped April 1, 1921, to J.R. Booth, Ottawa. To be delivered to Kenney Station, Ontario.

TS #165: *J.R. Booth No. 2*   This tug is identical to TS #164 except for Boiler No. 2501 and the West & Peachey slide-throttle valve. They were shipped together to the same destination.

TS #166: *J.R. Booth No. 3*   This tug is also identical to TS #164 except that it was shipped knocked down, (add $200) has Boiler No. 2502 and a Morrison throttle valve. Price — $6,800. Shipped January 25, 1921, to J.R. Booth, Ottawa. To be delivered to Kipawa, Quebec.

TS #167: *J.R. Booth No. 4*   This tug had the old machinery from Alligator #58, the *J.W. Hennesy*, installed in a new Alligator, converted to twin screw. It has Boiler No. 1275 and a Morrison throttle valve. Selling price was $3,387, f.o.b., Simcoe. Shipped April 4, 1921, to J.R. Booth, Ottawa. To be delivered to Kiosk, Ontario.

TS #168: *Big Eddy*   Standard-size tug, 10 by 42 feet. Dry-back Boiler No. 2503, 48 by 72 inches. Engine 9 by 9 inches. 5,000 feet of ⅝-inch steel cable. Morrison throttle valve. Anchor was shipped from Peterborough, Ontario. Price — $7,260 f.o.b., Simcoe. Shipped February 5, 1921, to International Nickel Company of Canada Limited, Copper Cliff, Ontario. To be delivered to Turbine, Ontario. By May 1923, owned by Spanish River Improvement Company. By June 1928, owned by Dominion River Boom Company, Limited. By May 1929, owned by Abitibi Power and Paper Company Limited.

TS #169: *Tom*   Standard-size tug. Dry-back Boiler No. 2507, 48 by 72 inches. Engine 9 by 9 inches. Powell-Gate throttle valve. Twin three-blade propellers — 30-inch diameter. Price — $7,260 f.o.b., Simcoe. Shipped March 22, 1921, to Continental Wood Products Company Limited, Montreal. To be delivered to Elsas, Ontario.

TS #170: *Dore*   Standard-size tug, 10 by 42 feet. Dry-back Boiler No. 2504, 48 by 72 inches. Engine 9 by 9 inches. Powell-Gate throttle valve. Twin 3-blade propellers, 30-inch diameter. Price — $7,260 f.o.b., Simcoe. Shipped March 22, 1921, to Continental Wood Products Company Limited, Montreal. To be delivered to Elsas, Ontario.

TS #171: *William M.*   Standard-size tug and engine. Dryback Boiler No. 1409, 48 by 72 inches. Morrison throttle valve. Machinery from Alligator #73, *Max* was used. It was overhauled, new shaft-bearing boxes and new drum braces installed, the old-style cable guide was repaired. New hull supplied. Price — $3,065 f.o.b., Simcoe. Shipped April 11, 1921, to Schroeder Mills and Timber Company Limited, Pakesley Station, Ontario. To be delivered to Ludgate Station, Ontario. By October 1927, owned by Gillies Brothers Limited, Braeside, Ontario. The *William M.* is currently to be seen on display at the Algonquin Park Logging Pioneer Museum, near Whitney at the east gate of the park.

TS #172: *Teddy Bear*   Large-size tug, 11 by 45 feet. Dry-back Boiler No. 2506, 48 by 72 inches. It has a West & Peachey slide-throttle valve. Engine 9 by 9 inches. Twin 34-inch propellers. Price — $7,535 f.o.b., Simcoe. Shipped April 5, 1921, to Abitibi Power and Paper Company, Limited, Montreal. To be delivered to Low Bush, Ontario.

TS #173: *Circle* — Large-size tug and engine, 9 by 9 inches. Dry-back Boiler No. 2522, 48 by 72 inches. Price — $7,535 f.o.b. Simcoe. Shipped May 4, 1921, to Abitibi Power and Paper Company, Limited, Montreal. To be delivered to Low Bush, Ontario.

TS #174: *La Tuque* — Standard size tug, 10 by 42 feet. Dry-back Boiler No. 2505, 48 by 72 inches. Engine 9 by 9 inches. West & Peachey slide-throttle valve. Price — $7,260 f.o.b., Simcoe. Shipped April 6, 1921, to St. Maurice Lumber Company, Trois-Rivières, Quebec. To be delivered to Lake Wayagamack, Quebec.

TS #175: *Dryden Paper Company, Limited, No. 2* — Large-size tug, 11 by 45 feet. Dry-back Boiler No. 2508, 48 by 72 inches. Price — $7,535 f.o.b., Simcoe. Shipped to Dryden Paper Company, Limited, Dryden, Ontario. To be delivered to Eagle River, Ontario.

TS #176: *Captain Jack* — Small-size tug, 8 by 37 feet. Dry-back Boiler No. 2457, 40 by 58 inches. Engine 7 by 7 inches. Powell-Gate throttle valve. 3,500 feet of ½-inch steel cable. Cast-iron drum and bevel gears, other gears made of cast-steel. Automatic cable guide, inboard drive. Three-blade propellers, 28-inch diameter. Cabin roof, felt-covered, false-decked. New-type smokestack. Price — $5,500. Shipped April 26, 1921, to St. Regis Paper Company of Canada Limited, Montreal. To be delivered to Oscalaneo, Quebec.

1922

TS #177: *Rae Holmes* — Standard-size tug. Boiler No. 2523, supplied with coal grates. Anchor not included, otherwise complete. 5,000 feet of ⅝-inch cable. West & Peachey slide-valve throttle, 1¼-inch twin safety valve. Automatic cable guide, inboard drive. Cabin roof, felt-covered, false-decked. Stationary 30-inch propellers. Coal-fired. Price delivered — $5,180. Shipped May 23, 1921, to Border Lumber Company, Fort Frances, Ontario.

1923

TS #178: *Alligator* — Large-size tug, 11 by 45 feet. Boiler No. 2587. Engine 9 by 9 inches. West & Peachey throttle valve. Twin 34-inch diameter, lifting-type propellers. Coal grates supplied. Cabin roof, felt-covered, false-decked. Price — $4,730 f.o.b., Simcoe. Sold less cable and anchor. Shipped February 27, 1923, to Brown Company, Portland, Maine. To be delivered to Bemis, Maine.

TS #179: *Pemluco* — Large-size tug, 11 by 45 feet. Boiler No. 2586. Engine 9 by 9 inches. West & Peachey throttle valve, 1¼-inch safety valve. 5,000 feet of ⅝-inch cable, 500-pound anchors. Cabin roof, felt-covered, false-decked. Price — $5,250. Shipped April 23, 1923 to the Pembroke Lumber Company, Limited, Pembroke, Ontario. To be delivered to Kipawa, Quebec.

TS #180: *Alice* — Small tug, 8 by 37 feet. Engine 7 by 7 inches. Boiler No. 2448. Powell-Gate throttle valve, 1¼-inch twin safety valves. 3,500 feet of ⅝-inch steel cable, 250-pound anchor, 24-inch diameter drum cylinder on winch. Toothed cable-guide drive wheel, twin 28-inch diameter, stationary 3-blade propellers. Coal grates. Roofs — felt-covered, false-decked. Standard bevel gears. Price — $3,767 f.o.b., Simcoe. Shipped to Austin & Nicholson, Chapleau, Ontario. Deliver to Dalton, Ontario.

TS #181: *Booster* — Small-size tug and engine. Boiler No. 2605. Powell-Gate throttle valve, 1¼-inch twin safety valve. Twin 28-inch diameter, stationary three-blade propellers. 3,500 feet of cable, 250-pound anchor. Spark arrestor in smokestack. 24-inch winch drum cylinder. Toothed cable-guide drive wheel. Coal grates. Roofs, felt-covered, false-decked. Standard bevel gears. Price — $3,767 f.o.b., Simcoe. Shipped to Hope Lumber Company Limited, Sault Ste. Marie, Ontario. This tug was built in 1923, but not shipped until March 28, 1924, to Ruel, Ontario.

TS #182: *John Morrison* — Large-size tug and engine. Boiler No. 2589, set facing forward. West & Peachey throttle valve, 1¼-inch safety valve, 5,000 feet of cable, 500-pound anchor. Twin 34-inch diameter, stationary three-blade propellers. Price — $3,450 f.o.b., Simcoe. Shipped, knocked down, on May 15, 1923, to Riordan Pulp Corporation Limited, Montreal. To be delivered to Ville-Marie, Quebec, via Haileybury, Ontario. Later owned by Canadian International Paper Company Limited, and renamed *C.I.P. No. 3*.

TS #183: *Edwards* — Large-size tug and engine. Boiler No. 2588. West & Peachey throttle valve, 1¼-inch safety valve. Twin 34-inch diameter, stationary three-blade propellers. 5,000 feet of ⅝-inch steel cable, 500-pound anchor. Coal grates. Price — $5,350 f.o.b., Simcoe. Shipped November 7, 1923, to Edwards Lumber and Pulp Ltd. Pembroke, Ontario. Deliver to Angliers (Quinze Lake), Quebec.

1924

TS #184: *Expanse* — Large-size tug and engine. Boiler No. 3020, set facing forward. 1¼-inch safety valve, West & Peachey throttle valve. 5,000 feet of Allan Whyte galvanized steel cable. 500-pound anchor. Twin 34-inch diameter, stationary three-blade propellers. Price — $5,420 f.o.b., Simcoe. Shipped April 14, 1924, to Riordan Pulp Corporation Limited, Montreal. This Alligator tug was wrecked in transit. It was returned to the West & Peachey factory and rebuilt at a cost of $1,594. It was reshipped on May 16, 1924, for delivery to Angliers (Quinze Lake), Quebec.

TS #185: *Sturgeon* — Large-size tug, 11 by 45 feet. Engine 9 by 9 inches. Boiler No. 3021, set facing forward. West & Peachey throttle valve, 1¼-inch safety valve. 5000 feet of Allan Whyte galvanized steel cable, 500-pound anchor. Twin 34-inch diameter three-blade propellers. Price — $5,420 f.o.b., Simcoe. Shipped April 14, 1924, to Riordan Pulp Corporation Limited, Montreal. Delivered to Angliers (Quinze Lake), Quebec. Later owned by Canadian International Paper Corporation, Montreal, and renamed the *C.I.P. No. 5.*

TS #186: Name unknown Standard-size tug. Boiler No. 3016. No hull, bow roller, cable or anchor were supplied. Otherwise, all equipment and machinery were included. Engine 9 by 9 inches. Automatic cable guide complete. Twin 34-inch propellers. Price — $3431 f.o.b., Simcoe. Shipped March 8, 1924, to Shevlin-Clarke Company Limited, Fort Frances, Ontario. Delivered to Flanders, Ontario.

TS #187: *Paddy of Allan Water* Standard-size tug, 10 by 42 feet. Boiler No. 3033. Engine 9 by 9 inches. West & Peachey throttle valve, 1¼-inch safety valve. Twin 30-inch diameter, stationary three-blade propellers. 5,000 feet of ⅝-inch steel cable. 500-pound anchor. Price — $5,050 f.o.b., Simcoe. Shipped to Alexander McDougall, Allan Water, Ontario.

1925

TS #188: *Seafoam* Standard-size tug. Boiler No. 1404. This was Alligator #72, rebuilt at Simcoe with a new hull and overhauled machinery, new automatic cable guide, winch-drum rudder-lifting type propellers installed. Price — $3,146 f.o.b., Simcoe. Shipped, knocked down, April 6, 1925, to Canadian Timber Company, Limited, Toronto, Ontario. Delivered to Glendale, Ontario.

TS #189: *Saginaw* Large-size tug, 11 by 45 feet. Boiler No. 3048. 5,000 feet of ⅝-inch steel cable. 500-pound anchor. West & Peachey throttle valve, 1¼-inch safety valve. 34-inch stationary propellers. Price — $5,600 f.o.b., Simcoe. Shipped, knocked down, on March 23, and April 3, 1925, to Hope Lumber Company Limited, Sault Ste. Marie, Ontario. Delivered to Glendale, Ontario.

TS #190: *Lake Superior Paper Company, Limited, No. 1* Standard-size tug, 10 by 42 feet. Boiler No. 3050. Bunks installed in bow of scow. 6,000 feet of ⅝-inch steel cable, 500-pound anchor. Twin 30-inch diameter, stationary propellers. West & Peachey throttle valve, 1¼-inch safety valve. Price — $5,150 f.o.b., Simcoe. Shipped on April 20, 1925, to Lake Superior Paper Company Limited, Sault Ste. Marie, Ontario. Delivered to Mile 163, Algoma Central Railway, via Franz, Ontario.

TS #191: *Champlain* Large-size tug, 11 by 45 feet. Boiler No. 3051. West & Peachey throttle valve. 5,000 feet of ⅝-inch steel cable, 500-pound anchor. Twin 34-inch diameter, stationary propellers. ⅛-by-12-inch steel strip placed along the sides at the water line. Price — $5,431 f.o.b., Simcoe. Shipped May 4, 1925, to the Champlain Logging Company Limited, Ville-Marie, Quebec. Delivered to Angliers, Quebec.

TS #192: *Ed Inwood* Large-size tug, 11 by 45 feet. Boiler No. 3047, set facing forward. Engine 9 by 9 inches. No anchor supplied. West & Peachey throttle valve, 1¼-inch safety valve. 5,000 feet of Allan Whyte galvanized steel cable. Twin 34-inch diameter, stationary three-blade propellers.

Price — $5,340 f.o.b., Simcoe. Shipped April 8, 1925, to Riordan Pulp Corporation, Limited, Montreal. Delivered to Angliers, Quebec. Later owned by Canadian International Paper Company. Renamed *C.I.P. No. 6.*

TS #193: *Tillicum* Standard-size tug, 10 by 42 feet. Boiler No. 3055. West & Peachey throttle valve, 1¼-inch safety valve. 5,000 feet of ⅝-inch steel cable. 500-pound anchor. Twin 30-inch diameter, stationary propellers. Price — $4,900 f.o.b., Simcoe. Shipped to John B. Smith & Sons Limited, Toronto. Delivered to Kenney, Ontario.

TS #194: *Relief* Large-size tug, 11 by 45 feet. Boiler No. 3059, set facing forward. Stock less anchor. Engine 9 by 9 inches. West & Peachey throttle valve, 1¼-inch safety valve. 5,000 feet of Allan Whyte galvanized steel cable. Twin 34-inch diameter, stationary propellers. Price — $5,300 f.o.b., Simcoe. Shipped September 29, 1925, to Riordan Pulp Corporation Limited, Montreal. Delivered to Témiscamingue, Quebec. Later owned by Canadian International Paper Company and renamed *C.I.P. No. 7.*

1926

TS #195: *Gertie* Large-size tug, 11 by 45 feet. Boiler No. 3073, set facing forward. Engine 9 by 9 inches. No warping anchor supplied. West & Peachey throttle valve, 1¼-inch safety valve. 5,000 feet of Allan Whyte galvanized steel cable supplied for additional $520. Twin 34-inch diameter, stationary three-blade propellers. Price — $5,240, delivered. Shipped April 20, 1926, to Riordan Pulp Corporation Limited, Montreal. Delivered to Angliers, Quebec. Later owned by Canadian International Paper Company and renamed *C.I.P. No. 8.*

TS #196: *Price Brothers Company Limited, No. 6* Standard-size tug, 10 by 42 feet. Boiler No. 3069. West & Peachey throttle valve, 1¼-inch safety valve. 5,000 feet of ⅝-inch steel cable. 500-pound warping anchor. Twin 30-inch stationary propellers. Price — $5,250 f.o.b., Simcoe. Shipped, knocked down, March 3, 1926, to Chicoutimi Pulp Company Ltd., "in Bankruptcy," Chicoutimi, Quebec. Delivered to Jonquière, Quebec. Later owned by Quebec Pulp and Paper Mills Limited, then by Price Brothers.

TS #197: *Price Brothers Company Limited, No. 7* Large-size tug, 11 by 45 feet. Boiler No. 3070. West & Peachey throttle valve, 5,000 feet of ⅝-inch cable, 500-pound anchor. Twin 34-inch stationary propellers. Price — $5,600 f.o.b., Simcoe. Shipped, knocked down, on March 3, 1926, to Chicoutimi Pulp Company, Limited, "in Bankruptcy," Chicoutimi, Quebec. Later owned by Quebec Pulp and Paper Mills Limited, then by Price Brothers.

PW #198: *Castor* Oversized tug, 11 by 55 feet, with pointed raked bow. Twin engines 7 by 9 inches. Dry-back Boiler No. 3076, 60 by 80 inches. 5,000 feet of steel cable. 500-pound anchor. Price —

$6,100 f.o.b., Simcoe. Shipped June 8, 1926, to Driving and Boom Company Limited, North Bay, Ontario. Delivered to Sturgeon Falls, Ontario.

1927

TS #199: *Crocodile* Large-size tug, 11 by 45 feet, with special pointed bow. Boiler No. 3074, set facing forward. Twin 34-inch diameter, stationary propellers. Price — $5,760 f.o.b., Simcoe. Shipped April 11, 1927, to Dryden Paper Company Limited, Dryden, Ontario.

TS #200: *Lake Superior Paper Company Limited, No. 2* Large-size tug, 11 by 45 feet, with raked, pointed bow. Boiler No. 3116. Twin 34-inch diameter, stationary propellers. Price — $5,600 f.o.b., Simcoe. Shipped April 28, 1927, to the Lake Superior Paper Company Ltd., Sault Ste. Marie, Ontario. By 1933, owned by Abitibi Pulp and Paper Company Limited.

1928

TS #201: *Lac Seul* Large-size tug, 11 by 45 feet. Boiler No. 3117, set facing forward. Boiler stationary, with overhead piping to engine, 1½-inch steam pipe, 2-inch exhaust pipe. Diamond-spark arrestor with screen and spark trap. Twin-34-inch diameter, stationary propellers. Steel gears throughout. Price — $5,400. Shipped April 5, 1928, to G.E. Farlinger, Sioux Lookout, Ontario.

TS #202: *Eli Johnson* Stationary Boiler No. 3195, set facing forward, overhead piping to the engine, 2-inch exhaust pipe, 1½-inch steam pipe. Engine cylinder 9⅛-inch diameter. Twin 30-inch diameter, stationary propellers. 5,000 feet of ⅝-inch cable. Price — $5,050 f.o.b., Simcoe. Shipped to J.A. Mathieu Limited, Rainy Lake, Ontario. Delivered to Fort Frances, Ontario.

1929

TS #203: *W.R. Moore* Stationary Boiler No. 3243, set facing forward. 1½-inch steam pipe, 2-inch exhaust pipe. Diamond-spark arrestor with screen and spark trap. 5,000 feet of ⅝-inch steel cable. 500-pound warping anchor. Price — $5,500 f.o.b., Simcoe. Shipped to the Canadian International Paper Company, Montreal. Delivered February 7, 1929, knocked down, to Clericy, Quebec, via Taschereau.

TS #204: *Amos* Boiler stationary, No. 3256, set facing forward. 1½-inch steam pipe, 2-inch exhaust pipe. Diamond arrestor with screen and spark trap. 5,000 feet of steel cable, 625-pound anchor. Price — $5,411 f.o.b., Simcoe. Shipped to Frank Blais & Sons Limited, Amos, Quebec.

TS #205: *St. Maurice No. 2* Standard-size tug, 10 by 42 feet. New Boiler No. 3244, built to be operated at a maximum of 120 pounds psi. Boiler stationary. This tug was a complete rebuild of Alligator #66 in Simcoe. She was purchased new in 1905. Selling price — $4,140 f.o.b., Simcoe. Shipped to the St. Maurice River Boom and Drive Company Limited, Trois-Rivières, Quebec. This tug was still in existence at Shawinigan, Quebec, in 1974.

1931

TS #206: *Charles Rowley Booth*   This was a complete rebuild of one of the J.R. Booth tugs. New hull and cabin wheelhouse was installed. 5,000 feet of ⅝-inch steel cable. The old lifting propeller equipment was changed to 34-inch diameter, stationary propellers. The selling price — $3,795 f.o.b., Simcoe. Shipped April 7, 1931, to J.R. Booth Ltd. Ottawa. Delivered to Kipawa, Quebec.

1934

TS #207: *St. Maurice No. 4*   Rebuilt hull 10 by 45 feet. Boiler No. 3257, set facing forward. Safeguard water gauge. Stationary 34-inch diameter propellers. 1½-inch steam pipes, 2-inch exhaust pipe. Price — $4,250 f.o.b., Simcoe. Shipped April 20, 1934, to St. Maurice River Boom and Drive Company Limited, Trois-Rivières, Quebec. Delivered to Grandes-Piles, Quebec. This was the last Alligator Warping Tug to be built by West & Peachey in Simcoe, Ontario. The abandoned remains of this tug are still located at Trois-Rivières, Quebec. It is thought to be a rebuild of Alligator tug #122.

Appendix E
Known Repairs to Unidentified Alligator Warping Tugs

West & Peachey, from early times of production of Alligator warping tugs, or scows, carried on an active business in supplying replacement parts and repairs to Alligators in need of such service. They would bring them in to their factory in Simcoe and carry out all work necessary, or, if the customer preferred, they would ship replacement parts to the site of the tug in question. If the customer wished, they would send well-qualified crews from the factory to the location of the Alligator needing the service and make the repairs or changes in equipment wherever the tug was working or located.

Detailed records of this kind of work, though they may have been kept at the time, are rarely available to researchers today. If the Alligator's number is known, the work done, or, shipment made, is recorded in the information on that particular tug. In many cases the tugs identity is not known. From original shipping records that remain the following information has been gleaned and is recorded here by date of shipment.

November 18, 1920:	Twin-screw machinery for an unknown Alligator tug was shipped on this date to Murray & Omanique Lumber Company, Barry's Bay, Ontario.
March 5, 1924:	New oak material supplied for hull of a twin-screw Alligator tug (name unknown). New 2⅛-inch shafts for 34-inch diameter, stationary propellers and two new rudders supplied. Steam engine repaired. A West & Peachey crew was sent to do the work for the Victoria Harbour Lumber Company Ltd. at Whitefish, Ontario.
January 15, 1925:	A complete supply of materials for a standard Alligator tug to rebuild the hull, cabin, and wheelhouse was shipped to St. Gabriel de Brandon, Quebec, on this date. A crew arrived from the factory in Simcoe to assemble it for the St. Maurice Paper Company Limited, of Montreal.

January 30, 1925:	Machinery to convert an unknown paddlewheel Alligator tug to a twin-screw scow with lifting propellers, plus complete material for a new hull, shipped on this date to Pratt & Shanacy of Midland, Ontario.
February 20, 1925:	Complete materials for rebuilding the hull of a large-sized paddlewheel Alligator tug was shipped on this date to Benney, Ontario. A West & Peachey crew was sent to assemble this new tug hull for the Spanish River Pulp and Paper Mills Limited of Sudbury, Ontario.
February 12, 1926:	All material shipped on this date for a standard-sized unknown Alligator tug hull to Ste.-Agathe-des-Monts, Quebec, for the St. Maurice Valley Corporation, Montreal.
August 25, 1926:	Materials to rebuild a large-sized hull, cabin, decks, and wheelhouse of an unknown Alligator tug shipped on this date, with all the parts to convert lifting type propellers to the stationary type of propeller. West & Peachey sent a crew from the factory to assemble this tug in Angliers, Quebec, for Riordan Pulp Corporation Limited, Montreal.
April 12, 1927:	All machinery to convert an unknown standard size paddlewheel Alligator to a stationary type twin-screw model was shipped on this date. A West & Peachey crew was sent to assemble this tug's equipment for Rochester & McKegg, Angliers, Quebec.
April 18, 1928:	All material to rebuild a small-sized paddlewheel Alligator tug's hull, cabin, decks, and wheelhouse shipped on this date. A West & Peachey crew was sent to assemble this tug at Nairn Centre, Ontario for the Spanish River Pulp and Paper Mills Limited, Sudbury, Ontario.

Appendix F
Alphabetical Listing of Alligator Warping Tugs

Alligator Tug Name	Number
Abitibi	PW #146
A. Ferguson	PW #93
Albert	PW #76
Algonquin	PW #59
Alice	TS #180
Alligator	PW #1 (Simcoe, Ontario)
Alligator	PW #13 (Trenton, Ontario)
Alligator	PW #65 (Tupper Lake, New York)
Alligator	TS #178 (Portland, Maine)
Amable du Fond	PW #8
Amos	TS #204
Amphibian	TS #111 (renamed Edwin Price)
Annie	PW #40
Ballantyne	PW #9
Baskatong	PW #25
Bay City	TS #92
Beaver	PW #11 (Lumsden Mills, Quebec)
Beaver	PW #48 (Waubaushene, Ontario)
Beaver	PW #61 (Rat Portage, Ontario)
Beaver	TS #103 (Callander, Ontario)
Beaver	TS #116 (Fort Frances, Ontario)
Beaver	TS #153 (Stackpool, Ontario)

Alligator Tug Name	Number
Belgique, La	PW #70
Bersimis	PW #101
Big Eddy	TS #168
Bonnechére	PW #7
Booster	TS #181
British Lion	PW #71
Bustikogan	TS #147
Captain Jack	TS #176
Castor	PW #79 (Ottawa)
Castor	PW #198 (North Bay, Ontario)
Champion	TS #109
Champlain	TS #191
Chandler	PW #137
Chapleau	PW #77
Charles Rowley Booth	TS #206
C.I.P. No. 1	TS #154
C.I.P. No. 2	TS #155
C.I.P. No. 3	TS #182
C.I.P. No. 4	TS #185
C.I.P. No. 6	TS #192
C.I.P. No. 7	TS #194
C.I.P. No. 8	TS #195
C.I.P. No. 9	PW #104
Circle	TS #173
Cleveland, The	TS #106
Coulonge	PW #47
Col. White	TS #145
Como	TS #159

ALLIGATOR TUG NAME	NUMBER	ALLIGATOR TUG NAME	NUMBER
Cook and Brothers	PW #56	Hamilton H.	PW #23
Crocodile	TS #199	Hardy	PW #32
C.S. Reid	PW #19	Hazlitt	PW #49
D. Lunam	PW #51	H.B. Shepard	PW #135
Dominion	PW #100	Hercules	PW #42
Dore	TS #170	H.H. Bishop	TS #83
Dreadnaught	PW #108	Holland and Graves	PW #43
Dryden Paper Company Ltd. No. 2	TS #175	Holland and Graves No. 3	PW #68
		Holland and Graves No. 4	PW #69
Durocher	PW #104 (Renamed *C.I.P. No. 9*)	H. Trudel	PW #3
		Hunter	PW #16
E.B. Eddy	PW #41 (Hull, Quebec)	James G.L.	TS #162
Eddy	PW #123	James R.	TS #152
Ed Inwood	TS #192 (Renamed *C.I.P. No. 6*)	James Thompson	PW #50
		Jessie	TS #129
Edith Hope	TS #141	J. Gwyne	TS #155 (Renamed *C.I.P. No. 2*)
Edwards	TS #183		
Edwin Price	TS #111 (See *Amphibian*)	J.J. McCarthy	TS #112
Eli Johnson	TS #202	John McLean	PW #54
E.L. and P. No. 2	TS #163	John McLean	TS #107
Emma	PW #37	John Morrison	TS #182 (Renamed *C.I.P. No. 3*)
Eunice	PW #88 (Renamed *Margaret*)		
		John W. Wells	PW #75
Expanse	TS #184	Joseph Taylor	PW #20
Fairy Blonde	TS #132	J.R. Booth No. 1	TS #164
Fisher	PW #90	J.R. Booth No. 2	TS #165
F.W. Avery	PW #30	J.R. Booth No. 3	TS #166
Gertie	TS #195 (Renamed *C.I.P. No. 8*)	J.R. Booth No. 4	TS #167 (See also PW 58)
		J.R. Booth No. 5	TS #121
George McPherson	TS #113	J.W. Hennesy	PW #58 (and TS #167)
G.H. Millen	TS #163 (Renamed *E.L. and P. No. 2*)	Kealy	PW #78
		Kegebongo	PW #34
Gordon	PW #64	Kenogami	PW #117
Gordon Mac	TS #91	Lac Ha! Ha!	PW #133

ALLIGATOR TUG NAME   NUMBER

Tug Name	Number
Lac Oureau	PW #18
Lac Seul	TS #201
Lake Superior Paper Company Ltd. No. 1	TS #190
Lake Superior Paper Company Ltd. No. 2	TS #200
La Tuque	TS #174
Laurentide Paper Company Ltd.	TS #85
Lion	TS #160
Lorne	PW #5
Lorne Hale	PW #28
Madawaska	PW #6 (Arnprior, Ontario)
Madawaska	PW #148 (Renfrew, Ontario)
Manitou	TS #138
Margaret	PW #88
Marjorie	PW #72 (see TS #188)
Marshay	TS #151
Mastigouche	TS #143
Matabitchuan	TS #121 (Renamed *J.R. Booth No. 5*)
Max	PW #73
McKinnon	PW#105
Metabachuan	PW #97
Mink	PW #33
Mississaga	TS #81
Muskoka	PW#15
Muskrat	PW #90
National	TS #150
Nellie	TS #84
Nimsongis	PW #22
Nipissing	PW #18
Northern	TS #98 (Renamed *Perley Holmes*)
North River	PW #10
O.F.P.	PW #127
Ohio	PW #29
Osaquaw	PW #99
Otter	PW #27
Otter	TS #131 (Renamed *Tommy Mathieu*)
Paddy of Allan Water	TS #187
P.B. & Company Ltd. No. 1	TS #115
P.B. & Company Ltd. No. 2	TS #130
P.B. & Company Ltd. No. 3	TS #136
Peck	PW #17
Pemluco	TS #179
Perley Holmes	TS #98
Pierre Dubois	PW #118
Pollux	PW #80
Pontiac	PW #53
Price Bros. Company Ltd. No. 6	TS #196
Price Bros. Company Ltd. No. 7	TS #197
Rae Holmes	TS #177
R.B. Eddy	PW #55 (Blind River, Ontario)
Reginald	PW #95
Relief	TS #194
R. Jackson	TS #96
Saginaw	PW #4
Saginaw	TS #189
Saguenay	TS #102
St. Anthony No. 1	PW #31
St. Anthony No. 2	PW #62

ALLIGATOR TUG NAME	NUMBER	ALLIGATOR TUG NAME	NUMBER
St. Donat	TS #156	Tom	TS #169
St. Maurice No. 1	PW #63	Tommy Mathieu	TS #131
St. Maurice No. 2	PW #66 (See TS #205)	Traveller	PW #45
St. Maurice No. 3	TS #67	Trent	PW #14
St. Maurice No. 4	TS #122 (See TS #207)	Tuque, La	TS #174
St. Maurice No. 5	TS #124	Victoria	PW #24 (Trout Creek, Ontario)
St. Maurice Hydraulic	TS #112	Victoria	PW #46 (Toronto, Ontario)
Company	(Renamed *J.J. McCarthy*)	Virginia	TS #126
Samson	PW #12	V.R.B. Company Ltd.	PW #82
Samson	PW #114	No. 2	
Seafoam	TS #188 (See PW #72)	Wabassee	PW #57
Sioux	TS 161	W.A. Christie	*TS #158*
Spanish Ranger	PW 21	Wawa	PW #93
S.R.L. Company	PW #125		(Renamed the *A. Ferguson*)
S.R.L. Company No. 4	TS #134	Wawaskesh	PW #52
Sturgeon	TS #185	Weslemkoon	PW #26
	(Renamed *C.I.P. No. 4*)	W.H. Carter	TS #110
Sweepstake	PW #44	William M.	PW #171
Teddy Bear	TS #172	Windermere	PW #128
Temagami	PW #74	W.J. Bell	TS #94
Tillicum	TS #193	W.J. Patterson	PW #140
T.J. Stevenson	TS #154	W.R. Moore	TS #203
	(Renamed *C.I.P. No. 1*)	W.T. White	PW #39

The following list of Alligator Warping Scows built by West & Peachey of Simcoe, Ontario, are recorded by number and type but no name for them can be found. They are, in sequence:

PW 2	PW 35	PW 36	PW 38
PW 60	? 86	? 87	PW 89
? 119	? 120	PW 139	TS 142
PW 144	PW 149	TS 157	TS 186

Notes

Introduction

1. R. John Corby, "The Alligator or Steam Warping Tug: A Canadian Contribution to the Development of Technology in the Forest Industry" in *The Journal of the Society for Industrial Archaeology*, Vol. 3, No.1 (1977): 15–42.
2. Donald MacKay, *The Lumberjacks* (Toronto: Natural Heritage Books, 1998).

Chapter 1: In the Beginning

1. Background information on the Native Peoples of the Norfolk County area is from the Dr. Wilfrid Jury Research Papers, University of Western Ontario. For more information on early Native Peoples' history in Ontario, see Edward S. Rogers and Donald B. Smith, eds. *Aboriginal History: Historical Perspectives on the First Nations.* Toronto: Dundurn Press in association with the government of Ontario, 1994.
2. From the Norfolk Historical Society Archives, Walsh Papers.
3. William Pope (1811–1902) was a cynical, well-to-do, twenty-three-year-old who left England in 1834 because he found the game laws there too restrictive, and immigrated to North America. He settled in the Long Point Country where he farmed, hunted, and painted the wildlife. He left over four hundred works of art, and, in 1917, fifteen years after his death, was touted as "The Canadian Audubon." A provincial plaque commemorating his achievements is located on Front Road just east of Port Ryerse. For more information on William Pope, see Harry B. Barrett, *19th Century Journals and Paintings of William Pope* (Toronto: M.F. Feheley, 1976).
4. From the diaries of Captain Alexander McNeilledge (1836–74) housed in the Norfolk Historical Society Archives of the Eva Brook Donly Museum in Simcoe, Ontario. For more information on Captain McNeilledge, contact the Port Dover Harbour Museum in Port Dover, Ontario, where a CD is available of a transcription of the diaries prepared by Judy Francis of Australia.

Chapter 2: The West Family in Norfolk County

1. Information on the West family from interviews of family descendants, John West's grandson Colonel D. Stalker, and others, by Clarence Coons in the 1970s and 1980s. Additional information was gleaned over a lifetime by Harry B. Barrett as a personal friend of the Stalker, West, and Skinner families, and as a past president of the Norfolk Historical Society (and a member since 1938).

Chapter 3: The West & Peachey Partnership, 1878

1. The information on the Peachey family is from interviews Clarence Coons conducted with the Peachey family when he was doing his research for this book in the 1980s. Harry B. Barrett confirmed this and acquired additional information from Barabara Peachey Wright, a granddaughter of James Peachey, and from other Peachey family members.
2. Information on the West & Peachey firm is taken from Clarence Coons's research and dialogue with both Colonel D. Stalker and John Quinsey, a great-grandson of John West, plus additional information Harry B. Barrett was able to add, given his position as a local resident of the area.
3. Background information on the West Montrose Metal Shingle was researched by Clarence F. Coons in the early 1980s.

Chapter 4: The Lumber Trade in Norfolk County Moves On

1. From Clarence Coons's research. It is likely that Clarence knew George S. Thompson personally, as they were contemporaries in the lumbering industry. It is equally likely that Clarence would have interviewed him for this work on the Alligator.
2. Information on the pointer boat is from Clarence Coons's research and from additional research by Harry B. Barrett and his interviews with Dave Lemkay of the Canadian Forestry Association. Lemkay is well acquainted with John Cockburn's grandson, Jack Cockburn.
3. Dave Lemkay of Pembroke, Ontario, is the general manager of the Canadian Forestry Association, Pembroke, Ontario, as well as manager, Special Projects, in the Science and Programs branch of Natural Resources Canada, Canadian Forest Service. Among other responsibilities, Dave oversees the naming of a town, county, or district each year as "The Forest Capital of Canada," for the Canadian Forestry Association.

4. For more information on the pointer boats, see Donald MacKay, *The Lumberjacks*, (Toronto: Natural Heritage Books, 1998), 129–30. See also, Bob Henderson, *Every Trail Has a Story: Heritage Travel in Canada* (Toronto: Natural Heritage Books, 2005), 182–83.

Chapter 5: Joseph Jackson and the Warping Tug

1. This information on Joseph Jackson comes from a combination of research by Clarence Coons and Harry B. Barrett's research and discusssions with Colonel D. Stalker and others.
2. From records dealing with the West & Peachey firm accessed by Clarence Coons during his research. See also the West & Peachey Collection in the Norfolk Historical Society Archives, Eva Brook Donly Museum in Simcoe, hereafter referred to as the West & Peachey Collection.
3. Good quality white oak grows in profusion on the Norfolk sand plain. West & Peachey bought white oak from local sawmills and later sawed it in their own mill on site.
4. This reference to the Clyde is to the design or type of boiler first designed and built along the Clyde River in Scotland.
5. From the West & Peachey Collection. The company requested testimonials from many of their customers.
6. *Ibid.*
7. Copies of many of these original West & Peachey patents are in the West & Peachey Collection.

Chapter 6: John West's Other Interests

1. It is believed that this Ronald Fire Engine may have been made in St. Thomas, Ontario. Anyone with specific information is invited to contact the author or the publisher.
2. To "stop at dead centre" meant that the piston would stop at the exact top of its stroke. When steam was next injected it would not move the drive shaft, as it would be pushing directly down on the cam, or it might move or turn it backwards, which could equally be a problem.
3. Information on John West's role as fire chief and mishaps in his life is from an interview with Colonel D. Stalker.

4. A retort is a large, heavy iron container with perforated sides that held a great many cans of produce as they moved through a tank of boiling water to be cooked. The West & Peachey Collection has photocopies of all these plans, drawings, and patents.
5. The quote from patent on the "Improved Road Making Sleigh" is found in the West & Peachey Collection.

Chapter 7: Evolution of the Alligator Warping Tug

1. The Moore Lumber Company testimonial is in the West & Peachey Collection.
2. In the West & Peachey Collection.
3. *Ibid.*
4. *Ibid.*

Chapter 9: The Gilmour Dynasty — Their Tramway and the Alligator

1. For more information on the Gilmour Company, see Gary Long and Randy Williams, *When Giants Fall: The Gilmour Quest for Algonquin Pine* (Huntsville, ON: Fox Meadows Books, 2003).
2. For more information on the Gilmour tramway, see Ralph Bice, *Along the Trail With Ralph Bice in Algonquin Park* (Toronto: Natural Heritage, 1993), 32–35.
3. Captain George S. Thompson, *Up to Date, or the Life of a Lumberman* (Peterborough, ON: n.p., 1895).

Chapter 10: Steamboats for South America

1. Author's note: The original letter in West's handwriting, dated October 28, 1895, is very difficult to read. I replaced dashes with periods and separated the content into paragraphs for ease of reading. The square brackets were inserted by West. Letter from the West & Peachey Collection.
2. John West's original letter, "To the Editor," is located in the West & Peachey Collection.
3. From discussions with Colonel Douglas Stalker.

Chapter 11: The Diverse Enterprises of West & Peachey, 1897–99

1. Author's Note: Alex Landon, my long-time good friend (we were classmates at the Ontario Agricultural College, 1945–49 and we both returned to farm in Woodhouse Township, Norfolk County, on our home farms) told me that his father kept records of logs cut in their Charlotteville Township (Norfolk County) woodlot.

2. The author's grandfather was W.H. Barrett.

Chapter 12: West & Peachey Enter the Twentieth Century

1. Author's Note: Clarence Coons recounted this story in his original manuscript. It was probably obtained in the early 1900s. I have heard Doug Stalker talk of his grandfather's Locomobile.
2. *Ibid.*
3. More stories told by Doug Stalker and collected over the years by both Clarence Coons and Harry Barrett.
4. A direct quote from Clarence Coons's research papers.

Chapter 13: The Alligator Warping Tug in Newfoundland

1. From the West & Peachey Collection.
2. *Ibid.*
3. For more information on John Waldie, see Kenneth A. Armson and Marjorie McLeod, *The Legacy of John Waldie and Sons: A History of the Victoria Harbour Lumber Company* (Toronto: Natural Heritage Books/Dundurn, 2007).

Chapter 14: Turn-of-the-Century Improvements and Modifications

1. Information on the general improvements and modifications to the structure of the Alligator taken from Clarence F. Coons's research.

Chapter 15: The Story of the Cavendish Lumber Company's Alligator Tug

1. The Scott timber limits, made up of 105 square miles in Cavendish, Anstruther, and Harvey townships of Peterborough County, were acquired by Scott in the 1840s. Due to a lengthy and costly legal battle extending into 1889, no cutting took place on these limits until they were bought by the Dickson Lumber Company in early 1890s. In 1893 this company bought the water-powered sawmill in Lakefield, Ontario. Late in 1893 they sold the Scott timber limits to J.W. Howry and Sons Lumber Company of Saginaw, Michigan, as described in this chapter.

Chapter 16: The Role of the Alligator in the Ottawa Valley

1. There are differing opinions as to whether the spelling should be McLaren or MacLaren. For more background on the Peter McLaren and his involvement in the

lumbering industry, see http://david.mclaren.name/lumber_days.htm, accessed October 30, 2009.

2. Information on Bud Doering is from a conference call involving Harry B. Barrett, Bud Doering, Dub Juby, Mary Campbell (mayor of McNab-Braeside), Tom Stephenson and Dave Lemkay on November 21, 2008. The call was made from the Valley Carver, Dub Juby's home overlooking the Ottawa River near Braeside. As well, Bud Doering and Dave Lemkay drove to Port Dover and Simcoe to allow Harry and Bud to have a face-to-face session on November 27, 2008. Meetings were held at Norfolk County offices, with a dinner session that evening at the Erie Beach Hotel in Port Dover.

Bud was engaged for over almost fifty years as woodlands manager for Gillies Brothers in the Temagami and Pontiac regions of Quebec, retiring in 1991 to become mayor for a few years of Horton Township near Renfrew.

Chapter 17: J.R. Booth — A Distinguished Ottawa River Client

1. For more information on J.R. Booth, see "John Rudolphus Booth: The Greatest Lumberman Canada Ever Produced," www.biblioottawalibrary.ca/connect/research/local/booth_e.html; see also John Ross Trinell, *J.R. Booth: The Life and Times of an Ottawa Lumber King* (Ottawa: Treehouse Publishing, 1998).

2. From the original preliminary manuscript researched by Clarence Coons.

Chapter 18: Timber Operations in Northwestern Ontario

1. For additional information on logging in the Fort Frances-Quetico Park area of Ontario, and Quetico Provincial Park in general, see Jon Nelson, *Quetico: Near to Nature's Heart* (Toronto: Natural Heritage/Dundurn, 2009), 34–36.

2. J.A. Mathieu Ltd. of Rainy Lake, Ontario, bought Alligator #202, the *Eli Johnson* in 1928. It was shipped to Fort Frances. In 1914, Shevlin-Clarke ordered Alligator #131, the *Otter* and changed the name to the *Tommy Mathieu*. While there may be a connection between the name of this tug and the name James A. Mathieu, a link could not be found. James A. Mathieu obviously switched from the steam tugs to the gasoline-operated Russel boats that were built in Fort Frances.

3. More information on Bill Bergman can be found at the John Ridley Research Library, Quetico Park Information Pavilion, French Lake. As part of his research for this book, Clarence F. Coons interviewed Bill Bergman in 1972.

4. This quote was taken from an undated account handwritten by Art Masden himself. Clarence Coons may have acquired it from a friend when he was visiting the Quetico area some twenty-five to thirty years ago.
5. *Ibid.*

Chapter 19: Some Alligator Accidents Over the Years

1. For more information on the French River and its turbulent rapids, see Toni Harting, *French River: Canoeing the River of the Stick-Wavers* (Erin, ON: Boston Mills, 1998), see also *Ontario Parks French River Map* (Copper Cliff, ON: The Friends of the French River Heritage Park, 2006).

Chapter 20: Technical and Operational Details in the Construction of Alligator Tugs

1. Information from the West & Peachey Collection, reasearch by Clarence Coons.
2. *Ibid.*
3. *Ibid.*

Chapter 21: The Alligator Warping Tug's Steam Engines

1. Specific information regarding the Alligator steam engines is from Clarence Coons's research on the West & Peachey Collection and other West & Peachey records. Today, the location of these papers is not known.

Chapter 22: The End of a Dynasty

1. Victor Darling and Mac Masson had been captain and first mate, respectively, of the *Seagull (II)* previously, the tug that hauled logs from Sturgeon Falls to Smith Island in Callander Bay. Both were veteran employees of John B. Smith & Sons. Masson was said to be a perfectionist and is reputed to often have had frequent vitriolic run-ins with his skipper, Victor Darling.

Chapter 23: The Russel Brothers' Gasoline-Powered Warping Tugs

1. Russel Brothers Ltd. established their machine shop in Fort Frances around 1914. Here they developed their steel, gasoline-operated warping tugs. They relocated to Owen Sound and operated there from 1937 to 1984. For more information on the company, see http://russelbrothers.com or contact the Owen Sound Marine and Rail Museum.

Chapter 24: The End of the Alligator Era

1. The cane presented to James Peachey on the occasion of the fiftieth anniversary of the West & Peachey firm is now in the possession of his grandson, Jim Peachey.

2. Tommy White was named Simcoe's Citizen of the Year for 1993. He was a well-known, deserving man who had contributed much to his community. He passed away a few years ago.

3. *Your Forests* is a forty-to-fifty-page, good-quality magazine, published three times a year since 1967 by the Ontario Ministry of Natural Resources. The major purpose was to maintain a link with private landowners and others interested in forest information, as well as printing a great many historical articles.

4. This write-up was produced by the Ontario Archaeological and Historic Sites Board for the dedication of the plaque by the Ontario Heritage Foundation in 1982. The last West & Peachey Alligator was said to be operating in Quebec in the 1960s. Russel boats and others were in use even later, and some of John West's original ideas are incorporated in landing barges of today.

5. This quote is the last paragraph of Clarence Coons's unfinished manuscript given to Harry Barrett by Dave Lemkay for rewriting and completion. The material is dated 1983.

6. William "Bill" Kirkwood was also an inventor. After the Second World War, many local homes were heated by the efficient coal-fired, self-feeding furnaces, designed and patented by him. These furnaces were named and sold as "The Thrifty Scot" because of their efficiency. As well, Kirkwood was well known locally as an accomplished naturalist and photographer. He was the only man to photograph the collapse of the Honeymoon Bridge from ice build-up in Niagara Falls.

Chapter 25: Aftermath

1. The information on the visit of the Piette girls is taken from an account written by Bill Yeager, curator of the Eva Brook Donly Museum, Simcoe, at that time. The account was found in West & Peachey Collection.

2. The Alligator that Ewan Caldwell painted had been abandoned by the McLachlin Brothers on the shore of a lake in Pontiac County, Quebec, in 1927.

3. The painting of the deserted Alligator was purchased directly from Ewan Caldwell. His ancestors were among the pioneers who opened up the Ottawa Valley timber trade with harvests of white pine in Lanark County. After serving in the Canadian Army from 1940 to 1945, Major Caldwell attended the University of

New Brunswick, graduating with a degree in forestry in 1948. He began his forestry career as a summer student at Gillies Brothers and Company at Braeside, eventually becoming woods manager for the company. When Caldwell retired from forestry in 1983, he was the Ottawa Division woodlands manager for Consolidated Bathurst. He died in 2001.

Today, this Caldwell painting hangs in the Ottawa home of Chris Lee, the former executive director of the Canadian Institute of Forestry. An image of this painting is on the back cover of this book, courtesy of *The Forestry Chronicle*, the Canadian Institute of Forestry journal that had featured the painting on the cover of its October 1992 issue.

Chapter 26: The *W.D. Stalker* — An Alligator Reborn

1. Tom Stephenson of Pembroke had once worked for the Gillies Brothers. He became interested in log marks and ultimately published a book on the log stamps.

Selected Bibliography

Books

Aldred, Diane. *Registered Timber Marks of Eastern Canada 1870 to 1984 — Les marques des bois de construction enrigistrées dans l'est du Canada 1870 à 1984.* Ottawa: Multiscience Publications Limited, in cooperation with the Canadian Forestry Service and the Canadian Government Publishing Centre, Supply and Services Canada, 1985.

Armson, Ken and Marjorie McLeod. *The Legacy of John Waldie and Sons: A History of the Victoria Harbour Lumber Company.* Toronto: Natural Heritage Books/Dundurn Press, 2007.

Gillis, Peter R. and Thomas R. Roach. *Lost Initiatives: Canada's Forest Policy and Forest Conservation.* Santa Barbara, CA: Greenwood Press, 1986.

Hughson, John W. and C.J. Bond. *Hurling Down the Pine.* Old-Chelsea, QC: Historical Society of the Gatineau, 1964.

Jackson, J. Barnwall. *The Lumberman's Timber Mark Guide: Facsimile of Timber Marks, by Order of Registration.* Montreal: G.E. Desbarats, 1873.

Kauffmann, Carl. *Logging Days in Blind River.* Blind River, ON: self-published, 1970.

Lee, David. *Lumber Kings and Shantymen: Logging and Lumbering in the Ottawa Valley.* Toronto: James Lorimer & Company Ltd., 2006.

Long, Garry. *Gilmour Tramway: A Lumber Baron's Desperate Scheme.* Huntsville, ON: Fox Meadows Books, 2001.

Long, Gary and Randy Whiteman. *When Giants Fall: The Gilmour Quest for Algonquin Pine.* Huntsville, ON: Fox Meadow Books, 2003.

Lower, A.R.M. *The North American Assault on the Canadian Forest.* Toronto: Ryerson, 1938.

MacKay, Donald. *The Lumberjacks.* Toronto: Natural Heritage Books, 1998.

_____. *Heritage Lost: The Crisis in Canada's Forests.* Toronto: Macmillan of Canada, 1983.

Price, Vernon, *Logging on the Schyan.* Burnstown, ON: General Store Publishing House, 1986.

Smith, Maurice D. *Steamboats on the Lakes.* James Lorimer & Company Ltd., 2005.

Tatley, Richard. *Northern Steamboats*: *Timiskaming, Nipissing & Abitibi*. Erin, ON: Boston Mills Press, 1966.

Taylor, Bruce W. *The Age of Steam on Lake Temiscaming*. Cobalt, ON: Highway Book Shop, 1993.

Trinell, John Ross. *J.R. Booth: The Life and Times of an Ottawa Lumber King*. Ottawa: Treehouse Publishing, 1998.

Whitton, Charlotte. *A Hundred Years A-Fellin': The Story of the Gillies on the Ottawa*. Ottawa, ON: Runge, 1943.

Journals/Magazines/Newspapers

Coons, C.F. "The John R. Booth Story." *Your Forests*, Vol. 11, No. 2 (Summer 1978).

Corby, John R. "The Alligator or Steam Warping Tug: A Canadian Contribution to the Development of Technology in the Forest Industry." *Journal for the Society of Industrial Archaeology*, Vol. 3, No. 1 (1977): 15–42.

Fowke, Edith. "Songs of the Northern Shantyboys." *Journal of Forest History*, Vol. 14 (January 1971): 22–28.

McKay, Donald. "The Canadian Logging Frontier." *Journal of Forest History*, Vol. 23 (January 1979): 4–17.

Mackey, Doug. "Alligators Plied Nipissing Waters." *North Bay Nugget*, March 2, 2001.

Phipps, R.W. "Across the Watershed of Eastern Ontario." *Journal of Forest History*, Vol. 9 (October 1965): 2–8.

Pross, A. Paul, ed. "Historical Memorandum of the Management of the Crown Lands." *Journal of Forest History*, Vol. 15 (April 1971): 22–29.

Websites

Briggs, Doctor Steve. "Russel Brothers Limited Online Archive" (http://russelbrothers.com).

Business and History: Gillies Bros. Co. Ltd. (www.lib.uwo.ca/programs/companyinformationcanada/ccc-gillies.html).

Druska, Ken. "Canada's Forests:A History" (www.foresthistory.org/publications/Issues/canforests.html).

Mackey, Doug. "A Closer Look at Lumber Baron J.R. Booth." Heritage Perspectives: A Column by Doug Mackey (www.pastforward.ca/perspectives/Oct_272000.htm).

Note from the Ottawa Room. "John Rudolphus Booth: The Greatest Lumberman Canada Ever Produced" (www.biblioottawalibrary.ca/connect/research/local/booth_e.html).

Index

About the Authors

Harry B. Barrett, a long-time resident of Norfolk County, is a noted naturalist, conservationist, and historian. Harry was the founding chair of the Long Point Foundation for Conservation, and is the author of several books on the local history of the Norfolk-Haldimand region of Ontario. He lives in Port Dover, Ontario.

Clarence F. Coons, now deceased, was a well-known professional forrester in Ontario. While growing up in Lakefield, Ontario, he heard many stories about the white-pine harvesting in the Trent Watershed and the "Alligators" at work. Clarence provided the original research for this book and Harry B. Barrett completed the work.

Of Related Interest

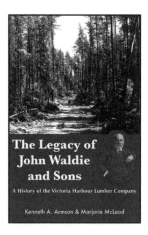

The Legacy of John Waldie and Sons
A History of the Victoria Lumber Company
by Kenneth A. Armson
978-1-55002-758-7
$22.99

A young Scottish immigrant who came to Wellington Square (now Burlington, Ontario) in 1842, John Waldie, founder of the Victoria Harbour Lumber Company, was identified as the second-largest lumber operator in Canada. Active in local and federal politics, and a friend of Sir Wilfrid Laurier, he invested capital in mills, people, and forests. Local history and genealogical connections are part of the Waldie story, headquartered at Victoria Harbour in Simcoe County. This little-known story provides insights into days of rampant entrepreneurialism, the world of the lumber barons, and the overall impact on our Ontario forests.

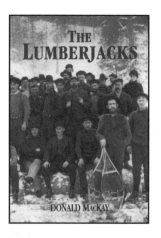

The Lumberjacks
by Donald MacKay
978-1-55002-773-0
$24.99

The nineteenth century spawned a unique breed of men who took pride in their woodsmen skills and rough codes of conduct. They called themselves lumberers, shantymen, timber beasts, *les bucherron,* and, more recently, lumberjacks, working in the vast forests of eastern Canada and British Columbia. Across the country, farm boys would go to the woods, lumbering being the only winter work available. Immigrants — Swedes and Finns more often than not — resumed the trades they had learned so well in the forests of northern Europe. They broke the cold, hard monotony of camp life with songs, tall tales, and card games. Donald MacKay allows us a glimpse into that moment in our heritage when men entered the virgin forest to carve out an industry from the seemingly endless array of pine, spruce, maple, and balsam fir.

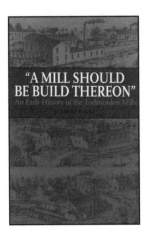

A Mill Should Be Build Thereon
An Early History of the Todmorden Mills
by Eleanor Darke
9780920474891
$16.95

It is difficult for Todmorden Mills Museum visitors to imagine that this site so close to the busy Don Valley Parkway was once home to an important mill. As early as 1793, Governor Simcoe recognized the industrial potential of this portion of the Don River. By 1795 Skinner's sawmill was under construction, initiating an era of technological development that spread beyond the valley of the Don into what was then Muddy York. Today, Todmorden serves to remind us of Toronto's industrial heritage and the spirit of the time.

MARQUIS

Marquis Book Printing Inc.

Québec, Canada
2010